What people are s

Heavy Radicals

Heavy Radicals is a concise and insightful history of a long-forgotten but vibrant radical movement. Leonard and Gallagher break new ground in revealing the extent to which law enforcement will go to infiltrate, destabilize and ultimately destroy domestic political organizations that espouse a philosophy counter to the status quo. To better understand the current state of domestic surveillance and political repression, from Occupy Wall Street to the Edward Snowden revelations, start with this little gem of a book.
T.J. English, Author of *The Savage City* and *Havana Nocturne*

In this masterfully written and extensively researched book, Aaron Leonard with Conor A. Gallagher offers a no-nonsense critical analysis of one of the most resilient, misunderstood, and controversial anti-capitalist organizations of the last fifty years. This book is a MUST READ for anyone invested in nuancing their understanding of revolutionary political struggle and unrelenting state repression in the United States.
Robeson Taj Frazier, Author of *The East Is Black: Cold War China in the Black Radical Imagination"*

Based on impeccable research, *Heavy Radicals* explores the rise of the Revolutionary Communist Party in the late 1960s and 1970s. Militant Maoists, dedicated to revolutionary class struggle, the RCP was one of many organizations that fought to carry on the 60s struggle for radical change in the United States well after SDS and other more well known groups imploded. Leonard and Gallagher help us to understand how the RCP's revolutionary ideology resonated with a small group of young people in post-

1968 America, took inspiration from the People's Republic of China, and brought down the wrath of the FBI.
David Farber, Author of *The Age of Great Dreams: America in the 1960s*

Meticulously researched, drawing on both internal documents hiding in plain sight and a wealth of information gained through laborious freedom of information requests, *Heavy Radicals* is a great example of history of the near past -- in examining how the FBI acted, we are better able to understand the methods employed in undermining dissent today.
Eveline Lubbers, Author of *Secret Manoeuvres in the Dark: Corporate and Police Spying on Activists*

In this untold and highly accessible history of Sixties radicalism, Aaron Leonard and Conor Gallagher expertly guide us through the world of the Maoists who picked up and maintained the activist cause well into the Seventies, long after others had collapsed. Fascinating!
Rick Shenkman, Founder and publisher of George Mason University's History News Network

Heavy Radicals: The FBI's Secret War on America's Maoists

The Revolutionary Union / Revolutionary Communist Party 1968-1980

Revised Edition

Heavy Radicals: The FBI's Secret War on America's Maoists

The Revolutionary Union / Revolutionary Communist Party 1968-1980

Revised Edition

Aaron J. Leonard
with Conor A. Gallagher

Winchester, UK
Washington, USA

JOHN HUNT PUBLISHING

First published by Zero Books, 2014
Second edition published by Zero Books, 2022
Zero Books is an imprint of John Hunt Publishing Ltd., No. 3 East St., Alresford,
Hampshire SO24 9EE, UK
office@jhpbooks.com
www.johnhuntpublishing.com
www.zero-books.net

For distributor details and how to order please visit the 'Ordering' section on our website.

Text copyright: Aaron J. Leonard, Conor A. Gallagher 2014

ISBN: 978 1 80341 317 4
978 1 80341 318 1 (ebook)
Library of Congress Control Number: 2022944391

All rights reserved. Except for brief quotations in critical articles or reviews, no part of this book may be reproduced in any manner without prior written permission from the publishers.

The rights of Author Name as author have been asserted in accordance with the Copyright, Designs and Patents Act 1988.

A CIP catalogue record for this book is available from the British Library.

Design: Matthew Greenfield

UK: Printed and bound by CPI Group (UK) Ltd, Croydon, CR0 4YY
Printed in North America by CPI GPS partners

We operate a distinctive and ethical publishing philosophy in all areas of our business, from our global network of authors to production and worldwide distribution.

Contents

Maoism in the US	xiii
Acknowledgements	xxvii
Note on Chinese Names	xxx
Preface	1
Introduction: The Way From San Jose	5
1 Foundation	10
2 SDS, the RU, and the FBI	34
3 Beyond the Student Movement	58
4 Protracted Urban War or Protracted Struggle?	86
5 People's China	110
6 Coalitions, Infiltrators, and Schisms	132
7 Sinking Roots and Making the Papers	160
8 The Short Leap from the RU to the RCP	183
9 The Final Split	205
10 After the Fall	224
11 Conclusion	245
Postscript	252
Appendix: Interview with Danielle Zora	253
Glossary of Organizational Acronyms	264
Bibliography	266
Endnotes	273
Index	338

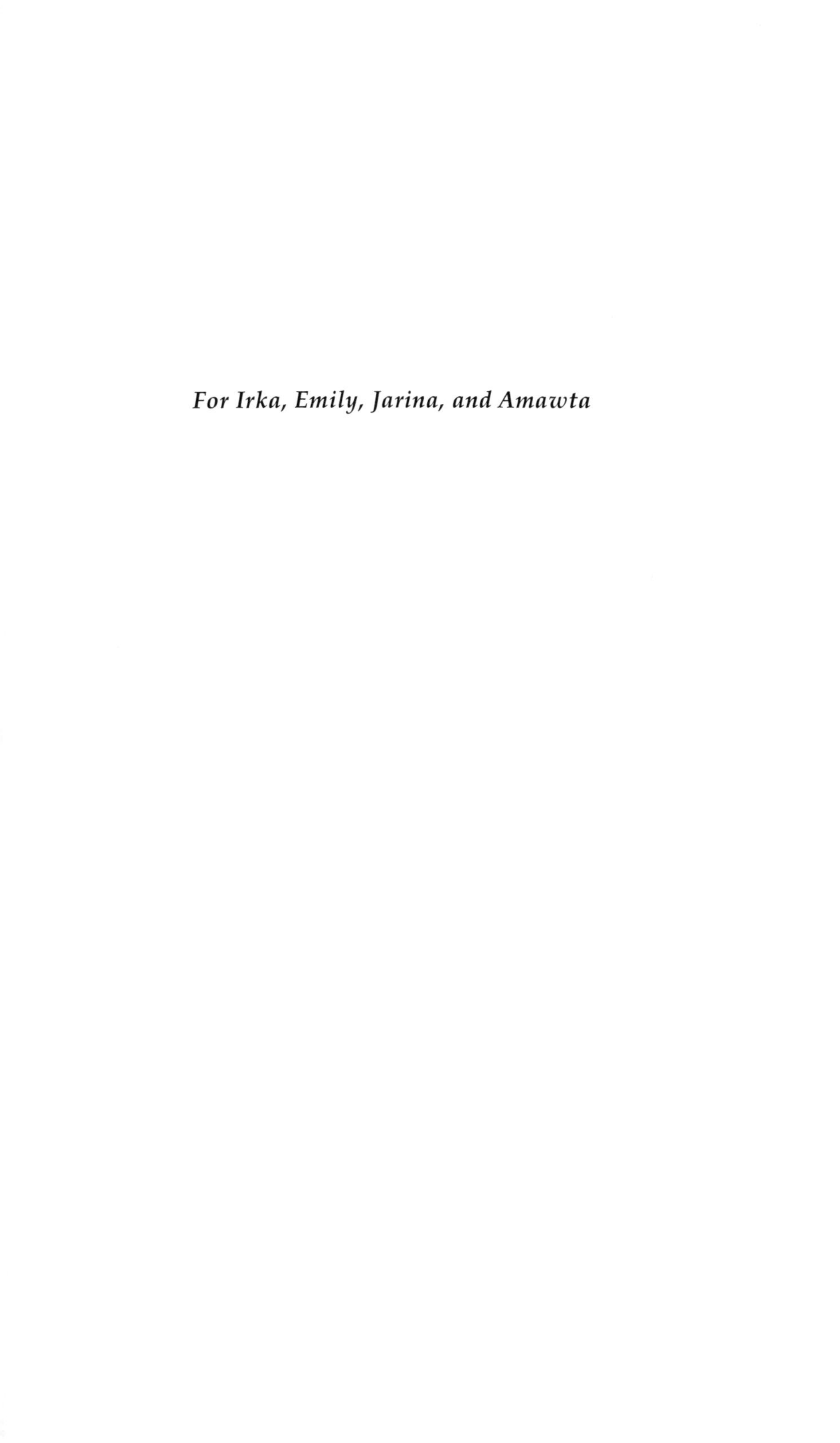

For Irka, Emily, Jarina, and Amawta

AARON J. LEONARD is the author of the *Folk Singers & the Bureau* and *Whole World in an Uproar: Music, Rebellion & Repression 1955-1972*. He has a BA in Social Sciences and History from New York University, *magna cum laude*. He lives in Los Angeles.

CONOR A. GALLAGHER is an educator, author, and researcher of US government repression of post-WW2 communist groups. He earned his BA from the CUNY Graduate Center and his master's from the University of Southern California. He currently lives in Italy. He supports Vélez Sarsfield.

Maoism in the US

One of the questions Conor and I confronted when we started working on *Heavy Radicals* ten years ago, and which still comes up, is why, in the twenty-first century, would anyone be interested in US Maoism. It is a reasonable question if one usually asked with an edge of mockery.

Driving the question is the fact that Maoism—the most animating revolutionary current of the late 1960s and early 1970s—has garnered only the barest mention in relevant US historiographies, the exception being Max Elbaum's *Revolution in the Air,* about which more in a bit. On the whole, however, to read the available history, one would think there was no significant gravitation to Maoism in the US.[1] This, in turn, has created a self-reinforcing situation where its absence from the historiography becomes evidence of its absence from history.

That is not to deny that, as a credible political philosophy, Maoism has taken a serious hit. This is especially true in China, where Mao is still canonized as a founding father, but his presentation is completely disconnected from any revolutionary history. However, given the power of certain of Maoism's cohering principles, and the fact that there are tens of thousands, if not millions, worldwide who still adhere to this interpretation of Marxism, it strikes us as highly negligent to minimize, or worse, omit, its legacy—to say nothing of its potential, remote or otherwise, for resurgence in an era where a younger generation are once again beginning to look to various forms of socialism.[2]

With that in mind, we thought a new edition of *Heavy Radicals* would be of some use. While we have not altered the book's text, aside from necessary grammatical, style, and spelling fixes, we offer this introduction with clarifications and elaborations on our initial discoveries.[3] Along with that, we include an appendix of an interview with one of the participants in the Revolutionary

Union's 1971 China visit, which offers a rare picture of Maoist China—or at least how it sought to present itself to international supporters—before it abandoned most of Mao's policies.

Richard Gibson, the CIA, and Donald H. Wright

Between *Heavy Radicals* and its follow-up, *A Threat of the First Magnitude*, it would seem we have written near all we could about the former RU leader and FBI informant, Donald H. Wright.[4] However, a new piece of evidence is worth noting. This comes by way of recently declassified documents of a former CIA asset, Richard Gibson, referred to by the code name "Sugar."

In the early 1960s Gibson, an African-American, worked for CBS News but also entered into left-wing politics, in his work with the Fair Play for Cuba Committee. In 1962 he quit that organization and repatriated to Switzerland in 1963, to work for the magazine *La Révolution Africaine*.[5] It was in this period that he reached out to the CIA to offer his services.

His CIA ties, however, seem to have been an open secret—or at least suspected—for some within the left, including for the RU's Bruce Franklin:

> According to this source [informant], BRUCE FRANKLIN in no uncertain terms described GIBSON as a CIA agent who was exposed as such and had to flee France lest he be killed. FRANKLIN stated that he had proof of GIBSON's affiliation with the CIA. LEIBEL BERGMAN on the other hand stated in no uncertain terms that BRUCE FRANKLIN's allegation was completely untrue, and that GIBSON had been thoroughly checked out when BERGMAN was in Red China and had been found to be all right.[6]

Despite Bergman's certitude, Franklin—who had lived in France—was correct, though both men, it should be noted, were conducting their argument, unbeknownst to them, in front of an FBI informant.[7]

Nonetheless, the released material on Gibson provides a compelling piece of evidence about Donald H. Wright. This by way of a report Gibson submitted to the CIA:

> A confidential source [Gibson] has reported that Donald WRIGHT of Chicago, born on 9 March 1936, traveled to Algiers to attend the First International Congress of Support for the Palestinian People held on 27-29 December 1969. WRIGHT is a member of the Black Panther Party and the Chicago Ad Hoc Committee for a Marxist-Leninist Party. WRIGHT met with Eldridge CLEAVER in Algiers.[8]

Gibson's memo had been forwarded to FBI headquarters, who then forwarded it to their Chicago and Denver offices with a cover note under the subject line, DN 447-S:

> Enclosed for information of Chicago and Denver is an informal CIA report dated 2/6/70 captioned "Donald Wright, Black Panther Party, Travel to Algiers." It is noted that the subject of this report is known to both the Chicago and Denver offices.[9]

The memo then notes, *"DN 447-S is identical to the subject of Agency* [CIA] *report dated 2/6/70"* [our emphasis]. In other words, the FBI is saying that the subject of the CIA report, Donald H. Wright, is *their informant*, code name, DN 447-S, referring to his informant codename for the FBI's Denver field office.[10] To date, this is the most direct confirmation of Donald H. Wright being an FBI informant we have obtained.

More on the "Ad Hoc Committee for a Marxist-Leninist Party"

As Gibson's characterization makes clear, Donald H. Wright identified himself as a member of the "Ad Hoc Committee," the

FBI-created Maoist group—an entity which we unearthed in *Heavy Radicals* and elaborated on in *A Threat of the First Magnitude*. While the National Archives has yet to release the voluminous AHC files—estimated to be between 15-17,000 pages—records released in accord with a Congressional order to make public material pertaining to the Kennedy assassination offer tantalizing new information about the scope of its operations.

The most shocking thing, to the degree the information is accurate, comes by way of an FBI memo relating to "Herb Block," an AHC member and FBI informant and seemingly key member of the AHC:

> 1.) A sensitive source [Richard Gibson] has reported that Leibel BERGMAN and Herb BLOCK share a deep detestation of the Progressive Labor Party (PLP). BLOCK stated that he was convinced that the PLP was secretly run by the CPUSA and that he (BLOCK) has learned that Fred JEROME's mother, Alice JEROME (a prominent member of PLP) had secretly attended a Party school in the Soviet Union after being publicly associated with the PLP.
>
> 2.) The main reason BLOCK and his wife wanted to visit China was to continue denunciations of the PLP. BLOCK is convinced that his previous communications with the Chinese about the PLP had some effect and that the PLP would shortly be "derecognized" by the Chinese.[11]

Here the PLP is portrayed, by way of an informant, as a tool of the CPUSA, and thus is being denounced to the Chinese, who are openly hostile to any communist group, such as the CPUSA, sympathetic to the Soviet Union

This is not the only example of Block spreading misinformation about the Progressive Labor Party. For example, Block had met with a Communist Party member, Gerald Kirk, and tried to recruit him into doing work for the AHC. However, Block was not aware that Kirk was also an FBI informant, who would later testify to Congress about his meeting with him.[12] In his testimony, he offered the following:

> I believe the Progressive Labor Party is a front for the ad hoc committee. I will give you a piece of information I got from the ad hoc committee. I also met a man from the ad hoc committee for a Marxist-Leninist party whose name may be an alias, he encouraged me if I wished to join to make up my mind yes or no. Once I joined, I would have to do quite a bit of work. And he said the Progressive Labor Party was some of their people, but many of the Progressive Labor Party just didn't know that.[13]

Allowing that Kirk may have misunderstood what Block was telling him, a picture emerges from these examples of an AHC informant creating a good deal of confusion—and bad blood—particularly in regard to the PLP. This raises all manner of questions, including what impact that had on everything the PLP was involved in, from its role in Students for a Democratic Society, especially in the critical years of 1968-1969, to its move away from Maoism in the same period.

While there is considerable fog surrounding those events, one thing we *can* shed light on is the actual character of the AHC. There was a question in our research, left hanging, about whether it was an actual organization, with certain members duped as to its true character and purpose. The AHC—by the FBI's account—was not an organization, but rather an initiative carried out by seven informants and their FBI handler(s). The most likely operational model, beyond their newsletter the *Ad Hoc Bulletin*, is that informants attempted to sow confusion and dissension by their recruiting and interacting with individual contacts. However, there is no evidence of organizational independence: hierarchy, meetings, editorial boards, etc.

This information comes by way of an FBI report discussing the phenomena of organizations operating more as a masthead than membership. As they write, there has been "a tendency of some relatively minute extremist groups to publicly project themselves as large membership organizations." By way of example, they offer "long-time communist Homer Bates Chase," operating "in almost solo fashion out of the Boston area as the New England Party of Labor (NEPL), where he is the Editorial Board of *Hammer and Steel Newsletter*. The report then cites other examples:

> The Committee of Correspondence of Seattle, "Antithesis" of San Francisco, the Committee for Political Studies of New York, the Maryland Socialist League, the California Communist League, the Cousins Coordinating Committee of Upstate New York are but representative of a number of organizations which in actuality are the instruments of one egotistically minded militant seeking to develop fraternal relationships with other extremists.[14]

All of which is interesting in its own right, but the FBI saw in this a further justification for the efficacy of their Ad Hoc Committee operation:

> For several years through the Ad Hoc Committee for a Marxist-Leninist Party, USA (AHC) investigation, involving the coordinated direction of seven Chicago informants, the Bureau has capitalized with excellent intelligence results upon the propensity of domestic and foreign extremists to accept alleged militant organization based upon their projected image as opposed to actual membership and activities. The AHC has established widespread contacts, both domestic and international, with a variety of extremists

> of left-wing, New Left, pro-Chicom [Chinese communist], Arab, and Negro extremist organizations.[15]

There is a lot to unpack here, not the least of which is that the AHC operation itself consisted wholly of seven informants, run out of the Chicago FBI office. Beyond that, however, is that the legitimation of groupings consisting of one or a handful of people, by the wider communist movement, played a role in legitimating the AHC. Rather than being seen as an outlier with no physical presence, it was seen as an actual organization.

The Scope of the Threat

In stark contrast to such marginal, even fictitious, operations, the RU/RCP was an actual national organization. As a result, the investigation undertaken by the FBI against them was massive—the largest carried out against any organization grouped within what came to be called the new communist movement.[16] While the Weathermen and others engaged in political violence garnered considerable, if not more, attention, that was because they were subject to criminal scrutiny. Unlike those groups, however, the RU/RCP was *not* the subject of a criminal investigation; it was their Maoist politics that made them a target.[17]

In that regard we have since obtained two reports by the Bureau, prepared for the US Attorney General which attempt to quantify the strength of the Revolutionary Union and then the Revolutionary Communist Party. The first was the Bureau's report for the year 1971, by an ailing J. Edgar Hoover. The report, an overview of all the FBI's work that year, included a section about a group he felt merited particular attention:

> The Revolutionary Union, organized in 1968, is a group with some 300 members which seeks to form a new domestic Marxist-Leninist party allied with the Communist Party

> of China and devoted to the teachings of Mao Tse-tung. It believes in violent revolution and open guerrilla warfare to overthrow the American government.[18]

Five years later, the Bureau continued to have its sights on what had become the Revolutionary Communist Party—a group, which by their own account, had more than doubled in size. Here is how FBI Director Clarence Kelly described the organization:

> The Revolutionary Communist Party was formed in October 1975, to replace the now-dissolved Revolutionary Union. Membership is composed of persons who had previously been in the Revolutionary Union. With approximately 750 members in some 30 cities, the party embraces Marxist-Leninist ideology as developed through the teachings of the late Chairman Mao Tse-tung.[19]

Kelly's report came at a time when the FBI was coming under increased scrutiny, this because of revelations from the exposure of COINTELPRO operations and their illegal efforts against the Weathermen. Within two years of this report, they would begin scaling back, then completely overhauling their domestic security operations. However, Kelly's language, as late as 1976, is indicative of how active their operations against the RU/RCP remained.

As for FBI estimates, while they seem an under-count, they are not an under-count by much—missing the mark by at most a few hundred. We say this based on reports from areas where Bureau informants appear to have done a pretty good job in identifying individuals in and around the RU/RCP, and comparing those counts with those of activists based in those cities at the time. When we published *Heavy Radicals*, we estimated the group's size as "well over a thousand cadre."[20] Given the new information and insights available, we would reduce that number to be between 900 and 1100 members.

This is important in and of itself, but also in assessing other organizations in the field.

The October League & Others

One thing we did not know much about when we initially published was the size of other groups in the new communist movement, though we tended toward the view that others in this milieu, while smaller, were at least operating on a similar plane. We have since obtained information that disrupts this view in significant ways.

It is largely understood, by those familiar, that after the RU/RCP, the October League was the next largest Maoist entity. We now have more information by way of the Bureau's October League file held in their Atlanta office. Here is how they characterized the group in 1974:

> The October League (OL) National Headquarters is located in Los Angeles, California. The OL currently has chapters in nine cities. Organizational structure set forth. OL membership estimated between 150 to 200 nationally. OL members in Los Angeles estimated at approximately 35.[21]

That same report went on to note that the group did not then have a national office, but rather operated out of leader Mike Klonsky's home. While OL eventually established an office in Chicago, and likely grew some after 1974, given the overall decline in social tumult and the tendency in this period for more cadre to leave than join, it is hard to imagine they grew by much. As for FBI estimates, while perhaps an under-count, in line with their projections for the RU/RCP, it would be a modest under-count.

Another group that comes across as smaller than we had assumed was the Communist League (CL) which would become the Communist Labor Party. We came by more information on that group via the FBI file of Joe Burton, an FBI informant who fronted a phony Maoist organization in Florida called the Red Star Cadre. Because Burton had contact with CL, his file contains information on that group's size and operation. Specifically, there is a January 1973 report on CL leader, Nelson Peery, speaking to an informant in his Chicago home. In the course of his conversation with the informant, who is not identified, Peery gave the group's size as "approximately 200 members"—use of the word "approximately," suggesting a membership under, rather than over, 200. The suggestion of a more modest size is reinforced when the report goes on to note its headquarters, like that of the OL, operated out of its leader's apartment.[22]

More modest than CL was the Puerto Rican Revolutionary Workers Organization (PRRWO). The group, which had evolved from the Young Lords Party, had mass appeal at the beginning of the 1970s but had in a few years dwindled in size considerably. According to PRRWO leader Richie Perez, by the mid-1970s it was "down to 40 people."[23]

Smaller still was the Black Workers Congress, which was never large, but due to splits and exits had shrunk considerably. According to an FBI informant, in September 1973 it had "less than 10 to 15 hard-core members."[24] While that number might appear as an exaggeration, the BWC file is both massive and meticulous, suggesting the head-count is more factual than fanciful.

Significantly, PRRWO and BWC had worked with the Revolutionary Union in the National Liaison Committee—an effort undermined by the informant Donald H. Wright—to join into a single entity. Given the modest size of PRWWO and BWC, had that effort been a success, it would have been a success mainly in the qualitative component of combining a few score Black and Puerto Rican cadre with the disproportionately white and Asian-American RU, but would have made only a modest impact on the group's aggregate size.[25]

Of course, all these estimates were subject to certain biases, but in the case of PRWWO and CL, it is well positioned members themselves offering the estimates. As for the FBI, while one ought to read their reports with sufficient skepticism, they were for internal, not public, consumption. As such, their aim was to serve the agency's larger mandate, which undue exaggeration, let alone fabrication, would undermine.

All that said, were this simply a matter of marginal political organizations operating in the larger terrain of US fringe politics, it would be hard to argue for giving them too much attention. However, it was the Maoist politics at the core, particularly of the RU/RCP, that made it significant. The RU/RCP may have been a small group in the US, but it was connected to a far more significant international trend.

Mao Zedong Thought or Third World Marxism?

Which brings us to the assessment of Maoism we find in Max Elbaum's *Revolution in the Air*. Given that book's influence—for the generations that have come up since that time and historians who source it—it has become the go-to reference for understanding the New Communist Movement.[26] As such, a few things need to be said.

Elbaum's work is helpful to a degree, in bringing a confusing array of information—the myriad groups, sects, and sect-lets—into a single, understandable space. Further, its non-sectarian tone, in contrast to the internecine sparring—often vicious and petty—among the various actors, reads as refreshing. However, in an important way, it comes up short.

The concept of "Third World Marxism," which is a principle at the core of the book, is problematic. Rather than adhering to such an outlook, the ideology of groups identifying as "new communist" was either drawing on the Marxism-Leninism of the Soviet model, or the Marxism-Leninism, Mao Zedong Thought of the Chinese Communists, or some combination of the two. Elbaum's notional term, which he describes as "a version of Leninism identified with the Third World Movement," simply did not exist.[27]

In actuality, it was Maoism that emerged as the most radical trend, and in turn, was the most appealing for those gravitating toward revolutionary communism in the late 1960s. *Revolution in the Air* acknowledges as much, but it does so in a confusing way:

> Maoism did provide the most elaborate framework available for early 1970s revolutionaries who were critical of the USSR, and it served as the new movement's strongest single reference point. But it did not, and could not, consolidate behind its banner all those who rallied to the perspective of Third World Marxism.[28]

While the first part of this passage is sound, the second reads as a tautology. Of course, the Maoist framework could not consolidate "all those who rallied to the perspective of Third World Marxism," because the latter was not a coherent thing. Beyond that, and more importantly, suggesting there was something other than Maoism animating the most radical communist elements contributes to the overall diminution of the role and presence of Maoism in that historic period.

The "China Franchise"

Finally there is the matter of China's support, or lack of, for any particular organization. While we held to the idea, one also put forward by the US government, that the RU had garnered the support of China, the situation appears to be more complicated.[29]

While China welcomed a delegation of the RU in 1971—and appears to have given it a privileged status (see appendix)—they did so in the context of a broad invitation to progressives and radicals in the United States. Aside from that, there is no evidence, one way or the other, of China endorsing any single group to act as its representative in the US in the period of roughly 1969 to 1976, after the PLP and China parted ways—though the RU was intimately involved in the US China Peoples Friendship Association, the organization that facilitated travel for those wanting to visit revolutionary China.

What we have found in released records from the FBI, to the degree they can be believed, is that China in the first years of the 1970s was pushing for all the groups on the left—regardless of the RU already operating as a de facto party—including the October League, forces around the *Guardian,* the Puerto Rican Revolutionary Workers Organization, the Black Workers Congress, I Wor Kuen, and others to unite into a single party. None of this is laid out in any type of smoking gun guidance, but rather comes via internal chatter garnered by informants.[30]

That said, the period of "party building" in the United States coincided with a period of high turmoil in China, one that saw Mao in declining health, major moves toward rapprochement with the United States—flowing in no small part from the heightened tensions, even war scare, with the USSR—and an attempt by more conservative forces within the Chinese Communist Party to regain control of Chinese society in the wake of the Cultural Revolution. All of which suggests an absence of unanimity of aim within the Chinese leadership on matters dealing with international fraternal organizations. While Mao Zedong would arguably have had the power to make such a call, it was likely not an issue occupying his attention as a priority. Indeed, given he was about to fete Nixon, holding off on such recognition might have seemed a better option.

In fact, it was only after Mao died, and right-wing forces reasserted full control, that the Chinese Communist Party—apparently keen to maintain some facade of Maoist continuity—anointed a specific proxy, this being the newly minted Communist Party (Marxist-Leninist), formerly the October

League. This was on display when a CPML delegation visited the country in 1977 and its leader, Mike Klonsky, attended a banquet where he shared a toast with Mao's chosen successor, Hua Guofeng.[31] Unfortunately for the CPML, it was a matter of getting to the party as it was about to break up. By the end of 1978 the press was reporting that Deng Xiaoping—by then the real power in China—"seems to be dragging the rest of China behind him on what looks suspiciously like a capitalist road."[32] By 1981, Hua would be fully pushed aside. As for the CPML, it dissolved that same year.

While the Maoist era of China is over, and the RU/RCP as it existed during that time, is no more—it is worth stating plainly something too rarely said. Despite the unrelenting capitalist triumphalism since the fall of the Soviet Union, in the larger sweep of history, it remains true that empires—and social-economic systems—rise and then they fall. What that means for the future is beyond our capacity to say, but it is far too soon to close the book on everything the twentieth century brought forward—there will be plenty of time for that as history fully clarifies itself. In the meantime, it is our hope *Heavy Radicals* can serve as a tool toward a greater understanding of that contentious, fraught, and ambitious era.

Aaron J. Leonard & Conor A. Gallagher
Spring 2022

Acknowledgements

Many people helped in the course of undertaking this project and I want to thank them. To Mat Callahan, who pointed me to the road and allowed me to draw a map on how to reach my destination. To Dave Pugh for his deep well of experience, memory, and unending generosity, without which this would be a story of only fragments. To Lincoln Bergman, who opened his home and his memory to me, giving a human picture to a critical character in our story. To Doug Monica for his generosity and insights. To Dennis O'Neill for his candor, irreverence, and willingness to introduce me to a realm beyond my grasp. To Page Dougherty Delano for sharing her precious insights and memories. To Marc Lendler, for his critical memory and for helping me expand the frame of my analysis. To Mark Rudd, for his insights on the metamorphosis of SDS. To Art Eckstein for his deep well of knowledge on the FBI. To Scott Harrison and his essential archival material on the Revolutionary Union and Revolutionary Communist Party. To David Morgan, for his insights and insightful dissertation. To Bill Drew for taking the time to talk, and to put down in writing his stark and rich experience. To the late David Sullivan, for having the foresight to see his papers as something more than the detritus of a time gone by. To the staff of Encyclopedia of Anti-Revisionism On-Line, especially Paul Saba, for continuing to rescue the bounty of material of the new communist movement from oblivion. To Leslie Thatcher and the staff of *Truthout* for printing what too few others will. To the faculty and staff at NYU's McGhee Adult Undergraduate program, particularly Ozan Aksoy, Simon Davis, Taj Frazier, Clif Hubby, Kathleen Hulley, April Krassner, and Larry Menna, who walked me through the doorway toward new ways of thinking. To Heather Thompson, who I met only briefly, but to lasting effect. To the staff of the NYU's Tamiment Library and Robert F. Wagner archives, and their depository of radical United States history that is indeed a treasure. To Zero Books, and the wonderful people who make it a reality, for having the confidence to take on this project, especially Tariq Goddard, Tamar Shlaim, Liam Sprod, Dominic C. James, Catherine Harris, Mary Flatt, Nick Welch, Stuart Davies, Trevor Greenfield, and John Hunt. To the former RU and RCP comrades who called up a time in their lives that remains both essential and unsettled and shared their thoughts and memories with me—they know who they are, but likely do not know how essential they were to this project. To Hunter McCord, Ben Slater, and Alan Yee, whose reading and insights allowed me to go past the limits of my own constrained vision. To Brandon Prince for his essential research and support. To Laura Freeman for her advice and abiding friendship. To Jolie Gorchov and Anji Taylor, for their example and their friendship. To Conor Gallagher, who took this project into the stratosphere with his relentless tenacity in prying secrets from the hands of the secret-keepers and his penetrating insights; this would be a far lesser book without him. And finally, to my partner, Irka Mateo, for her keen ear, keener insight, and illuminating joy and humanity, I am fortunate beyond words. Of course, assistance and support do not connote agreement with my particular views and analysis, and in the end, I am solely responsible for the book's content, analysis, and any shortcomings.

AJL

Along with those acknowledged above, the following individual is worthy of praise: Kathleen Gallagher, who received countless FOIA letters and documents, scanned and emailed them while I was out of the country, and without whom this project would not have been possible. Jim Wolpman was generous in mailing me a copy of the Mid-peninsula Free University FBI file he had attained. I must also acknowledge the following archives that were immensely helpful in retrieving and reproducing documents Stanford University's Hoover Institution on War, Revolution and Peace, and the Department of Special Collections and University Archives, the New York Public Library's Archive and Manuscripts, and the Schomburg Center for Research in Black Culture, the University of Missouri's Archives, the University of Washington's Special Collections, Temple University's Urban Archives, Duke University's David Rubenstein Rare Books and Manuscript Library, Wayne State University's Walther P. Reuther Library, the City Archives of Portland, Oregon, the Chicago History Museum, the State Historical Society of Missouri Research Center, and the National Archives and Records Administration.

CAG

Note on Chinese Names

We have used the Pinyin naming structure for Chinese names in the text. In any quotes we have retained whatever form, Wade-Giles or Pinyin, contained in the original.

Pinyin	Wade-Giles
Beijing	Peking
Deng Xiaoping	Teng Hsiao-ping
Guomindang	Kuomintang
Hua Guofeng	Hua Kuo-feng
Jiang Qing	Chiang Ching
Lin Biao	Lin Piao
Liu Shaoqi	Liu Shao-chi
Mao Zedong	Mao Tse-tung
Xinhua	Hsinhua
Zhou Enlai	Chou En-lai

Preface

The impetus for this book began forty years ago. At the time, I was a 16-year-old, radically inclined high school student who had recently formed an organization in my hometown in upstate New York. The group was named the "Stoned Rabbits Peoples Party," based on the subject component of our school symbol, a rabbit being pulled out of a magician's hat. As for the stoned aspect, it speaks for itself. The SRPP, like more than a few groupings at the time, was looking to Maoism, among others, as an ideology to try to resolve the universe of questions the previous decade had thrown up. As part of our efforts to break beyond the bounds of our small town, in 1975 we sent off to New York's China Books and Periodicals and obtained two critical pieces of literature: a copy of *Revolution* newspaper and the Revolutionary Union's newly released *Red Papers 7: How Capitalism Has Been Restored in the Soviet Union and What this Means for the World Struggle*. *Revolution,* dated October 1975, had a blaring headline announcing the founding of the Revolutionary Communist Party, USA. Thus began a decades long relationship with the RCP, from working with its unemployed organization, to being part of its youth group, to writing for its newspaper. It is a relationship that with the crystalline clarity of hindsight, should have ended a good deal sooner than it did—which is a story in its own right—but alas this is not a memoir, rather an attempt at a much needed first-pass at a history of this organization.

My direct participation with the group began in May 1976. Thus, my connection begins two-thirds of the way into the story of which I write. Everything before is reconstructed by direct research. The period from 1976 on, however, has the benefit of my having been a participant observer. Regardless, given the amount of time that has passed, the fading of memory, my embedded biases of the time, I draw only sparsely from that experience, and instead rely as much as possible on the ample documentation, witness interviews, and other sources, to reconstruct the major events.

I talked to many people in the course of researching and writing this book. Given their varying associations with a Maoist organization having as its stated aim leading a mass revolutionary uprising, quite a number agreed to speak, but on the condition they not be named. In those cases, I refer to them obliquely in the endnotes. I have also exercised discretion in referencing formerly secret FBI documents, naming only RU/RCP members who have elsewhere been identified in the public record as having been associated with the group. That allowed for, as the reader will see, most of the information collected comes from documentary and archival material. As helpful as it was to speak to actual people, in the end, the record was more reliable than any individual's memory—regardless of how clear some of them were.

One further note on documentary sources. What my collaborator, Conor Gallagher, and I discovered in researching this book was that there was quite a wealth of material "hiding in plain sight." For example, we found critical files on William Hinton in an online collection of documents pertaining to an FBI background check of R. Sargent Shriver, the former US diplomat and Vice-Presidential candidate. We came across an informant report coinciding with an RU delegation visit to China among a collection of documents released by the National Archives in regard to the The John F. Kennedy assassination. We also found critical FBI-RU memos in an archive of the Liberation News Service housed in the Temple University library. All of this material was available before our various Freedom of Information requests began trickling in. The relative ease in discovering formerly secret material is testament to the sheer quantity of records on this group and the dearth of research.

That said, there were still quite a few responses by the FBI to our requests that certain files either did not exist, had been destroyed, were "reported missing," or were unavailable due to a "catastrophic flood" at a particular facility. In one instance where we requested CIA material on Vicki Garvin, the wife of RU founder Leibel Bergman and a prominent activist in her own right, we were told, "the CIA can neither confirm nor deny the existence or nonexistence of records responsive to your request."[1]

On the whole, however, we were able to learn a great deal. In that regard, what follows will be revelatory, not only for those coming to this subject brand new, but even for those with extensive knowledge. There remains, however, much yet to uncover.

In taking on this project, a number of people questioned whether there was any value in giving attention to a US Maoist organization whose best days were decades in the past. This seemed to have more to do with the generally bad opinion of the group on the part of some former members and others who encountered it along the way, than with any demonstrable insignificance. But if it were just the matter of assessing Maoism in the US in that period, this would be a lesser book, relevant with its own specific lessons, but a much drier story. However, it was the interaction of the group with the secret police in the United States—which itself was highly political—that ultimately animated this undertaking. Conor and I began this project after the Chelsea Manning case became public, but before Edward Snowden's revelations, and before the various police measures against the Occupy Movement began coming to light. What is clear through those and many other examples is that the understanding of how determined, organized resistance and political repression are intimately intertwined remains a current and relevant problem. While the particular actors and repressive agencies have shifted as the tumultuous time of the Sixties fades into the ever expanding past; there are in the contradictions, methodologies, and challenges, certain things that stand as universal. In that regard, this is a book more about the present and the future than the past.

Aaron Leonard
September 2014

Introduction

The Way From San Jose

Guerrilla-like we hide our giant hate,
Take refuge in a silence, forest dark.
We light another cigarette and wait;
Hold back the arrow though we see the mark.
Will we know when to answer to alarm?
Will we remember how to lift an arm?
— Frustration, Leibel Bergman, 1962.[2]

It is felt that the magnitude of the threat by RCP and its front groups to accomplish its aims or [sic] organizing and overthrowing the United States Government by force and violence warrants constant vigil so that we may fulfill our responsibilities for domestic security.
— Federal Bureau of Investigation, Internal Assessment, September, 1976.[3]

Richard Nixon liked crowds, so it was natural, having just finished speaking inside the San Jose Civic Center, that he bounded outside, eager to greet the people waiting for him. To get the proper adulation, he climbed atop his limousine and thrust his arms up in his trademark V for Victory gesture. Suddenly, to the shock and panic of those charged with protecting him, eggs, rocks, and bottles started coming at him. This was not the anticipated friendly campaign crowd, but rather an assembly of anti-war demonstrators, 3,000 strong, who had come out to denounce Nixon for his continued and escalating prosecution of the war in Vietnam. According to a witness, people were so incensed by Nixon's flashing what they interpreted as the peace sign that "several rocks just missed his head!"[4]

The small contingent of San Jose Police, about 60 in all, there to protect the President were suddenly in a panic. It was strictly touch and go as the demonstrators continued to harangue, encroach on his car, and toss missiles in his direction, while police scurried to get him in the car and off the scene. According to Police Chief Ray Blackmore, Nixon "was on the car for three or four minutes—maybe only two minutes—but it seemed to me like two years."[5]

The next day, papers across the country blazed with headlines about Nixon's harrowing encounter. The *Village Voice*—referring to Nixon's close call with a crowd in Venezuela in 1958—drew the global analogy: "President Nixon experienced a sort of domestic Caracas incident."[6] Columnist Mary McGrory opined, "[t]he President has been looking for trouble from the 'radical few,' and they have been spoiling for a showdown with him. Now it has happened."[7]

Though it drew people from all over northern California, the key organizer of the action was a relatively small, newly formed Maoist organization: the Revolutionary Union—who until recently called itself the Bay Area Revolutionary Union. Though not much heard of outside the Bay Area, the RU was already a high-profile target of the police and FBI. As someone on the scene that day later explained, the "cops certainly were concerned about the RU, they raided the houses of several San Jose RU members the night before the demo and kept folks locked up until the demonstration was over."[8] Though ultimately unsuccessful in preventing the RU's participation, the fact that authorities were able to act in such a modestly preemptive way was a result of the FBI's already having informants inside the group. One of those being Lawrence "Larry" Goff, who told the press after the demonstration that the Revolutionary Union, "had about 50 members in his chapter," in San Jose and "was the main organizer of the incident."[9] It was in this way, in October 1970, that the Maoists of the RU were introduced to the larger world.

* * *

The RU/RCP's roots lay in the most important struggles of the Sixties. Its leaders emerged from the anti-HUAC protests, the Free Speech Movement, the Peace and Freedom Party alliance with the Black Panthers, and the struggles in the final year of SDS, among other key events of the time. These individuals in turn formed an organization that went from a handful of youthful Maoists, former Communist Party USA members, and China-philes, to become a national organization with between 900-1100 cadre, and many thousand active supporters.[10]

By 1971, while groups such as the Black Panthers and Weathermen were in disarray, retreat, or disintegration, the Revolutionary Union, the forerunner of what would become the RCP, was ascendant. While some of the more sensational actions of these other groups had captured the imagination of portions of the youth population, it was the RU/RCP that was arguably the largest inheritor of Sixties radicalism. In September 1975, *Los Angeles Times* reporter Ellen Hume ran a profile on radicalism in the Seventies singling out the RU. The article's title was, "The 'heavy' radicals—The intellectual cadre plant ideas not bombs; terrorists considered least important to cause."[11] The message being that Sixties radicalism had not evaporated in 1969, but rather had passed its legacy on, in a more sophisticated form, into the next decade.

As the Seventies hit its stride, the RU/RCP became a fully articulated national organization. In 1976, the FBI penned an assessment. It was a report that was as direct, given the relative obscurity of the group, as it was surprising. According to the FBI, the RCP and the organizations most closely associated with it were, "A threat to the internal security of the United States of the first magnitude."[12]

In turn, the group was a priority focus of the Bureau. In researching this book, there is now an abundance of previously unreleased and unexplored FBI documents—including un-redacted informant files, unexamined COINTELPRO documents, and thousands of pages of previously unreleased FOIA material. From its very beginning, this grouping was the focus of the FBI and its contacts, including people like 'labor' columnist Victor Riesel, who wrote pieces specifically targeting the RU/RCP in direct collusion with the FBI. It was also the object of an array of covert operations and dirty tricks: setting organizations against each other, sending of poison pen letters, falsifying documents, fomenting splits, setting up phony communist collectives, using provocative comic books and cartoons, informant infiltration, deportation proceedings, planting of phone taps, putting microphones in apartments, break-ins to steal membership lists, and more.

Amid the shifting terrain of the crisis-wracked Seventies, these newly minted Maoists sent cadre to factories to immerse themselves in major US industry. In a few short years, they had an established presence in the steel plants across the US, the mines of West Virginia, auto plants in Detroit, meatpacking centers of Tacoma, Chicago, Milwaukee, and dozens of other greater and lesser industries. They were at the heart of militant labor struggles, particularly in the wildcat strike movement in the West Virginia coalfields. Along with this, they inspired and led dozens of chapters of the university based Attica Brigade/Revolutionary Student Brigade. They politically led controversially—Vietnam Veterans Against the War, and were a critical force behind the highly influential, US-China Peoples Friendship Association.

In the wake of the death of Mao Zedong and the corresponding turn in China from a socialist toward a market economy, a major schism took place. The group broke into two pieces, one later merging with other organizations, the other continuing on in name, but as a much different organization, with a significant diminishment in membership and influence.

The story of the Revolutionary Union/Revolutionary Communist Party is an essential piece of Sixties and Seventies history. It is a narrative in opposition to the standing mythology that all who became radicalized in that time quickly returned to the mainstream or spent the ensuing years dealing with the consequences of having attempted direct "blows against the empire." It is also, consequentially, the story of the Draconian repressiveness of the FBI—undertaking one of its biggest projects of the period. In short, it is a large piece of Sixties and Seventies history that needs to be put into place.

Chapter 1

Foundation

I do everything I can to merit the respect of my children and I don't think I could get that kind of respect by cooperating in any way with [the] history, purposes, and many of the crimes committed by this committee.

— Leibel Bergman testifying to the US House of Representatives, Committee on Un-American Activities (HUAC), San Francisco, 1960.[13]

There were several people at the University of California interested in forming an organization to aid victims of United States aggression [in] Vietnam. We felt that this was the least we could do in terms of making protest against what our Government was doing to the people of Vietnam and in order to show the American people and people across the world that all Americans do not, that the American people do not back this Government's vicious, criminal war in Vietnam.

— Steve Hamilton, testimony in front of the House Un-American Activities Committee, August 1966.[14]

In 1968, revolutionary communism appeared to be dead as an organized force in the US. Of course, there were an assortment of communist organizations in existence; there was the old Communist Party USA (CPUSA), which had long ago abandoned even the pretense of a revolutionary strategy. There was also an array of splinter groups, fragments of fragments of quasi-religious sects broken off from larger organizations—in the manner of Joan Didion's essay, *Comrade Laski, C.P.U.S.A. (M.-L.).*[15] There were a number of Trotskyist groups, such as the Socialist Workers Party and the International Socialists, but for all their ambitions, they were constrained by the fact that their politics had never achieved practical political power. And there was the anomaly of the Progressive Labor Party, a grouping with roots in the CPUSA, that seemed to embrace revolutionary Maoism but by 1968, was heading in another direction.

Much of the writing about the Sixties seizes on this state of affairs to then dismiss or ignore any role of revolutionary communists in that transformative era. Just as the popular mythology of the McCarthy era is today one of government authorities "seeking reds hiding under the bed," i.e., jumping at shadows, so too the dominant Sixties narrative is one of a delusional J. Edgar Hoover, chasing a largely non-existent communist subversion. That the state of the communist movement in the US was fractured and in disarray in 1968, however, did not mean there were no revolutionary communists, or that new ones were not emerging, quickly. Given the historic role such communists played in many important struggles of twentieth-century America—regardless of what one thinks of that ideology—this was no small matter. It was the communists who usually first arrived at the point of controversy and militant opposition, if not outright resistance. In this, they stood out for their catalyzing effect of moving the goal posts of protest and dissent in more radical directions.

Though they had no corresponding party, the most radical elements of the old Communist Party *did* exist, and indeed had been set free from the constraints of their former organization. At the same time, the student movement was engendering—often in concert with these older leftists—a new generation of Marxist-Leninists, more radical than the generation that had preceded them. Many of these militant radicals, who were turning to Maoism, saw armed revolution as their immediate objective in the not far-off future; the threshold to cross before attempting socialism in the US. It can be debated how realistic this was, but these young Maoists *were* serious about forging a doctrine for revolution, with all that involved—the exaggerated posturing that pervaded certain quarters in this period does not erase this basic fact.

While this phenomenon has been overlooked and ignored by too many writers and historians, this was not so on the part of the state authorities who gave a great deal of attention to such forces, even in their incubating incarnations. From their standpoint, they had a legal predicate and an official obligation to "pay some attention," and attention they paid. But they did more than that. They responded proactively in order to undermine, fragmentize, and neutralize such forces—systematically breaking laws they were ostensibly sworn to uphold in the process, all in a feverish rush to get ahead of such organization. For them, this was not an abstraction or the product of delusional thinking, but at least in potential, an existential threat.

To understand where this came from; including how the anti-communist consensus in US society seems to have lost much of its power in the late Sixties, and in turn brought forward a new wave of communists, chief among them the Revolutionary Union, it will help to start with a look at the key individuals at the heart of the formation of the RU—individuals who embraced this ideology either as renaissance or revelation, all swimming in the roiling waters of 1960s America.

Leibel Bergman

Any story of the RU/RCP must necessarily start with its organizational and political architect, Leibel Bergman. Bergman was born in Grand Forks, North Dakota in 1915, of pious roots—descended from "an unbroken line of Hebrew high priests and rabbinical scholars."[16] By any measure, he was highly intelligent. He attended the University of North Dakota, where he earned a degree in mathematics at the age of 19, then went on to work as a Chief Statistician of the North Dakota State Planning Board. Along the way he joined the Communist Party, though it is unclear precisely when, though the FBI says it was in 1937.[17]

During the late 1930s, Bergman traveled throughout the Midwest and East Coast as a party member, organizing packing house and other workers, and advocating for communism. When the Second World War broke out, he joined the US military, consistent with the CPUSA's position of defending the Soviet Union and defeating Hitler's Germany. His actual military service was directed at the chief focus of the United States, Japan. He served five years in the US Army, primarily as an Army-Air Force navigator.[18]

After the war Bergman settled in San Francisco where he worked for many years in a drop forge factory, was a Party union organizer, and published a militant newsletter called *The Scriber*. In the 1950s, he and other comrades were put on trial by the national leadership of the Communist Party, reprimanded for pushing forward too fast, and several were expelled. Although Bergman was not expelled, the incident was a foretaste of a larger break.[19]

Bergman's relationship with the Party would ultimately end over the matter of how to view Josef Stalin—the precipitating event being Nikita Khrushchev's 1956 speech criticizing Stalin. Khrushchev—who had been a loyal party functionary throughout Stalin's rule—denounced Stalin for the purges in the late 1930s and the "Cult of Personality" built around him.[20] He went on to advocate a more conciliatory and non-revolutionary view of realizing a communist future. For those who had stuck with the Communist Party, through the famines during collectivization, the show trials and the Great Purge of 1937-38, the alliance with Hitler's Germany in the wake of the Molotov-Ribbentrop Pact, this was too much to bear. Attacking Stalin pushed the limits of the rationalizations that had kept people loyal to this communism. How they fell out in this was untidy, some continuing despite the CPUSA's latest line shift, others decisively breaking with it, but not with its overall legacy. Others would become staunch anti-communists.

The changes in Soviet policy and doctrine would also lead, by the early 1960s, to a major schism between the Soviet and Chinese Communists. The reason for the split is a matter still being excavated by historians. On the surface, the Chinese accused the Soviets of revisionism and accommodation with imperialism. However, the nationalism and ambitions of both countries, to say nothing of larger geopolitical concerns, were huge consequential factors.[21] Regardless, the split was earth shifting. These two countries had born the brunt of human casualties in World War II—the Soviets beating back the bloodiest foreign invasion in human history, while the Chinese Communists played a critical role in the defeat of the Japanese, before defeating their former wartime ally the US-backed Guomindang. The alliance between the two socialist countries after the War was a huge fly in the ointment of plans to "organize the economic resources of the world so as to make possible a return to the system of free enterprise in every country"[22] that was envisioned by the United States. As a result, the US resorted to a policy of "containing" communism, a euphemistic expression for brandishing their superior nuclear power and the implicit threat of its use, as a Damocles sword over any who challenged their interests. In this respect, China, under the leadership of Mao Zedong, in many ways, offered a more formidable challenge to the US than the Soviet Union. The following from 1956 gives a sense of why:

> Now U.S. imperialism is quite powerful, but in reality it isn't. It is very weak politically because it is divorced from the masses of the people and is disliked by everybody and by the American people too. In appearance it is very powerful but in reality it is nothing to be afraid of, it is a paper tiger. Outwardly a tiger, it is made of paper, unable to withstand the wind and the rain. I believe the United States is nothing but a paper tiger.[23]

Leaving aside Mao's elements of hyperbole, the audacious tone was in marked contrast to that of the more accommodating and bureaucratic Soviets. For a time in the 1960s and early 1970s, Communist China would be seen by many in search of such things as a potential alternative to the capitalism of which the US was now the chief representative.

The changing definitions of Marxism-Leninism by the Soviets and Chinese in the period after Stalin's death would also lead to a split of communists internationally—including the exit of a good number of the more radically inclined who were still in the CPUSA. Among them was Leibel Bergman, who would write a long paper critical of Khruschev's speech at the 20th Party Congress, and who was inclining more toward the Chinese position.[24]

It was against this backdrop that Bergman, in 1960, was summoned before the House Committee on Un-American Activities (HUAC). The Committee was collecting information on the Communist Party's Northern California District. Bergman's testimony was non-cooperative and defiant:

> Mr. Willis. I order and direct you to answer the question.
> (The witness conferred with his counsel.)
> Mr. Bergman. After that explanation, I still fail to see pertinency. I want to remind the committee that I am here against my will. I do not sympathize with this committee.
> Mr. Willis. You said that before.[25]

Bergman's testimony came at a point when a certain section of the left and progressive movement was pushing back against the Red Scares and the witch hunts of HUAC. Organized defiance was the order of the day for these hearings, with union leaders, Communist Party members, and students—infused with the activist sensibility of the civil rights movement—mobilized to oppose the hearings. Bergman's testimony occurred on May 13,

1960, the day of the now famous "HUAC riot"— "riot" more precisely being the police measures against the crowd of largely student protestors. Many of those students, who came from UC Berkeley, were violently ejected from the hearing by police using water hoses and billy-clubs.[26] That event, in turn, would become a foretaste of the political activism that would soon convulse California, especially its campuses.

While HUAC was poking around into the old Communist Party's influence, Bergman himself was moving on. On leaving the CPUSA, he had become a founding member of the Maoist-inclined Progressive Labor Party, (which had started out as the Progressive Labor Movement in 1963).[27] However, he quickly became disenchanted. "He found its leadership style flamboyant and publicity seeking, rather than concentrating on the quiet class analysis and careful, long-term working class organizing in key locales that he and others advocated."[28]

In this period, his wife Anne—herself a communist whom he had married while in the military—contracted multiple myelomas, a form of bone cancer. In 1963, she died at the age of 47. It was also in this period, unbeknownst to Bergman, that he was being considered for prosecution under the Smith Act, a law that made it illegal to advocate the overthrow of the US Government, as seen in FBI's David Ryan's testimony:

> Q. And to your knowledge was any prosecution under the Smith Act ever brought against Mr. Bergman as a result of that consideration?
> A. I don't believe the indictment was filed. Part of the reason being that Bergman wasn't around.[29]

Unfortunately for the US Government, he had left the country in July 1965, having made a fateful trip with his two sons to live in China. He went ostensibly to teach English, as what the Chinese called a "foreign expert," but he also went to learn about the

Chinese revolutionary experience. It was in China that he met the African-American activist Victoria "Vicki" Garvin. Garvin, herself a former Communist Party member,[30] was an important figure in the African-American community of the day. Among other things she had helped coordinate the historic 1964 tour of Africa by Malcolm X.[31] Bergman and Garvin fell in love and were married in China in a Red Guard ceremony in 1966. In 1967, he returned to the US—Garvin would follow a few years later. With him, he brought not only decades of experience in organizing and in sparring with the forces of domestic repression, but also firsthand experience in the dizzying events underway in China.

Leibel Bergman with Chinese friends in the People's Republic in the mid-Sixties. Also in the picture is Vicki Garvin, longtime African-American activists and Bergman's wife. Courtesy of Miranda Bergman and Lincoln Bergman, for the Victoria Garvin estate.

The San Francisco he returned to, however, was not the one he left. In Berkeley, the respectful and peaceful protest in support of civil rights had transformed into such things as the confrontational Free Speech Movement. In Oakland, which bordered the UC California college enclave, a new organization called the Black Panther Party for Self Defense had been created. It was quickly having an electrifying effect among Black people who had hit the limits of non-violent protest. Finally, the movement against the Vietnam War was fully underway, embraced by students and liberal intelligentsia throughout northern California, including at Stanford University.

With this, the FBI, which had been watching Bergman for

decades, was continuing to keep a close eye. Writing some years later, they would accurately point out that the "history of the RU in many ways has paralleled the movements of Leibel Bergman." They then, however, proceeded to map out a conspiratorial scheme that seems a mix of fact and fantasy—with the exact lines blurred:

> In July 1965, Bergman traveled to Peking, China and did not return to the United States from Communist China until August 1967. Upon his return to the United States, Bergman told select individuals that his reason for returning to the U.S. was that he had promised his friends (Chinese) that he would do a job for them. He stated the struggle between the U.S. imperialists and China would continue for many years and because of the struggle it must be recognized it is necessary for us to make plans for the future 20 to 30 years from now. Because of this, Bergman stated a youth cadre must be selected, trained and held in reserve for utilization by China in 20 to 30 years.[32]

According to the FBI, Bergman felt "this cadre must be selected from the most promising youth in the U.S." It then offered, without corresponding evidence, "[t]he selected youth would be trained in China and would not necessarily be those who are best known in the left wing world."[33] In this estimation, the Chinese and Bergman, would be puppet masters behind the emerging radical generation. It makes for an intriguing narrative, one containing elements of both truth and absurdity. In the end, it missed the more overarching reality. What was taking place in the Sixties was shaping individuals and transforming them in ways that no one had any control over. The young radicals Bergman would meet and begin working with are a case in point.

Steve Hamilton

Steve Hamilton, unlike Leibel Bergman, did not have a

particularly religious pedigree, yet his initial life-inclination was to follow a spiritual path. As things developed, that did not work out so well.

Hamilton was born in 1944 in the Watts neighborhood of Los Angeles. His father had worked on an assembly line at General Motors, a job that led to his contracting lead poisoning, the fallout of which led to his spending ten years in Camarillo State Mental Hospital in Ventura County, where he endured among other things, shock treatments.[34] The younger Hamilton's mother supported the family by working at a Firestone tire factory.

When Hamilton graduated high school, he won an American Baptist Church scholarship to Wheaton College, an evangelical school in Illinois. He attended Wheaton from 1962-1963,[35] but decided it was not for him. In 1963, he made the fateful decision to transfer to the University of California at Berkeley, where he matriculated as a history major.

His enrollment in Berkeley coincided with the initiation of the Free Speech Movement. In September 1964, the University administration, citing rules that only allowed the Republican and Democratic Parties to solicit on campus, announced it would strictly enforce a ban on all other activity. What ensued was a resistance that would send shock waves across the country. At Berkeley—and soon most every major campus in the US—the acquiescent, pliant, post-war anti-communist apathy was soon shattered. For the remainder of the academic year, sit-ins, protests, and mass arrests ensued. In a defining moment of the Free Speech struggle, Mario Savio stood before students assembled in Sproul Plaza on December 3, 1964, and told the crowd

> [t]here is a time when the operation of the machine becomes so odious, makes you so sick at heart, that you can't take part; you can't even passively take part, and you've got to put your bodies upon the gears and upon the wheels, upon the levers,

> upon all the apparatus, and you've got to make it stop.[36]

Hamilton was one of those who entered Sproul Hall after Savio's speech, where hundreds of other students began a sit-in in protest of UC policies. He, along with 800 others, were arrested. Hamilton himself was later found guilty of trespass and resisting arrest.[37]

In the wake of the Free Speech Movement, Hamilton became part of the Maoist-inclined Progressive Labor Party. This, in turn, put him under the direct scrutiny of the FBI, who opened a file on him in April of that year. In it, they recommended he be added to their Security Index. This was a list of people to be closely monitored by the Bureau and literally, rounded up in case of a national emergency—a kind of preventative detention *cum* concentration-camp construct, that was a mainstay of the Bureau in the Hoover years.[38] (Three years later Hamilton, by then a member of the RU's Regional Executive Committee, had his ADEX status upgraded to Level II.)[39] Hamilton as an anti-war student associated with a communist organization was a threat to be closely monitored, as can be seen in the following:

> Subject registered with Dean of Students Office, University of California (UC) Berkeley, California, for the fall of 1965 as president of the May 2 Movement and president of the Medical Aid for Vietnam Committee.[40]

Here one sees not only the FBI scrutiny but also the apparent cooperation of University authorities. This was only the beginning of the attention given to Hamilton.

As a result of his activity, UC Berkeley dismissed Hamilton in 1966—ostensibly for manning an unauthorized literature table.[41] That, however, was not the end of his troubles. In August 1966, Hamilton along with Jerry Rubin of the Vietnam Day Committee (VDC), George Ewart and Stephen Cherkos, of the PLP and the VDC, Stephen Smale, a math professor from UC Berkeley and part of the VDC, Stewart McRae and Anatole Anton of the Stanford anti-war movement, and Windy Smith, part of the VDC and DuBois club,[42] were all subpoenaed by the US House of Un-American Activities Committee looking into "Assistance to Enemies of U.S. in Times of Undeclared War."

The hearings were, in turn, an occasion for an early anti-war demonstration. Protestors outside the hearings demanded "Hands off the Antiwar Movement" and "Bring the Troops Home."[43] They were also accompanied by a statement of support, printed in the *New York Review of Books,* signed by prominent intellectuals such as Robert Lowell, Saul Bellow, Julian Bond and others.[44] For his part, the 22-year-old Hamilton's testimony was uncompromising, and insistent on making larger political points:

> Mr. Pool: Are you a member of the Progressive Labor Party?
> Mr. Hamilton: As I was starting to say before, because of my experiences with the regents of the University of California and with the local Oakland-Berkeley power structure and the university administration and their attempt to stop civil rights activity in the Berkeley area, Berkeley students, and because, you know, of my experience with the war, with looking at the war in Vietnam and seeing that this is not a war which is in any sense in the interests of the American people, you know, I tried to figure out whose interest this war is [in]; and it became very clear to me that it was in the interests of the corporation bosses who make the profits from this war.[45]

This was duly noted in his FBI file—which contained the full transcript of his testimony along with the notation "Testimony set forth revealing HAMILTON's attitude and testimony and expulsion from hearing."[46]

Despite the arrests, surveillance, and subpoenas, Hamilton's commitment and determination only increased. By late 1966 he had left the PLP and become active in Students for a Democratic Society—at a time when that group was turning more attention to anti-war work. Hamilton himself was consumed with how to take the anti-Vietnam War effort to a more effective level.[47] As historian Michael Foley points out, Hamilton along with Lennie Heller, "independently arrived at the same idea for a draft resistance movement," in what would come to be called "The Resistance."[48] One result would be a national Stop the Draft Week in October 1967. As part of the week, Hamilton sent a telegram to California Governor Ronald Reagan, reflecting the level of resolve and frustration that was beginning to characterize the overall anti-war movement: "Debate has accomplished nothing; the war must be stopped." This was not idle talk, as his note made clear: "We plan to shut down the Oakland Induction Center."[49] In the course of the protest that took place, hundreds, including Hamilton, were arrested.

In the wake of the protest, he and six others, who would come to be known as the Oakland 7, were singled out for prosecution. They included Jeff Segal, a former anti-draft coordinator for SDS, Mike Smith who had worked in the Free Speech Movement and with the Student Nonviolent Coordinating Committee (SNCC) in the South, Terry Cannon, also an organizer for SNCC and who also helped found the influential Bay Area newspaper *The Movement*, Frank Bardacke, who taught political science and was an activist in the Berkeley radical community (and would join the RU for a brief time), Bob Mandel who had worked with SNCC for two summers, and Reese Erlich, of the Peace and Freedom Party.[50] In aggregate they were a cross-section of the anti-war movement (though pointedly all-male), many with roots in the struggle of the civil rights movements. The specific charges brought by the Alameda County district attorney's office against the Seven claimed they had conspired "to induce others to commit the misdemeanor of trespass" along with

Six members of the anti-war "Oakland Seven." From l-r, Steve Hamilton, Bob Mandel, Reese Erlich, Terry Cannon, Frank Bardacke, Mike Smith. (Jeff Segal not pictured.) Courtesy of ©Baron Wollman

interfering with police.[51] The *New York Review of Books* noted the Orwellian irony: "Under a California Statute, conspiracy to commit a misdemeanor is a felony."[52] The Seven were eventually acquitted, but remained in the sights of the ruling authorities.

As for Hamilton, the more he engaged in this work, the more strongly he advocated that the movement get beyond a moral call to do the right thing. His aim became one of raising a revolutionary movement with a corresponding mass base that could fundamentally change things.

> [Hamilton] wrote a blistering column in *New Left Notes* [SDS's newspaper] in which he condemned what he saw as middle-class elitism at work in the Resistance, "I don't think moral witness on our part can have any concrete effect on those who cannot afford to make a moral witness... No revolution is built on bad conscience, but on the organizations of those who are exploited.[53]

Such statements were exemplary of the fact that by 1968, Hamilton had gone well past the confines of militant student activist, and was by then embarking on a new project, the creation of a new revolutionary organization. To that end, he, along with a fellow Berkeley student, Bob Avakian, and one other person, moved to Richmond, California to undertake efforts to organize the working class. The formation of the Bay

Area Revolutionary Union would follow soon after.[54]

Bob Avakian

To the degree the RU and its successor the RCP are known today, it is closely linked with the person of Bob Avakian. Of all the original key members, he was the youngest, arguably the most unyielding, and in the end the most tenacious in holding to the dogma of the group that would continue on. While others under discussion here have their own particular association with the historical moment known as the Sixties, it is Avakian who exemplifies a critical link between the Revolutionary Union and what was then the most radical organization of its day, the Black Panther Party.

Robert Bruce Avakian was born on March 7, 1943, in Washington, DC. He came from a middle class family. His father Spurgeon "Sparky" Avakian, was the son of Armenian immigrants, an Alameda County Superior Court judge, and a strong advocate of racial equality.[55] His mother Ruth, had an English background, and worked raising the family.[56]

The younger Avakian attended Berkeley High and graduated in 1961. In the fall of that year, he entered UC Berkeley as an English major. Due to a kidney disease his undergraduate time was disrupted, but he was in school during the critical period of the Free Speech Movement, where he was arrested at the Sproul sit-in, along with Steve Hamilton and hundreds of others.[57] Avakian was also an early activist against the war in Vietnam and was part of the Vietnam Day Committee.

In contrast to Hamilton, Avakian's political radicalism appears to have come on more slowly. For example, when the VDC's office was bombed in 1966 and a subsequent demonstration turned into a confrontation with the police, Avakian's more restrained position was noted in the press. As one report explained he "was sharply critical of the VDC for failing to tell participants in the demonstration Tuesday night of the possibility of a confrontation with police."[58] Such positions, however, were wildly in play as others, more radical, exerted influence on him.

This can be seen in his working for *Ramparts* magazine—which began in 1966. *Ramparts* writer, Robert Scheer, in particular had a big influence, "a positive one in radicalizing me," as he recounted.[59] *Ramparts* had started out modestly enough as a Catholic literary quarterly in 1962. By the mid-1960s, however, it had become a major voice in the emerging anti-war, Black power, and wider radical movement. It was *Ramparts* that was responsible for early exposures of the CIA's covert work in support of the South Vietnamese government.[60] Also, during the peak of US involvement in Vietnam, it ran the highly provocative cover of a Green Beret, Donald Duncan—a story Avakian contributed to—in full uniform, with the title "I Quit."[61]

Ramparts also had on staff Eldridge Cleaver, who was able to gain parole due to the magazine's assistance. Cleaver too would have a major impact on Avakian. Avakian tells the story of seeing a poster of Mao in Eldridge's apartment and asking him why he had it, to which Cleaver reportedly replied "Because Mao Zedong is the baddest motherfucker on planet earth;"[62] a comment consistent with Cleaver's outsize personality and corresponding bravado.

It was in this period that Avakian continued to work the mechanisms of the system for the changes he felt were needed. In 1967 he was a candidate running for Berkeley City Council, as part of the Community for New Politics. Though he ultimately lost, he garnered 10,499 votes. During the campaign, his slate posted two campaign billboards with a pointedly anti-war message. The billboard company (ADVAN), in turn censored the billboards, eliminating the line that read "Oppose the War," and leaving only the lines "Create Jobs and Lower Taxes." Avakian with the support of the campaign, got up on a ladder for a photo op, and repainted the anti-war slogan onto the billboard.[63] This marked a final foray on his part into electoral politics. According to Avakian, Cleaver told him, "Well, now you've got that all out of your system. You had your fling with reform politics. So now you should get all the way into revolution."[64] While Cleaver himself never hewed too close to his own advice, for Avakian it was a turning point.

The organization Cleaver was part of, the Black Panther Party for Self Defense, was formed in 1966 by two students from Merritt College in Oakland, Huey Newton and Bobby Seale. Their organization concentrated a militant, even revolutionary, Black Nationalism, unlike anything ever before seen in the US. The first point in their Ten-Point program stated explicitly "We want freedom. We want the power to determine the destiny of our black and oppressed communities."[65] This was not bluster; the Panthers' inaugural activity was to conduct armed patrols of the police in Oakland. This immediately brought them into direct conflict with law enforcement, but also brought them national notoriety.

While their Ten-Point program was relatively straightforward, their overall politics were never as clear; embracing everything from Marxism Black Nationalism to anarchism, though revolutionary Black Nationalism would appear to have been their unifying theme. As a result, the organization could have Newton, whose thinking went through numerous shifts, proclaim the group "dialectical-materialist,"[66] but also put forward something he called "intercommunalism," claiming "[s]ocialism will not exist anywhere in the world, because for socialism to exist, a socialist state must exist, and since states do not exist, how can socialism exist?"[67] Or it could have Seale state: "Now one might say he's a socialist or a communist, on the contrary, I'm a Black man trying to get some of the wealth out of this country."[68] As for Cleaver, his views tended more toward action and all that implied. Politically, he would come to extol the virtues of the lumpen (or criminal) class in opposition to the working class, a highly fraught strategy, to say the least.[69] Such a range of thinking created a situation where the *idea* of the Panthers—disciplined organization, the notion of a larger revolutionary unity, and a willingness to be theoretical—was far more powerful than the *actual ideas* of the Panthers. This was to prove critical in limiting their ability to go forward.

Given his ties with Cleaver and others in the BPP, Avakian would be at the center of the coalition of the Peace and Freedom Party and the Black Panther Party. Building off of Robert Scheer's 1966 campaign in which he nearly unseated Rep. Jeffrey Cohelan in a Democratic Congressional Primary as part of the "New Politics" movement,[70] the Peace and Freedom Movement (later the Peace and Freedom Party) was founded in 1967. Both Avakian and Steve Hamilton had joined the group, along with a number of former Free Speech Movement people, with Avakian becoming statewide coordinator.[71] It was Avakian and Scheer, along with others, that approached the BPP about forming a coalition, which was announced on December 22, 1967.[72] In fact when the alliance between the two was announced, it was Bobby Seale and Bob Avakian who spoke on behalf of the two groups at a rally at Hunter's Point.[73]

The PFP would undertake a number of highly charged and wildly contradictory political campaigns. Among them was running Eldridge Cleaver for President in 1968.[74] The thinking behind the campaign being an apparent combination of symbolic protest, revolutionary proclamation, Black Nationalist manifesto, and a means to popularize the Free Huey! campaign—Newton having been jailed for the killing of an Oakland police officer.[75] The confused campaign was embodied in the statement of a BPP member: "If we win we'll paint the White House black and then burn it down."[76] It was through this alliance with the PFP that Cleaver in particular sought to broaden the support base for the Panthers. This at a time when they were, though not even two years old as an organization, besieged by state authorities on several fronts.

Avakian went on to be a featured speaker at the famous Free Huey! rally held on Newton's birthday in February 1968, sharing the podium with H. Rap Brown (later Jamil Abdullah Al-Amin), Stokely Carmichael (later Kwame Ture), Ron Dellums and others.[77] At the rally he was welcomingly introduced by Cleaver as someone who, "[h]as worked diligently on behalf of brother Huey." Avakian's speech captured the reverence many white radicals had for the Panthers:

> I wouldn't be on this stage. We wouldn't have been at the Oakland Induction Center if it weren't for the courageous people, the masses of people, and the leaders who led and participated in the Black liberation struggle all these years, because they're the ones that taught us. They're the ones that forced us to face the reality of what America and this system was all about. And in this sense, we say, not only are black people a vanguard but they are an inspiration. We don't expect them to liberate us, we have to do that for ourselves. But they have inspired us to begin that struggle to end this imperialist, racist, colonial system once and for all.[78]

On the one hand, Avakian's statement reflected a great deal of deference to the Panthers' place as the vanguard of the revolutionary movement within the US. There is, however, in the closing a suggestion of something new emerging, which would eventually go much farther politically than the Panthers were ever able to go.

Avakian's association with the BPP was also leading to his own type of trouble—albeit modest in comparison. He spent 30 days in jail in the fall of 1968 after getting caught by police with an American flag that had been taken down by demonstrators during the opening of Newton's murder trial in Oakland [79]—

Avakian being on hand after having helped form the Black Panthers' Legal Defense Team.[80]

While Avakian's influences were wide ranging—from *Ramparts* to the Panthers—his critical relationship is the one he developed with Leibel Bergman. As he later wrote, Bergman was "someone who would play a very important role in developing me fully into a communist and in lending more ideological clarity to our efforts in forming the organization that we did form in the Bay Area late in 1968."[81] In this, whatever Avakian had been before then, would soon be overshadowed by what was to come.

Bruce Franklin

The last in this list of key figures is H. Bruce Franklin, a critical character in the overall ferment on California's campuses and the larger intellectual community. Franklin was also a bridge generationally between Bergman's counter-intuitive embodiment of the "greatest generation" and that of the youthful Hamilton and Avakian. He was a "grown-up" of sorts, but not an elder.

Howard Bruce Franklin was born in the Flatlands section of Brooklyn in 1934. His father started work as a runner on Wall Street and went on to hold various white-collar positions. He also was active in the local Democratic club, but according to his son, as "the only Jew in the neighborhood, he couldn't get elected dogcatcher."[82] His mother had attended Cooper Union in New York to train as a commercial artist and later worked for a time as an advertising artist, then as a clerk in the art and supply departments at the Abraham and Strauss department store.

The younger Franklin attended a Friends Quaker school in downtown Brooklyn. Despite the liberal inclinations of the Quakers, the fact that he was growing up at the height of the Cold War, for him, meant being staunchly anti-communist. He describes how one of his earliest jobs was at the Mayfair

Photofinishing Company in Brooklyn, where the owners were secret Communist party members. Their subterfuge was something that rankled him, though he did credit them to an extent: "No one who belonged to the Communist Party during the Korean War and the witch-hunts of the forties and fifties can be considered a complete coward."[83]

In 1951, he began attending Amherst College where he also enrolled in the Air Force ROTC, this to ensure that he wouldn't be sent as a foot soldier to fight in Korea. He studied English at Amherst, graduating in 1955, which in turn set his future academic course. Before continuing, he was compelled to active duty in the Air Force, first with a refueling squadron and later as a squadron intelligence officer. This experience was part of a certain awakening. As he notes, one of his "main jobs in SAC intelligence was to prevent anybody in the United States from knowing that the Soviet Union had no ability whatsoever to deliver a nuclear attack." This, as he explained, was due to their inadequate bomber fleet and inability to refuel planes on long distance missions.[84] Such insights cut against the reigning Cold-War philosophy of Mutual Assured Destruction that determined the US's nuclear policy—and the concomitant arms build-up. It was this knowledge that was accruing as Franklin returned to academia at the threshold of the Sixties.

In 1961, he completed his doctoral dissertation on Herman Melville at Stanford, at which point he was offered an assistant professorship—the first time in 33 years a graduate student had been asked to stay on. He remained until 1964, when he moved east to take on a teaching position at Johns Hopkins. He then went back to Stanford in 1965, where he was granted tenure in 1970, a position that would be short lived. It was at Stanford that Franklin found himself at "ground zero" of the University military-research complex's peculiar concentration in California.

Stanford had been late to the game in garnering large defense contracts. During the Second World War, its main role was as a training center for officer candidates and military specialists. In 1946, it attempted a change in direction, with then Stanford President, Donald Tresidder creating the quasi-autonomous entity, the Stanford Research Institute. The role of SRI was to contract and carry out defense research.[85] With increasing US involvement in Vietnam, Stanford would thus find itself at the vortex of US weapons production. Its military research, in turn, would figure prominently in the radicalism that sprung to life on that campus.

Bruce Franklin's entry into radicalism began when he and his wife Jane joined the Stanford Committee for Peace in Vietnam, a group oriented toward "militant non-violent protest." Franklin tells of how in January 1966, a worker from United Technology Center secretly let him and a few other anti-war activists know that UTC had just received a subcontract from Dow Chemical to develop an improved type of napalm, Napalm-B, a thicker gel that would "ignite more reliably, burn more intensely and stick more tenaciously."[86] He describes how he was part of a delegation who went to nearby Sunnyvale, where UTC had its main office. They confronted Barnett Adelman, a scientist and President of the company, who candidly justified the production of the weapon to them:

> "After all," he said, "our business has suffered a great deal from the [Vietnam] war. Our main work is in long-range liquid-fueled space rockets. These have no immediate military application. The Defense Department has taken away all our funds for these rockets because of Vietnam. So we have no choice. Even if we didn't want to work on napalm, we would have to, just to stay in business."[87]

It was in the context of confronting head-on the limits, indeed the futility, in reasoning with those fully enmeshed in such a military-economic paradigm—that Franklin edged toward more and more radicalism.

It was at this time that he also began to look past the more scholarly writers he was steeped in and studied Marx, Engels, and Mao Zedong. It was also in this period, in the wake of the napalm campaign of 1966, that the Franklins traveled to France. In a later profile in the *New York Times Magazine,* he explains the impact of the trip:

> Paris, was the critical experience. "Jane and I became Marxist-Leninists while we were in France ... We'd been quite active in the anti-war movement here, provided some leadership and so on and by the time we left the United States in 1966 we considered ourselves revolutionaries, but we didn't really know what that meant and we hadn't studied any theory to speak of. During that year in France we had the opportunity to work with young people from many countries, including Vietnam, who had quite an influence on us. When we came back to this country we were Marxist-Leninists and we saw the need for a revolutionary force in the United States."[88]

It was in the larger Palo Alto area that Franklin would work with the Peace and Freedom Party, as well as the student-oriented Peninsula Red Guard, based in Palo Alto and comprised of the Franklins and Stanford students.[89] But it was on the Stanford campus that he made his biggest mark. Young, charismatic, and intellectually sophisticated, Franklin would exert a great influence on those around him. He would be responsible for radicalizing no small number of the undergraduate and graduate students he came in contact with.

While the four people profiled above were critical figures in the formation of the RU, with Bergman standing out, it would be wrong to limit the group's creation and early evolution to them. Here one would need to add Jane Franklin and Mary Lou Greenberg of the Peninsula Red Guard, Vern Bown, an ex-CPUSA member and old comrade of Bergman, as well as Larry

Harris, Gertrude Alexander, Barry Greenberg, and a number of others who never publicly identified themselves as part of the RU. It was these forces that would form the Bay Area Revolutionary Union in the spring of 1968.

From the beginning the group had a strong percentage of women cadre and leaders. It was the case, however, that this was a mainly white group—though it would draw in some Latino and Asian-American cadres. The absence of Black and other non-white ethnicities, in the early days especially, appears to have to do with a strategy of the new organization seeing itself, at some point, merging with other organizations, rather than recruiting such forces directly into their organization.[90]

Regardless, what those who initiated the RU held in common was a connection to critical events of the time: the Cultural Revolution, the defiance of HUAC, early and aggressive anti-Vietnam War work, and bold support for the Black Panther Party. Individually and collectively, they represented a strain of radicalism that was more disciplined, more theoretical, and more strategically inclined, than most of the other trends in operation at the time.

It was in this way that they entered the pivotal year of 1969, about to confront the collapse of the most important student organization in existence in the US.

Chapter 2

SDS, the RU, and the FBI

The program of SDS has evolved from civil rights struggles to an anti-Vietnam War stance to an advocacy of a militant anti-imperialist position. China, Vietnam, and Cuba are regarded as the leaders of worldwide struggles against United States imperialism whereas the Soviet Union is held to be revisionist and also imperialist.
— FBI Internal assessment of SDS, April 1970.[91]

The [RU] emerged as a hard political pole within the National Collective [of SDS] which represented the logical conclusion of at least one aspect of the collectives' own internal development. The entire National Collective came very rapidly to reflect the political influence of the RU.
— Jack Weinberg and Jack Gerson, Independent Socialists, September 1969.[92]

The standard script of Students for a Democratic Society reads something like this: it arose in the early Sixties full of youthful idealism, got down to the hard work of joining with the civil rights movement, transitioned to anti-war activism, became increasingly radical, then self-immolated in sectarian squabbling with a small, hard core of Weathermen going off into a brief foray of infantile terrorism, while the rest of the organization faded away. It is a tight narrative, with a strong beginning, middle, and end. There is, however, a problem. Two huge pieces are left out: the emergence of the Revolutionary Union and its critical influence within the grouping, and the FBI's aggressive and elaborate efforts to destroy the organization.

SDS's roots lay in the turn of the century America Student

League for Industrial Democracy, the student arm of the League for Industrial Democracy.[93] This was an organization, mainly focused on socialist and progressive education, founded by Norman Thomas, Upton Sinclair, Jack London, and other socialists of the turn of the century United States.[94] In 1962, in an effort to broaden its appeal, it changed its name to Students for a Democratic Society and its founding conference issued a statement named after its place of authorship: Port Huron, Michigan. Drafted during a particularly dark period of the Cold War, it was a broad call for students to form a "New Left" and step into activism:

> As students for a democratic society, we are committed to stimulating this kind of social movement, this kind of vision and program on campus and community across the country. If we appear to seek the unattainable, it has been said, then let it be known that we do so to avoid the unimaginable.[95]

The grouping—formed amid the civil rights movement, revolution in Cuba, and the US intervention in Vietnam—caught fire in the imagination of the US student population. By 1969 it had a membership estimated at around 100,000, (though dues-paying members were considerably fewer), and was active on over 300 campuses across the United States.[96]

The group's rise coincided with an unraveling of significant parts of the post-war US social order. Perhaps most significantly, the war in Vietnam, which did not follow the path of earlier efforts, i.e., the unquestioned victory of World War II, or even the stalemate of Korea. Worse, a relatively quiescent population was replaced by a determined anti-draft and anti-war movement, an opposition that largely caught authorities off-guard.

The result was that local and national police—in an effort to stop the impact of determined opposition—responded to SDS and like-minded organizations with oftentimes brutal repression. This, in turn, had a catalyzing effect in generating more determined opposition. The following incident, from what is largely agreed was a police riot during the Chicago Democratic Convention of 1968, is illustrative:

> The defiant kids began a slow, orderly retreat back up Michigan Avenue. They did not run. They did not panic. They did not fight back. As they fell back they helped pick up fallen comrades who were beaten or gassed. Suddenly, a plainclothesman dressed as a soldier moved out of the shadows and knocked one kid down with an overhand punch. The kid squatted on the pavement of Michigan Avenue, tried to cover his face, while Chicago plainclothesmen punched him with savage accuracy. Thud, thud, thud. Blotches of blood spread over the kid's face.[97]

Such incidents, repeated scores of times, along with a more profound loss of faith in the legitimacy of the ruling structures, had a radicalizing effect. By 1969, most of the leading elements of the organization were no longer looking to have their voices heard; "Part of the way with LBJ" gave way to "Ho Ho Ho Chi Minh! NLF is gonna win!" They turned to revolutionary ideology—including revolutionary communism in myriad forms and interpretations—as both a philosophy and a course of action.[98] Given its prestige and size, all of this was concentrated within SDS, but it was not tidy. Many different groups were represented, all pushing to a degree their own agendas. There were Trotskyists, representatives of the old Communist Party, anarchists, and there were Maoists. The Maoists, in particular, broke two ways: The Progressive Labor Party, which had formed from remnants of the old CPUSA, and there was the RU, which was brand new.

The Progressive Labor Party

Though they likely did not know it at the time, the Progressive

Labor Party (PLP) which had assumed the mantle of the key Maoist organization of the US, was moving quickly to the margins. It had recently adopted contrary positions around two of the biggest fault line questions of the day. First, the PLP now put forward a position condemning Black Nationalism, which was at odds with the one animating an entire generation of Black youth and their large body of radical white supporters. Second, the PLP denounced the National Liberation Front, which was leading the armed struggle in South Vietnam and served as inspiration for many revolutionaries in the US.

Regarding the first point, the PLP self-critically assessed that:

> [b]ecause we supported the resistance of nationalists like the Muslims and Robert Williams, we viewed them as generally good. We failed to understand that nationalism is reactionary, and that this is the main aspect.[99]

Regarding the second point, the PLP reasoned that:

> [w]e regard this as a principled concession to nationalism because it is within the framework of a serious fight against imperialism. If not for the anti-imperialist struggle there would be no reason for the concession.[100]

These were bewildering concepts to the politically uninitiated and unacceptable ones to certain of the politically sophisticated. To make matters worse, the PLP, working in SDS as the Worker Student Alliance, then tried to take over organizational control of SDS.[101]

Enter the Revolutionary Union

There is no public record of the moment when the RU formed. According to Bob Avakian:

> At a certain point, we decided that we needed to form some kind of an organized group, not just in Richmond but more broadly in the Bay Area. So I wrote up a position paper, which we took around to other people, and it became the basis of discussion and the basis of unity, more or less, for drawing people together—originally just a handful—to form some kind of a group.[102]

Steve Hamilton puts the inspiration down to "the grandiosity created by a few too many beers one evening."[103] More substantially, he describes the RU emerging from the more radical elements of the Peace and Freedom Party, anti-war activists, "a few ex-PL people and even a few ex-CP and ex-PL veterans, and student groups from the peninsula."[104]

While both explanations offer a broad strokes picture, neither answers basic questions about the group's origins. But while Avakian and Hamilton's recollections are vague, there is another account available that is quite precise: the detailed reports of an informant sitting on the then newly formed RU Executive Committee.

Present at the Creation

In the early years of the Revolutionary Union, Steve Hamilton was seen by the FBI as a key leader. He was watched, his whereabouts constantly noted, and the Bureau sent any records relevant to his RU activity to his file. Amid his personal profile, notes on public meetings he attended, and the constant updating of his address, is a cache of files: reports from an informant, who reported on Hamilton and other RU members as it was just beginning. In it, we have an extensive and detailed record—albeit one through the eyes of an informant—of the very beginnings of the RU.

The earliest entries of the file begin with an initial report based on a discussion with the informant and J. Edgar Hoover's instructions on how to proceed with what he clearly saw as an early coup against the RU. Initially, Hoover proceeded with caution:

> Because the information set forth above comes from a single source and because the revolutionary character of this organization has not been corroborated by any other source to date, no report is being submitted at this time.[105]

His temperance, however, was backed up by aggressiveness: "It is realized that we must endeavor to penetrate this organization with other live member sources"—something it appears they were rather quickly able to do.[106]

Along with due diligence on the informer, Hoover put a high priority on the RU:

> [B]ecause of the radical and covert character of the RU, and its reported fanatical nature, the organization and its membership must be afforded expeditious investigation and all pertinent information must be disseminated to the Department and interested agencies at an early date.[107]

With an eye toward the future, he stipulated that "characterizations of the RU and Bergman, [be] prepared, in a manner to protect informants, sensitive techniques, and operations."[108] Further, he decreed that RU members "be promptly recommended for inclusion, where not already added," to the Security Index.[109] A few months later, he was more explicit:

> [I]n each instance you should endeavor to determine if the member has engaged in firearms or guerrilla warfare training. If such is the case, the individual's Security Index card must be tabbed indicating Priority I (six month reporting) under the provisions of the Priority Apprehension Program. Also,

> Security Index cards of individuals identified as members of the RU Area Executive Committee and who, as such, are considered members of the Executive Committee of the three RU Locals, should be tabbed for Priority I.[110]

The informant was quickly giving the Bureau insight into the group:

> He [the informant] advised that the group was formed around January or February 1968, and he feels that Leibel Bergman and Bruce Franklin, a professor at Stanford University, were instrumental in organizing this group. He stated that he started attending when it had its third meeting, which was held in April 1968.[111]

All deference to Franklin aside, the informant also says "Bergman appears to be the dominating factor." As he explains, Bergman wants to see "the Revolutionary Union grow into where it becomes a national organization which would be synonymous with the Chinese Communist Party in the United States."[112] Bergman's vision was apparently well grounded. Even at this early point, the group had at least 20 members in three different collectives. As the reports accumulated, it became obvious the group was growing rapidly.[113]

Those informant reports, often running to several single-space typed documents, outline everyone in attendance at meetings, their physical descriptions personal details, and the positions they take in political debates. They also note which particular collective each belongs to, e.g., San Francisco, East Bay (Richmond) and Palo Alto (Stanford).

All this was in the context in which the RU had hit the ground running. Though it was not yet public, throughout 1968 it was working aggressively to set up left-wing caucuses within the Peace and Freedom Party as a way of extending its organizational reach. The Executive Committee meetings are replete with discussion of the PFP, and the need "to strengthen the radical caucus and to extend its control over PFP."[114] Some of the results were quite good; for example Bruce Franklin reported "that the Palo Alto group controls Peace and Freedom movement of San Mateo County and PFM of Santa Clara County."[115] This work would continue for at least the next year and appears to have been a crucial source of early RU expansion.

The aim, however, was not simply to strengthen the shoots of their group, but to challenge their main nemesis in Maoism:

> He [the informant] pointed out that Progressive Labor Party apparently has taken over the Peace and Freedom Party and that LEIBEL BERGMAN does not like to see PL take over as he thinks this is a dangerous group opposed in some manner to his philosophy of Maoism. [SOURCE] stated that the caucus, which he mentioned, comprised of individuals connected with the Revolutionary Union is actually the largest small group within the Peace and Freedom Party and up until this point no one realizes this factor except naturally the BERGMAN group."[116]

The RU was thus apparently contending with the PLP from the start, and saw it as an obstacle to its own expansion.

Ironically, one of the big issues occupying the early group is the matter of when to "surface," and who should be an open representative versus who should conceal their membership. Bergman seemed most vociferous in holding back, arguing "consistently against the RU surfacing and indicated that he would favor a minimum surfacing via publications with a few public spokesmen." Regardless, even if the group did surface, he would "stay in the background."[117] For his part Avakian was feeling the strain of already having been in the public eye:

> [Avakian] mentioned the feeling of being alone out in front with no one behind him. He said that STEVE HAMILTON and BRUCE FRANKLIN had also mentioned that they had this feeling, and FRANKLIN specifically mentioned that he had received threats of death and injury. AVAKIAN stated that the three of them felt cut off and isolated from the rest of the RU membership.[118]

The informant notes "the pressure of publicity" was affecting public members who "have had no particular experience with this kind of pressure and do not know how to cope with it."[119] The irony is that the FBI already had a comprehensive knowledge of the *entire* organization. As for Bergman being in the background, he was arguably the most surveilled of anyone. His covert status afforded him only the anonymity of not being known publicly as part of the RU, while the FBI related to him as its driving force. This situation would not improve anytime soon. By September 1968, the record suggests a second informant in the RU:

> The investigation of the RU members must be conducted in a most circumspect manner to protect the identities of SF 3169-S, SF 3117-S as well as the highly sensitive Leibel Bergman intelligence investigation.[120]

Indeed, by early 1969, FBI records show reports on the Executive Committee sourcing two different informants.[121] Regardless, the RU *would* surface and insert itself aggressively in the SDS controversy.

The RU Meets SDS

The RU formation, such as it was, came at a pivotal time in SDS, and they were not standing aside. SDS was a critical organization for any grouping that wanted to fuse with the most radical elements among students and attempt to win them to Maoism. As a result, when SDS held its National Council meeting in Austin, in March 1969, the RU sent Bob Avakian, Barry Greenberg, Marv Treiger and one other RU person, to try to influence things.[122] It was in Austin that the conflicts within SDS were becoming sharply drawn. Factions were emerging, which would rip the group first into two, then three parts: the doctrinaire Marxist-Leninists of the PLP, the (soon to be) terrorist faction of the Weathermen and the new Maoists, of which RU would become the largest.

The RU, by all accounts, was well received at the meeting. They would later report that SDS leaders read the RU "Statement of Principles" and agreed with it: they "read the anti-brainwash paper [see below] and that this was an excellent paper and should be published without any changes."[123] Even rival groups vying for influence acknowledged the RU's success. For example, the Socialist Workers Party wrote that "[a]t the 1969 Austin SDS national council meeting; one could hear Bob Avakian give an eloquent polemic in defense of black nationalism and the right of self-determination against PL's anti nationalist economism."[124] The Independent Socialist Club put things more directly, "The handful of RU members who showed up at the Austin meeting for all intents and purposes walked away with it."[125]

The Red Papers

It was on the heels of Austin that the RU published *The Red Papers,* an outline of a strategy for revolution that was clarifying for certain radical minded youth. As one former SDS member (who joined a post-split SDS formation), and who would later join the RU, wrote, "I received *The Red Papers* in my first year of college—I read it until I had memorized it and the pages were worn."[126] It would become arguably the organization's most influential document.

The Red Papers opened with a major statement titled "Against the brainwash ... a defense of Marxism-Leninism." It put forward the position that "[w]hatever we accomplish against the monster, from inside the monster, creates favorable conditions for all the struggles of the world's peoples."[127] This was in contrast to other trends that applauded national liberation as a certain end in itself. Instead, *The Red Papers* suggested a mutually reinforcing relationship between national liberation worldwide and revolutionary struggle within the US proper. In this it took a cue from Mao Zedong: "The evil system of colonialism and imperialism arose and throve with the enslavement of Negroes and the trade in Negroes, and it will surely come to its end with the complete emancipation of the Black People."[128]

Among the more striking and controversial elements of the document was its defense of Soviet leader Josef Stalin (he is pictured on the cover along with Marx, Engels, Lenin and Mao):

> Stalin is the bridge between Lenin and Mao theoretically, practically, and organizationally. The successes of the world proletarian and people's movements are a part of our history, and they are our successes, they are the successes of our class. The mistakes and errors must also be ours. We admit the mistakes of our class and its leaders, try to correct them or, failing that, try to avoid repeating them. But we will not disassociate ourselves from these errors in the opportunist manner of many bourgeois intellectuals and armchair "revolutionaries."[129]

This was mandatory for any group wanting to align itself with Maoism. The schism between the Soviet Union and China had as one of its critical components whether or not to uphold Stalin.

As we will see in the next chapter, the RU's position on Stalin came with its own internal controversy, however, by the time of the publication of *The Red Papers,* their position was set. The

RU defense was big on assertion, but thin on substance. They protested that "we are still being bombarded with bourgeois propaganda about how ruthless Stalin was in suppressing opposition"[130]—as if the ruthlessness, leaving aside anti-communist exaggeration, was somehow a fabrication.[131] Such defensiveness would characterize the group's approach to this matter throughout its existence.

That taken into account, to the rare degree *The Red Papers* and the RU are mentioned in SDS's history it is usually in relation to the defense of Stalin exclusively. A telling example is Kirkpatrick Sale's seminal *SDS*. That book's acknowledgement of the *The Red Papers* comes in a footnote: "SDS leaders and publications quoted Mao and Lenin and Ho Chi Minh more regularly than Jenminh Jih Pao [China's *People's Daily*], and a few of them even sought to say a few good words for Stalin."[132] Such an account overlooked that the RU and others in the new communist movement were upholding Stalin in the way the Chinese Communists were, that is, critically. This comes through in Mao's own off-the-record statements, which reveal, in their own problematic way, an acknowledgement and rejection of the violently repressive methods of Stalin. For example, Mao wrote, "[Stalin] didn't deal with this matter well at all. He had two aspects. On the one hand, he eliminated genuine counter-revolutionaries; this aspect was correct. On the other hand, he wrongly killed a large number of people, important people, such as delegates to the Party Congress."[133] Mao and the Chinese Communist Party had a highly contentious relationship with Stalin and the Soviet Union that only grew more complex when Stalin's Soviet successors—with their own agenda—attacked Stalin.[134] The Chinese position on Stalin was highly problematic, but it was not a simple-minded embrace. This was true for China and true for the emerging Revolutionary Union.

The FBI Works the Contradictions

One of the most striking things included in *The Red Papers* was the sharp polemic against the Progressive Labor Party. It took on what it felt were its most egregious positions. First, decrying their lack of support for the National Liberation Front:

> PL has been openly attacking the government of the Democratic Republic of Vietnam and its leader Ho Chi Minh with particular venom, along with the National Liberation Front of South Vietnam, as betrayers of the Vietnamese people.[135]

The Red Papers also criticized the PLP's position on the Black Panther Party, taking particular issue with a PLP article headlined "Panther Shot, Nationalism Guilty." The RU was incensed

> [t]hat these revolutionary nationalists, these heroic martyrs of the revolution, were responsible for their own death. It really makes your skin crawl.[136]

From the RU's standpoint, the PLP polemic in *The Red Papers* was a matter of fulfilling a political obligation; people drawn in or confused by the PLP needed to be set straight and this was critical for the revolutionary movement to advance. There was also the unacknowledged factor, having to do with their own legitimation; there could not be two pre-eminent pro-Chinese, Maoists organizations in the US. Leibel Bergman, according to an informant, appears to have been particularly passionate in this:

> Leibel Bergman was vehement in his condemnation of PL and argued strongly that it is necessary to attack and destroy PL as being the party in the United States, which represents the Chinese Communist line.[137]

What the RU does not seem to have fully appreciated was how fraught this was in regard to the Bureau's efforts. The informant on the Executive Committee was keeping the FBI apprised of the RU's work in regard to the PLP as the following from March, 1969 shows:

> It was felt that this is a most important paper in that it is necessary to expose the PLP as not following the true line of the Chinese Communist. It was the feeling of those preparing this paper that the PLP must be destroyed and that the RU must take a leading role in this effort.[138]

There had, according to the informant, been some dissension on this matter, but by April, "[a]ll of the members of the Executive Committee are now strong for the attack on PLP."[139]

With such intelligence the Bureau was in a strong position to drive even more of a wedge between the PLP and the RU.

One of the things they suggested was to "forward copies [of *The Red Papers*] to one or several of the addresses listed in the PLP publication," with the aim of "additional disruption."[140] The Bureau, however, did not limit themselves to working with the documents at hand. A few days before the June 1969 SDS national meeting, an article appeared in the *Chicago Tribune* that claimed an "underground communist organization is expected to vie for control of the radical Students for a Democratic Society." The group in question, according to the paper, had emerged after a "year of secret organizing" in the Bay Area, its name the "Revolutionary Union."[141] The article reported that the RU "used its booklet to criticize the Progressive Labor Party which has been accused by SDS leaders of receiving operating funds from the Chinese communist government." The piece also explained that the PLP would attempt to take over the organization. It ended with the prescient caution: "Federal and local authorities who have been watching closely the activities of

SDS believe that the factional infighting at the convention could lead to the formation of new revolutionary student groups."[142]

This article was not mainly the result of journalist Ronald Koziol's legwork. The ghostwriter, if you will, was the FBI, which internally would take direct credit. As they wrote in a memo, the piece "resulted from the Bureau authorized contact by SAC M.W. JOHNSON with REDACTED *Chicago Tribune*," i.e. the Bureau gave the reporter the information. They also bragged that it "[a]ggravated a tense situation and helped create the confrontation that split SDS."[143] In another memo, they express satisfaction in limiting the RU's influence: "Mike Klonsky, national secretary, SDS, was extremely irate with the article particularly with the association of REDACTED [likely Avakian] with the Revolutionary Union." The same memo noted that, "there was widespread discontent among the delegates to the SDS national convention with [the] politics of the RU and their attempt to 'take over SDS.'"[144] All in all the Bureau appears to have measured this a success.

It is worthy of a side note here that the Bureau was not just working the RU–PLP rift in targeting the RU at this early date. They toyed with using the RU's own writings against them:

> We can slightly alter RU publications, have them reproduced by the laboratory and distributed in great numbers to Marxist, Black militants, SDS, left publications, etc. throughout the country. By altering the publications, we can distort the political line of the RU, in fact, turn it into a revisionist line in a subtle manner.[145]

This missive is particularly striking in its level of sophistication, and as we will see, telling of the advanced level of *political warfare* that would be leveled at the RU.

COINTELPRO

Such ideas were categorized by the Bureau as a "counterintelligence" initiative; this being the FBI's euphemistic terms for efforts that deliberately, secretly, and often illegally, worked to undermine organizations beyond the monitoring, infiltrating, and accumulating of legal evidence.

They specifically had a campaign to destroy the New Left, which included SDS. While groups such as the PLP and the RU were not themselves "New Left" (they were communists),[146] their interaction with forces in that realm greatly blurred the boundaries. In this respect, it is worth looking at the Bureau's statement on their COINTELPRO-New Left. It is rare for a smoking gun to appear in history so fully articulated, but in the case of the FBI's New Left Counterintelligence Program (COINTELPRO) there is little left to the imagination:

> Our Nation is undergoing an era of disruption and violence caused to a large extent by various individuals generally connected with the New Left. Some of these activists urge revolution in America and call for the defeat of the United States in Vietnam. They continually and falsely allege police brutality and do not hesitate to utilize unlawful acts to further their so-called causes. The New Left has on many occasions viciously and scurrilously attacked the Director and the Bureau in an attempt to hamper our investigation of it and to drive us off the college campuses. With this in mind, it is our recommendation that a new Counterintelligence Program be designed to neutralize the New Left and the Key Activists.[147]

The same document explained in direct terms that the purpose of the program was to "expose, disrupt and otherwise neutralize the activists of this group and persons connected with it."[148] This was a broad and open-ended internal mandate for the Bureau to go after anyone they categorized as part of this trend, activity that was on full display as SDS met for what would be its last convention.

Chicago June 1969

The final convention of SDS, as indicated above, was ultimately a fractious event in which no one walked away a winner. Ostensibly, the defining struggle was between the PLP and the rest of SDS. The PLP was organized and politically savvy on how to operate and had the foresight to send enough members to the Chicago meeting to vote themselves into power through use of a simple majority. Against them was a coalition known as the Revolutionary Youth Movement (RYM), an entity that itself would split into two: RYM I and RYM II.

The RYM as a whole supported the National Liberation Front in Vietnam and the Black Panther Party in the US. However, on matters of strategy for revolution in the US—and this was a critical thing SDS leadership was arguing over in those days the RYM was split. This would eventually manifest itself as two irreconcilable strategies for revolution, but that would come later.

The national leadership of SDS, who came to be identified as the RYM I faction, would go on to become the Weathermen. Most histories of SDS disproportionately focus on that grouping—though it was neither the largest part of SDS nor its longest lasting part. Reading their initiating manifesto, "You Don't Need a Weatherman, today one sees an absence of a more thought-out strategy. In their view, "[w]inning state power in the US will occur as a result of US military forces overextending themselves around the world and being defeated piecemeal."[149] The basis for revolution would mainly come from without. In the meantime, they argued that

> [t]he most important task for us toward making the revolution, and the work our collectives should engage in, is the creation of a mass revolutionary movement, without

> which a clandestine revolutionary party will be impossible. A revolutionary mass movement is different from the traditional revisionist mass base of "sympathizers." Rather it is akin to the Red Guard in China, based on the full participation and involvement of masses of people in the practice of making revolution; a movement with a full willingness to participate in the violent and illegal struggle.[150]

They saw themselves as a "division of the International Liberation Army," which would contribute "to the many Vietnams which will dismember and dispose of US imperialism."[151] The approach today reads as a rather confusing work in progress—vague statements about a mass revolutionary movement counterposed with a clandestine party and revolutionary violence.

For its part, according to the Executive Committee informant, the RU early on thought there might be a basis to work with this grouping:

> In discussing the Weatherman Group (DOHRN group), the general feeling on the part of the Executive Committee was that this group is pretty good and that the RU should work with them. The RU felt that many of the proposals as to the new organization of SDS set forth by the Weatherman Group in New Left Notes were actually the same proposals that had been made by the RU.[152]

The actions and strategy the Weathermen adopted, however, would soon render any possibility of the two working together as moot.

In contrast to this, the RYMI II faction, which included the RU in a more traditional Marxist way, advocated the role of the working class. The RU view particularly, saw their role as more than a support apparatus—even an armed one—for revolutionary forces internationally and oppressed populations within the US. Theirs was a view that there was preparatory work for revolution to be done among this base and other sections of society, short of immediate violent revolutionary action. Particularly for the RU, there was an element of waiting in the Maoist sense of "gaining time to increase [the] capacity to resist while hastening or awaiting changes in the international situation and the internal collapse of the enemy, in order to be able to launch a strategic counter-offensive."[153] Contained here was a long-term view, less anxious and more strategic. This helps explain why the scholar David Barber, who sharply disagreed with the RU, wrote that, "*The Red Papers* nevertheless represented the future of where most of RYM II were headed."[154]

With such contending philosophies as a backdrop, the convention got underway. Things did not proceed smoothly, breaking down in chanting and counter-chanting over issues high and low. For its part, the Revolutionary Union scored an initial victory before things fully fell apart. The RU, despite opposition, was able to successfully put forward as a speaker a student and US citizen who had been part of the Chinese Cultural Revolution.[155] Chris Milton was an 18-year-old RU member who had lived in China while in high school and had joined a group of Red Guards in Beijing when the Cultural Revolution broke out in 1966. While his convention speech is not available, a 1969 interview where he talked about his experience at a Beijing high school is. In it he describes firsthand exchanges between conservative and radical forces and the mix of embrace and co-option taking place. When asked by the *Movement* newspaper why the Chinese Communist Party allowed such things, he said that the Central Committee

> was prepared to trust the masses, even though they made mistakes. If you got millions of people moving you know damn well that somebody is gonna fuck up sometimes. The issue was to try to politicize people through their own

> experience. Allow people to experiment. This was especially important to the youth.[156]

Leaving aside the deeper complexities and controversies about the Cultural Revolution, what comes through in Milton's description is a sense of youth revolt going on in the world's most populous country. The RU and others aligned with the RYM II forces were looking for something on which to base a revolutionary model and saw many attractive things in the radicalism on display in China. It was in this context that Milton's experience was welcomed by a certain element at the convention.

For the Bureau—which was monitoring the convention closely—Milton's experience was a matter of communist propaganda, albeit one they had to admit was striking a chord. According to a post-convention report by the Bureau, after an introduction by RU member Marvin Treiger, Milton gave a presentation

> laced with pro-Chinese communist sentiment, and in closing he called on all present to show solidarity with the CPC by displaying red bands. All except PLP forces responded to this request. The PLP objected on the grounds that MILTON was attempting to upstage PLP forces.[157]

The level of friction increased with the appearance of two Black Panther Party representatives who took the opportunity to talk about "pussy power"[158]—a reference to Eldridge Cleaver's convoluted view of women's empowerment. In a 1968 speech at Stanford, Cleaver referred to women as having "the power to bring a squeaking halt to a lot of things that are going on and we call that, pussy power."[159] The Panther statement at the SDS convention created no small amount of chagrin and anxiety, leading those in the house to chant and catcall against its blatant sexism.

The ultimate split at the convention, however, came after a Black Panther Party representative issued a challenge saying SDS "will be judged by the company it keeps and the effectiveness with which it deals with factions within its organization."[160] This, in turn, led to the whole of the RYM walking out and resolving to expel the PLP. For all intents and purpose this was the end of SDS.

The RU's final imprint on the convention came after he PLP and the RYM had become factions meeting separately. The RYM grouping set about electing their leadership. The Revolutionary Union fielded Bob Avakian for National Secretary, along with Lyn Wells (not an RU person) as National Education Secretary. Avakian's ticket lost out to the national office's Mark Rudd and Bill Ayers (both of whom would become prominent Weathermen). Avakian was, however, elected to the National Interim Committee.[161] Pyrrhic as it would turn out to be, the Revolutionary Union—in sending only a token number to the convention, and not having been a sizable force in the group before then—had obtained a position at the center of the organization.

One final aspect of the split in SDS, that appears to have flown past most historians, is how particularly the FBI was involved in events. Not only did the FBI work to exacerbate divisions before the convention, they specifically advised their informants to vote a particular way: "[a]ll REDACTED informants were instructed to support the National Office faction in SDS against the PLP faction." The reason? "PLP control of SDS would transform a shapeless and fractionalized group into a militant and disciplined organization."[162]

They also had an estimation of the consequences:

> The convention did result in a split of the SDS with the result that PLP was required to form its own "rump" organization; the SDS as the mainstay of the New Left Movement is

> now seriously divided and, to this extent weakened; and the National Office fraction is gradually being forced into a position of militant extremism which hopefully will isolate it from other elements of the libertarian community and eventuate its complete discrediting in the eyes of the American public.[163]

From the Bureau's standpoint, it was better for SDS to come under National Office control, because the turn toward violence would make them easier to neutralize. This is a strikingly different read on the terrorist current that emerged in this period. The FBI apparently favored such things—because they were easier to destroy—over more entrenched political organization.

In the case of the Weathermen, this was more or less borne out. After the convention, in October 1969, the Weathermen organized what would be their last public protest. The Days of Rage was an action, that by most every account was a travesty. It was to have been a massive effort to "Bring the War Home." As one poster advertising the action proclaimed, "During the 1960s the American government was on trial for crimes against people of the world. We now find the government guilty and sentence it to death in the streets." The demonstrations included, among other things, several hundred Weathermen breaking windows and destroying other property in Chicago's wealthy Gold Coast section. It ended in a confrontation with thousands of police and a proportionately massive number of arrests.[164] It was an undertaking which Chicago Black Panther leader Fred Hampton described as "Custeristic." The Days of Rage would become emblematic of the perils of go-it-alone voluntarism (in the philosophical sense, that the will is fundamental in determining events). Specifically, it meant 290 arrests, most of which were for disorderly conduct, but included 25 charges of resisting arrest, several charges of aggravated battery, and one charge of attempted murder.[165]

As for the Progressive Labor Party/Worker Student Alliance, they took control of the name SDS, and had modest success in leading struggles against ROTC recruitment on campuses in Columbia and Berkeley at the beginning of the 1970s. Overall, however, they would become increasingly marginal.[166] Standing in opposition to the central issues animating politicized youth—the struggle in Vietnam and defense of the Black Panther Party in the face of increasingly violent confrontations with the authorities—had a limited appeal.

This was made worse by the Bureau, who continued to exacerbate divisions between the RU and the PLP, attempting to stress their relations—such as they were—with the Chinese:

> Because the RU and the PLP are in obvious competition both in the domestic political areas and in seeking support of the Chicoms [Chinese Communists], it would appear to be to the Bureau's advantage for the current dissension between the two organizations be accelerated.[167]

To that end, they suggested a scheme wherein their offices in Chicago, New York, and San Francisco would prepare a series of articles, under the name of "Will B. Outlaw"—the pen name of Bruce Franklin —"attacking the PLP." They further suggested these be circulated widely "including to Communist China." Noting "Franklin's style of writing could be readily reproduced as he has authored a number of articles in his own name."[168]

Such schemes aside, the collapse of SDS is an ugly moment that stands in Sixties history as a train wreck. The most prominent student organization confronting the Vietnam War and racial injustice was reduced to tatters; a critical instrument for meeting the challenges yet to come was no more. The Revolutionary Union, however, unlike the PLP and the Weathermen, had come through this experience with an expanded political prestige and the basis for organizational expansion. It would in short order become the very thing the Bureau had tried to thwart in opposing the PLP's takeover of SDS—a disciplined organization of militant domestic Maoists.

Chapter 3

Beyond the Student Movement

Mr. Avakian shouted at [Weatherman Howard] Machtinger: "If you can't understand that white workers are being screwed too, that they are oppressed by capitalism, before they are racists, that just shows your class origins. To which Machtinger replied, "that just shows your race origins."
— News report on the Weatherman War Council," December 1969.[169]

In Richmond we are looking toward a radical community organization made up of people working in local factories, the unemployed, and some local high school and junior college students. It will be organized on the basis of an open radical political perspective and posture, working class identity and with the dual purpose of "serving the people" (helping people with everyday problems), and getting across some political understanding to our people.
— "Serve the People, Learn From the People, Become One With the People." Steve Hamilton, *Movement,* January 1969.[170]

Having navigated the rift in SDS, the RU was entering deeply uncharted waters. At the core of much of the struggle in SDS was whether or not there was a base within the US working class for revolution, or if the main potential came from outside. The RU had a clear strategy in answer to this, and they would move forward at an accelerated pace to implement it.

In December 1969, Bob Avakian attended the Weatherman "War Council" in Flint, Michigan, where that grouping was in the process of deciding to go underground. At the meeting, as the above quote highlights, the conflict between two views was sharply drawn. Avakian's memoir doesn't discuss the Flint meeting but does recount a trip he made to New York that "may have been after the SDS convention," the purpose of which was to talk with some of the Weathermen about what was needed for the revolutionary movement. In Avakian's recollection, the trip was at the prompting of Leibel Bergman, who suggested "Why don't you go back there and make Marxist-Leninists out of these people?" As events unfolded, things had already moved beyond that, or as he wrote, "they were set on a certain course and nothing that I said was going to convince them or did convince them to turn to a different course."[171] The course he is referring to is what is popularly known as terrorism, the strategy of violence to advance political aims.

Bergman had been intent on trying to win over the more radical elements of SDS, however, he was mindful of the perils given the evolving strategy of those associated with this trend. This can be seen in the following court testimony, from the FBI's David Ryan:

> Bergman is a principled, dedicated Marxist-Leninist revolutionary for many, many years. He is dealing with some debutante-type revolutionaries, people he characterizes as unprincipled, people who are not working class.
>
> Bergman is concerned because of what he called "the unprincipled conduct" of these people. These people, he is concerned, will bring the wrath of the law down on his apparatus. They will do this during the period that he is most trying to consolidate his forces.
>
> He consistently avoids these types and is trying to search out those principled Weathermen people, those that will be subject to discipline.[172]

Ryan's testimony was focused on establishing Bergman as a dangerous Chinese Communist intelligence agent, but here he appears to acknowledge something about Bergman that he felt important. The Weather-people would garner a lot of media attention during their brief political life and even more in its aftermath. However, because of the nature of their strategy, they quickly found themselves a priority target of law enforcement and were on the defensive from the moment they began.

Meantime the RU continued to work within the remnants of SDS, sending Mary Lou Greenberg, Bob Avakian, Steve Hamilton, and Bruce Franklin to the RYM II convention in Atlanta at the end of November 1969. The RU appears to have played a pronounced role at the convention, with Franklin and Avakian—according to an informant—being prominent speakers at the event. For her part, Mary Lou Greenberg would unsuccessfully run for a spot on the RYM II steering committee.[173]

All RYM activity aside, the RU was mainly putting its energy into creating its own organization—though the politics they were adopting was taking them on their own problematic course. That course included no small amount of trying to recreate the model of the 1930s Communist Party, which Bergman, Vern Bown and Gertrude Alexander, among others, were steeped in. This was on display when Avakian spoke at the Black Panther National Revolutionary Conference for a United Front Against Fascism, in July 1969.

The conference appears to have come at a time when relations between Avakian and Eldridge Cleaver were chilled—which was emblematic of the changes going on within their now two distinct organizations. In the previous year, Avakian had been slotted to be Cleaver's "mother country campaign manager" for his Peace and Freedom Party Presidential bid, with his name even appearing on election promotional material.[174] By the fall of '68 things seem to have changed:

> BOB AVAKIAN, formerly very close to the BPP will not even speak to CLEAVER because CLEAVER did not accept PEGGY TERRY, suggested by the radical caucus, as his

running-mate.[175]

By the time of the Panther conference, things had gotten worse. According to the informant on the RU's Executive Committee, Bob Avakian and Marv Treiger had initially proposed "that the RU boycott the UFAF and denounce it as reactionary"[176] because of the growing influence of the Communist Party USA within the organization:

> During the discussion of the BPP, it was mentioned that two articles that were to have appeared in the BPP paper, "The Black Panther" concerning Communist China, Hsin Hua articles, were washed out by DAVID HILLIARD and the Panthers are not carrying any news of Red China. It was the general feeling that the revisionists (CP) are now strong in the Black Panthers.[177]

Bob Avakian speaking at the "Conference for a United Front Against Fascism." Oakland Auditorium July 19th, 1969. Courtesy of KPIX

In the end, Avakian did attend the conference, and his speech was widely applauded by many on the left. The 26-year-old Avakian's speech contained a fair amount of rhetorical jargon, ("the primary ideological content of American fascism is racist white supremacist genocide.")[178] but it also called up the imagery of the Thirties, "We're going to get the ILWU to stop scabbing on the Vietnamese people and stop loading munitions ships."[179] This workerist stance would soon come to characterize the emerging Revolutionary Union.

Richmond

The attempt to apply this worker-based model, amid the

shifting sands of the late Sixties, was most clearly on display in the RU's efforts in Richmond, California. At the end of 1967 Steve Hamilton, Bob Avakian, and one other area activist had moved to the relatively industrial area of Richmond. According to Hamilton, this was with a "generalized commitment and optimism in regard to 'integrating with the working class.'"[180] Initially, they focused on building ties in the community, particularly working with the young workers they were meeting and introducing them to projects undertaken by the Black Panther Party. They also worked with a local section of the Peace and Freedom Party around issues such as community control of police and fought for a militant perspective within an anti-poverty agency.[181] As Hamilton wrote at the time:

> The more actively political people today are student-intellectuals and a majority of these are from petty-bourgeois usually professional families. Many are appalled that the working class people, even its youth, have not learned the things about American society that they have learned in the last few years.[182]

Hamilton's piece appeared in the radical newspaper the *Movement*, which the San Francisco FBI called "the most influential mass newspaper of radical youth."[183]

The RU was also working with a youth group in Richmond, called the "Young Partisans,"[184] which "patterned its demands after those of the Black Panther Party," something Congress noted with sufficient concern."[185] With the formation of the Revolutionary Union, the Richmond collective worked with this group, issuing joint leaflets and doing other common work; some members of the group would end up joining the RU.[186] While the Young Partisans offered a certain receptive base, according to Hamilton, the workers they "met and the ties established in plants came to be considered more steady and reliable." In contrast, the youth were "less rooted, often unemployed." As Hamilton recalls, the Young Partisans "became the vehicle for a more adventurist [i.e., violent] approach," as can be seen in their own writing in which they proclaimed that "people, we find, are ready for STP — Serve the People. Stomp the Pig." And

> [t]he Young Partisans are part of a people's army—just part of the beginning. We understand that if we want to change this country we will have to move from one level to a higher level—from trashing to picking up the gun.[187]

This was a view consistent with the fairly wide appeal of the readiness to "get it on" among radical youth of the time—though it contained no small amount of posturing.

The Standard Oil Strike

The RU's effort to support a strike by the Oil, Chemical and Atomic Workers Union is exemplary of their path-breaking efforts in the working class. Here was a strike ostensibly about wages and other basic union demands but played out amid tepid union support and Standard Oil's strikebreaking effort of importing scab, non-union labor. It also took place amid a larger societal upsurge, the police rampage at the Democratic Convention the previous summer, a violent effort to break a strike at San Francisco State College demanding Third World Studies, and ongoing protests against the Vietnam War. When the Richmond strikers found themselves being beaten and maced by police on their picket lines, some made profound connections. One striker remarked:

> We believed what we read in the newspapers. Now we know what kind of coverage we have been getting from the press, and I think we should be finding out what's happening from the people actually involved and we should be supporting

> them, just like they have supported us.[188]

The fact that students, on four separate occasions, stepped up to support the strike seriously bolstered the effort, nearly shutting the giant refinery down and "introduced an aspect of uncertainty, which continually keeps the company off balance fearing for its refinery." It also questioned some of the deeply held assumptions about Black people and their confrontations with police. As one worker noted, "[l]ast time there was a riot in North Richmond I was afraid to come to work; next time I'll be right there in the riot."[189]

For their part, the RU was popularizing the experience and drawing out their own lessons:

> A strike, when it is not a token tactical ploy in 'labour-management relations', is in many ways like a miniature revolution. Struggle, instead of collaboration, is the order of the day. The old individualistic ways of solving, blunting, or avoiding contradictions and confrontations give way to collective ways of facing them and fighting.[190]

In this way, the RU saw themselves shaping a model of how to build a base among the working class; one that went beyond the constrained parameters of trade unionism, envisioning such work crossing a bridge toward a revolutionary movement.

In turn, the authorities watched this closely. The FBI's chief journalistic conduit in the Bay Area, Ed Montgomery, reported on a May 1969 SDS event held at New York University where Bob Avakian spoke about the RU role in the strike. According to Montgomery, "Avakian said they brought in 300 to 400 students who joined the picket lines" and "were able to politicize the strike."[191] Montgomery was doing more than reporting here—he was letting larger elements of the ruling structure in on something of concern. As we will learn, this would not be the last time he took on this role.

Confronting the Stanford War Machine

While working to shift its base toward the working class, the RU continued to be immersed in the upsurges roiling the campuses. In that respect, their work at Stanford University stands out. Depending on which side of the divide you were on, Stanford between 1968 and 1970 was either a place of exhilarating protest or, in the words of its former President Richard Lyman, "pretty much a descent into hell."[192] Unlike its Berkeley neighbor to the north, Stanford was not convulsed by political turmoil until later in the Sixties. However, its privileged and relatively isolated position would also be shattered. This was concentrated in the struggle against the military research being carried on by the Stanford Research Institute (SRI).

Stanford University Students protest invasion of Laos outside the Computation Center at Pine Hall, February 1971. Associate professor of English H. Bruce Franklin argues with a police Captain. Courtesy of Jose Mercado/Stanford News Service.

A seminal moment at Stanford came when a coalition of campus radicals and activists—including SDS and a group called the Peninsula Red Guard (many of whom would join the Revolutionary Union)—challenged the Stanford trustees in an open meeting. Lyman, who was Stanford's seventh president, and the man brought in to quell the out-of-control situation[193] on the campus, would later describe events:

> At a meeting in Memorial Auditorium in March 1969, a group of trustees appeared for the purpose of answering questions, hearing the demands and charges of the radicals, and responding to them. But trustees were totally unaccustomed to having to account for their motives, and they made a feeble showing. By the end of the meeting, the group Students for a Democratic Society (SDS), which was crumbling elsewhere in the country, was back in business at Stanford.[194]

The feeble showing Lyman refers to had to do with their admitting to things they ought not have publicly admitted to, as can be seen in the transcript, reprinted in the underground newspaper, the *Peninsula Observer*.

> [Student] Rupert: Seymour Hirsch, in what I understand is a definitive study called *Chemical and Biological Warfare* attributes the Newport, Indiana Chemical plant, which produces Sarin, a version of nerve gas, to your corporation; and further checking on that by David Ransom of the *Peninsula Observer* got a clarification and an affirmation from one of the public relations men in your office in San Jose. So either the book or your P.R. man is wrong, or in fact it's true.
> [Trustee, William Hewlett, of Hewlett-Packard]: I'm amazed by the accuracy and reliability of your sources, but I happened to check with the president of FMC [Corporation], whom I consider superior to your sources, and he says that they are

> *not* making nerve gas at the present time.
> Floor: Have they *ever* made nerve gas?
> Hewlett: The answer is yes. They were asked to build a plant, which they built and operated at the request of the government and they turned that plant over to the government about six months ago.[195]

Two of those at the center of the students forcing such an admission were David Ransom and *Observer* editor Barry Greenberg—then a Stanford graduate student—both of whom would become part of the RU. Also in the room challenging the trustees were two SDS members who would later become part of the RU, David Pugh and Bill Klingel, then undergraduates.

In the wake of that meeting on April 3, there was a mass meeting involving some 700 people that drew up demands that Stanford abandon classified research for the US government. This would be the beginning of what became known as the April 3rd Movement.[196] Six days later there was a sit-in/occupation at Stanford's Applied Electronics Laboratory (AEL), where

> [h]undreds of students [were] involved in small working committees. Up to 1000 attend[ed] general meetings, broadcast live over KZSU. Bobby Seale, Chairman of the Black Panther Party, [spoke] at AEL. After the Judicial Council [threatened] discipline, 1400 students sign[ed] a Solidarity Statement that they, too, are part of the occupation![197]

The occupation ended after the faculty promised "to end classified research."[198] Things, however, did not improve for university officials. The following year, in the spring of 1970

> [p]olice were summoned repeatedly to Stanford, and there were running battles between police and rock-throwing demonstrators. Substantial damage was done to university

> buildings. For a time, many buildings were blockaded and classes canceled, even when the students enrolled in them wanted to meet. The school year ended in chaos.[199]

Amid the radical forces of SDS and the Peninsula Red Guard was the critical character of English professor H. Bruce Franklin. Franklin served as a political mentor to these students, much to the chagrin of Lyman, who would recall being "put off by his summoning his regular classes to meet at the sites of demonstrations." In Lyman's estimate, this abused the rights of "his captive audience, who had enrolled to study Melville, after all, not Mao."[200]

As a result of all this, Franklin and others around the emerging RU were the focus of direct and covert attention by authorities. This can be seen in the case of one of the characters hanging around the Stanford scene at the time.

Tom Mosher was typical of a certain radical, always primed and ready for action. He was nicknamed "Crazy Tom" by some who came in contact with him because of his volatility. This can be witnessed in an incident in July 1969. Mosher had gone to a party at Franklin's house to celebrate the acquittal of several radicals who had been "charged with fomenting a street riot in downtown Palo Alto." Attending the party were not only the defendants, but three of the jurors who had voted to acquit them. The guests were talking, dancing, and drinking wine, when, "Mosher slapped a juror who was dancing with [his wife] Mary," at which point Bruce Franklin jumped in. According to Steve Weissman, a former Stanford student, "[a]fter the punch up, Franklin cooled to Mosher, telling his comrades not to trust the lunatic."[201]

As for Mosher, he claimed, "I may be crazy, but I'm not a pig."[202] His mental state aside, Mosher *was* working for federal law enforcement. As he would later testify in front of a US Senate Committee, he had been an FBI informant from June 1969 to May 1970.

> Mosher: Upon my return to the West Coast in 1968, I found the same sort of sentiment I experienced upon my return to the Chicago area from Cuba. At that point in the bay area numerous white groups had associated themselves with the Panthers and had begun taking their political lead from the Panthers.
>
> [Senate Investigator] Tarabochia: Would you care to elaborate on the names of the groups you remember?
>
> Mosher: Yes. The Bay Area Revolutionary Union, which subsequent to that period became a national Marxist Leninist organization, had in depth, ongoing relations with key members of the Black Panther Party.[203]

Mosher had a specific reputation as a provocateur, but as noted earlier, the FBI had early on infiltrated the RU's leading structure.

The FBI was also targeting specific individuals with dirty tricks. This can be seen in an effort aimed at RU member Chris Milton. On April 17, 1969, Milton went to the Oakland Induction Center after being ordered to appear for induction. At his appearance he was joined by the "Chris Milton Defense Committee," which included Bob Avakian and Barry Greenberg and other RU members and supporters. The FBI, in a memo relating to Milton's appointment, assessed that it was "[a]n excellent opportunity to discredit REDACTED within the RU"—the redaction most likely being Milton. What they proposed was to imply that Milton had been "blowing off his mouth to Army officials." The memo, from J. Edgar Hoover, suggested a note be drafted on "appropriate stationery" and sent to the RU's public address. It stipulated that this should be unsigned, but worded "to indicate it is written by a disgruntled serviceman at the Induction Center." The text of the anonymous letter reads:

> Friends
> If you're wondering why REDACTED has dodged induction, its [sic] because he has a big mouth. He is blabbing to the intelligence guys about a "dictatorship" in Peking, your Rev Union and guns and even the Panthers.
> I can't wait to get out but he wants on the payroll without uniform.[204]

This was a popular FBI method that was termed "snitch-jacketing," wherein the Bureau or their operatives would circulate rumors that a dedicated member of an organization was in some way working for the other side. In this way, the FBI was trying to cast suspicions and create an atmosphere of apprehension and mistrust, and were also trying to alienate certain members, drive them out of the organization, and/or provoke harm toward them.

What is striking is how quickly the Bureau started attacking the RU and got informants in place. While the complete scope of penetration in this early period is yet to be revealed, two agents who also early on penetrated the group are instructive.

The Goffs

Lawrence "Larry" Goff did not fit the profile of a typical Sixties radical, but then again before the Sixties who did? Born in Kalamazoo, Michigan in 1941, he was not a bookish type. After graduating high school, he joined the Navy as an enlisted man, where he served from 1959 to 1963. He then went to work as a machinist in Michigan and later as a pipe fitter in Texas. In late 1965, he became a missionary, and traveled with his wife, Betty Sue, to Mexico, Nicaragua, Costa Rica and Panama. Betty Sue had come out of Mississippi and her stepfather had been a career Navy man. In Panama, the Goffs lived for two years with an indigenous tribe, but in 1968 they came back to the US and settled in San Jose, California, with Larry becoming a minister for a Church of God congregation. He supplemented his income—to support their four children—as a machinist and a gunsmith. Goff and his wife would take on one other responsibility. In 1969, they began working as FBI informants in the Revolutionary Union.[205]

The story of the Goffs is well documented. It is known largely because in October 1971 they appeared before the US House of Representatives Committee on Internal Security (HISC), formerly the House Committee on Un-American Activities (HUAC), to testify on what they knew about the RU, where there they were greeted as "two patriotic citizens."[206] The combination of their testimony, the internal RU documents they put into the record (which were extensive), and the organizational methodologies they disclosed, was a stunning reveal.

The Goffs began their penetration of the RU in late 1969, before the organization had fully matured. Larry Goff made his way into the RU by working with an organization called the Radical Action Movement—which the RU also worked with—based at San Jose State College. "Mr. Goff feigned an interest in the programs and projects of RAM,"[207] and it was through this work and because of his working-class background—to say nothing of his military background—that he was able to obtain membership in the organization. Not only did he become an RU member in a relatively short period of time, he became chair of one of the two San Jose workers collectives and in turn a member of the RU local executive committee.[208] That same month he was selected to be on the security committee due to his experience with weapons, and since he had taken courses in police science at San Jose City College[209] (one of his tasks on the security committee being to prevent infiltration).[210] As a result of his skills as a machinist, he was also repairing weapons of RU members and passing along the serial numbers to the FBI.[211]

With his new status, Goff was able to in turn "recruit" his wife in July 1970.[212] A subsequent informant report, perhaps from Larry Goff himself, appears to recount the process:

> REDACTED requested collective authority to recruit his wife into the RU. REDACTED pointed out that while she is completely new to Marxism-Leninism and revolution, she is making progress under his direction and is reading the *Peking Review* every week. It was decided that REDACTED will recruit his wife and that she will initially attend meetings of the Workers Collective.[213]

Through their positions, the Goffs had access to a wide swath of the organization, its security protocols, its internal documents, and up to a point, its leadership structure. In hearings before Congress in June 1971, they were presented with name after name of alleged RU members to which they dutifully confirmed their membership. Further, as Larry Goff testified, "I attended one of the central committee meetings in which I met other parts of the organization from the East Coast, Chicago, Detroit and other RU collectives..."[214] In other words, he had access to the RU's top leadership.

Larry's testimony was also telling of the government's concern regarding radicals in the military—this in the context of the undeclared war in Vietnam not only going badly, but generating a good deal of opposition by those called on to fight the war:

> Mr. Ferry: Let me ask you a basic question. What is their [RU] policy toward the draft?
> Mr. Goff: Their policy toward the draft is to give counsel to those being drafted as far as RU members are concerned. If a person receives an induction notice—which we are familiar with because this happened while we were members of the organization—first of all they would determine this person's usefulness, would he be more useful in the Armed Forces or would he be more useful here.[215]

In other words, the RU was not only opposing the US's war

in Vietnam, they were keen to work within the military to undermine that effort. Larry recounts the decision-making process after a collective leader had been drafted:

> [A]nd the collective agreed 100 percent that he should go into the Armed Forces because of his usefulness, because he is an expert at causing—he was an expert in riots and demonstrations. I personally witnessed that he could control whole crowds of people to go over and trash a building or I mean break windows. They thought he would be good because he could be so effective in the Armed Forces.[216]

Goff's testimony was also a window into the seriousness and commitment of the RU, albeit in a refracted and unintentionally humorous way. At one point, Goff spoke to the discipline of the group compared to his Navy boot camp training, which he felt was "mild [compared] to the type of discipline I received in the Revolutionary Union."[217] For her part, Betty Sue seems beside herself on certain things, as can be seen in the following:

> One night we had a 6-hour meeting just on the contradictions of what makes a cup stay together; they get down deep into it. That seems ridiculous, but it is not; everything is completely thought out, why even you have thoughts and things like this. It is completely a Godless doctrine.[218]

That aside, and allowing for the Goffs' exaggeration and embellishment, their testimony was raising a specter among the Congressmen, not only the RU position on the draft but also their position on weapons. Larry Goff testified extensively about the target practice carried out by RU members and spoke at length about weapons he claims to have seen. There is, in short, a recounting of the RU's logical view, that if there were to be a revolution, it would involve guns—though in this they do seem to have stayed within the legal limits in place. Larry, however, made much about the RU buying weapons at gun shows:

> The RU would furnish them the money. I recall one trip to Los Angeles where I believe it was over $1,500 was spent on arms and ammunition. They get them from the gun shows that come in the area.[219]

This likely refers to a trip carried out after a meeting, which he himself attended, as can be seen in the following

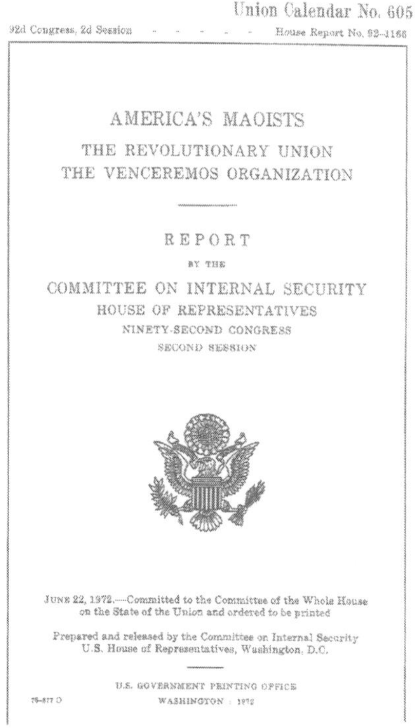

Union Calendar No. 605

92d Congress, 2d Session - - - - - - House Report No. 92–1166

AMERICA'S MAOISTS

THE REVOLUTIONARY UNION

THE VENCEREMOS ORGANIZATION

REPORT

BY THE

COMMITTEE ON INTERNAL SECURITY

HOUSE OF REPRESENTATIVES

NINETY-SECOND CONGRESS

SECOND SESSION

June 22, 1972.—Committed to the Committee of the Whole House on the State of the Union and ordered to be printed

Prepared and released by the Committee on Internal Security U.S. House of Representatives, Washington, D.C.

U.S. GOVERNMENT PRINTING OFFICE

78-877 O WASHINGTON : 1972

Cover of House Internal Security Committee Report on the Revolutionary Union and the Venceremos Organization. US Government document

informant report (the same one that talks about recruiting his wife) "REDACTED is going to attend a gun show in Los Angeles over the coming weekend and he wanted orders for weapons from members of the collective."[220] Regardless, Goff, as the RU's "gunsmith," was hardly a passive force.

Yet with all their conflicts and provocations, the Goffs' time in the RU was short-lived. The trajectory of the Sixties being such that it quickly moved beyond what they could sustain. Their ultimate demise came in the wake of an internal struggle over the role of violence in the revolutionary movement (see Chapter 4) and their concern about continuing to expose their children to this experience. However, the intelligence they passed on before that point was nothing short of devastating. Had there been no other FBI operatives infiltrating the RU at the time—and there were others more highly placed—what the Goffs offered up on the emerging organization was vast, detailed, and highly damaging.

The Stalin Split

While FBI infiltration presented one kind of challenge for the emerging organization, internal political struggle presented another, though the two were never that far apart.

In its official political history, the RCP outlined the key struggles it had navigated up to what would be its watershed year of 1977. For the RCP—much like their model, the Chinese Communist Party—they saw their history as one of a succeeding process of "two-line" struggles, each struggle strengthening their political outlook and resolve, regardless of cadre lost in each struggle.[221] It is no irony then that the first of these was over the question of whether to base itself on Marxism-Leninism, Mao Zedong Thought itself; or instead some type of what they referred to as "American exceptionalism," i.e., the "laws" of Marxism do not apply to the US because of its unique character.

At the core of the struggle was the matter of how to assess

Josef Stalin. According to the RCP, "[a] handful of petty-bourgeois radicals who had joined up with the RU because it seemed like "the thing to do," "couldn't support" "that butcher" Joseph Stalin. In their view:

> The struggle against this group, while in one sense not very intense or deep-going, did play an important part in helping the RU to consolidate around the stand of basing itself on the fundamental principles of Marxism-Leninism, and to publish *The Red Papers 1* on that basis.[222]

While this summation captures in broad strokes what was going on, it obscures that the RU was either going to be a group based on supporting the Chinese model of communism or it was never going to get out of the starting blocks. The controversy was centered in the East Bay branch of the Revolutionary Union, where Bob Fitch and five other RU members began raising objections to the group's position on Stalin. The drama can be seen in the FBI informant's account: "Larry Harris is very concerned over a split which has developed in the East Bay Local of the RU over the question of Stalin."[223] The debate that had broken out had become heated to the degree that

> [a]ny discussion of MAO Tse-tung was avoided at the meeting and, according to Harris, GERT ALEXANDER became so angry that she left the meeting and said she would never be back.[224]

This was a crisis not because a small number of RU members were pushing it, but because the organization, still in its infancy, had not consolidated its position. The Executive Committee informant reported "Bergman told Harris that at the Executive Committee meeting Avakian was not on the right side." Also, according to Harris, "Steve Hamilton at the present time is neutral in this matter and not voiced any opinion, pro or con." For Harris (and Bergman) the position in opposition to Stalin, and by extension Mao, was a non-starter.

> HARRIS feels that if things come to a head and one must make a choice they can't follow the road of FITCH, namely to take a position in opposition to MAO. He does not feel they can take this position.[225]

Of course, the group did ultimately settle this, upholding Stalin—which along with Mao was their raison d'être. This embrace of Stalin, albeit a critical one (as discussed in the previous chapter), would be a millstone around the group's neck, impinging on their future development, always having to reconcile its politics within the greater communist narrative in which people like Stalin sat. Yet the RU and the RCP took it on with zeal. An account by journalist Ed Montgomery of a speech by Bob Avakian at New York University in 1969 is exemplary.[226] Montgomery reported, "[w]hen he spoke of raising the banner of Stalin 'right in the heartland of bourgeois imperialism' a voice from the audience corrected him 'Comrade Stalin.' Avakian accepted the correction amid applause."[227] This matter of discussing Stalin with a certain bluster was not unique to Avakian. Within the RU and the larger new communist movement there was a great deal of posturing, even machismo, in invoking Stalin, which seems to have stood in for (or stood in the way of) a more critical understanding of his role and legacy. The fact that Montgomery seized on this is hardly surprising; it was an easy shot. It is also not surprising that the matter would be among the first the RU would set hard policy on.

Some years later, Steve Hamilton, speaking from the perspective of having left the RU, reflected on the struggle:

> The RU had its first split when some of the East Bay people,

> ex-student movement intellectuals, detected a tendency almost immediately to accept wholesale the "tradition" that they labeled "Stalinism." This trend was opposed and labeled rightist and these people left the RU. In the intervening years I've also come to be generally critical of much of this "tradition" and aware of the strength of the tendency toward dogmatism.[228]

Hamilton candidly admits that he was one of those who labeled this stance "rightist," at the time, further noting that, "if the RU leaders had the flexibility from the beginning to deal with this sort of criticism the subsequent history might have been quite different."[229] This was not, however, what developed. Rather, it would become exemplary of an uncritical and/or defensive adoption of positions from the Chinese and Russian revolutions, which would hold long-term consequences.

Marv Treiger

No sooner had the RU navigated that internal struggle than another one broke out. According to the RU, soon after the publication of the initial *Red Papers*, a small group in the RU, headed up by Marv Treiger, criticized the RU's position on the United Front, women's liberation, and the matter of how Black liberation would be achieved in the US. The jargon of the controversy was steeped in COMINTERN language, and included parsing out distinctions between "monopoly capitalism and imperialism." It also included differences on how to address actions by the recently emerged Weathermen. In the RU's words, the Treiger faction sought to:

> Cover up their own social-pacifism and fear of revolutionary struggle, they blasted the RU for refusing to join with them in publicly condemning the Weatherman group from SDS as "enemies of the people" at that time.

> And they charged the RU with "male chauvinism" because it didn't join with them in tailing behind petty-bourgeois tendencies of the women's movement.[230]

Treiger himself appears as politically mercurial, having been in the Communist Party in Los Angeles in the mid Sixties, before embracing Maoism. Then, after quitting the RU, he joined something called the California Communist League, which in turn led him to the Communist Working Collective. By the early Seventies, having exhausted Maoism, he turned to Trotskyism, joining the Spartacist League, which he too left amid controversy. In general, Treiger's presence in organizations was surrounded by turmoil and divisive debate.[231] While the differences with him were no doubt real, the fact that things seemed to have quickly gotten into a polemical framework was indicative of things to come within the RU.

There were in this, however, hints of the Bureau manipulating things in the background. Buried in the archives stored at NYU's Tamiment Library of former RU member David Sullivan are two documents from that period that suggest another player in this struggle. The items in the file are a political cartoon and an accompanying manuscript written to appear as if the Liberation News Service (LNS), the highly influential radical news service of the time, distributed them. The manuscript is by-lined, "Marv Treiger"—though its actual author is unclear.

Among other things, it tells a story of RU members Leibel Bergman and Davida Fineman who had recently traveled to the Middle East. It suggests that the trip was undertaken in order to aid US government agencies and to secretly support Israel. As evidence the article points out that Fineman's father had been involved in similar activity previously: some "digging and cooperation from knowledgeable friends disclosed he was a co-conspirator in a court case involving illegal trafficking in arms and personnel in Israel in 1968." By any reading, the point of the piece was to impugn the integrity of Bergman and Fineman, using guilt by association: "At best Bergman is an inept dupe of Israelites; at worst their agent." As for the cartoon, it shows a caricature of Bergman holding a racist Chinese mask and a Red Book, while an Israeli helicopter fires at an unnamed target above him with the mock Yiddish text"Yust read dat little Red Book!"[232] In the context of the struggle between the RU and Treiger, such material would seem an effort to toss lighter fluid on a small fire. Ted Franklin, who worked with LNS at the time, recalled seeing the item in 1970 or thereabouts. "Somebody sent LNS a copy and we passed it around as an item of curiosity. It was certainly not published by LNS, but the source was a mystery to which I recall we came to no resolution. We never published sectarian denunciations of factions within the movement."[233] The cartoon and text would seem good exemplars of the wisdom of that policy.

While authorship of the cartoon and article cannot be stated to a certainty, there are some clues. First, Treiger himself had already written a political polemic against the RU, the terms of which were clear, and did not go into *ad hominem* attacks on Bergman, in stark contrast to the fake LNS article. More than that, the FBI seemed keenly aware of the fake article and was eagerly awaiting its publication:

> Information has been made available to the Bureau that Liberation News Service recently prepared a special news release concerning the Revolutionary Union (RU) and its leader, Leibel Bergman. The release reportedly based on the writings of Marv Treiger, a disgruntled former member of RU, and is an attack on Bergman. Offices receiving this communication should remain alert to any publication of this article, and alert your sources for any information concerning this exposé.[234]

Less than two weeks after that memo, another FBI missive considered publishing an illustrated history of the Revolutionary Union "in comic book form which would ridicule the RU and its leader, Leibel Bergman." The idea was to make it appear as if another progressive publication had issued it, or as the memo outlined, used "the same printing ink, paper, format, or styling of a New Left-type publication such as 'Ramparts,' 'The Movement' or a publication of the Progressive Labor Party."[235] The Bureau, in other words, was eager to deploy cartoons and comics as a way of disrupting the RU and targeting Bergman.

Joining Collectives

All this was playing out at a time when the Revolutionary Union was moving away from being a local Bay Area entity to a national organization. Bob Avakian writes in his memoir of how in the spring of 1970, Leibel Bergman suggested that he and some others in the RU "drive around the country and link up with and win over all these revolutionary forces throughout the country."[236] This was in fact a national organizing tour, which included Avakian, Bergman, Jane Franklin and Barry Greenberg.[237] It was both hugely successful and hugely surveilled.

Before the tour, the informant on the Executive Committee was keeping the Bureau apprised of the RU's attempt to leverage its contacts into organizational ties:

> [T]here is a RU sister collective in Chicago working close to the RU, distributing the Red Papers and maintaining contact with individual leaders of the RU. It also came out that there is one sister collective in Los Angeles, which is distributing the Red Papers and which also keeps in touch with the RU leaders... They are not guided by the RU and they are not represented on the Executive Committee.

On the tour itself, evidence of the FBI comes in the form of an article by Ron Koziol, the same Chicago journalist who had written the FBI story about the RU attempting to take over SDS. In his article, Koziol cited unnamed investigators reporting on the fact that RU recruiters "were seen in Chicago, Elmhurst, Melrose Park and Waukegan (the RU would go on to form chapters in both Waukegan and Maywood)."[239] He then pointedly notes that the RU is "considered by authorities to be as dangerous as the Weatherman faction of the Students for a Democratic Society." The article also includes a very specific account of the tour's itinerary:

> Many of the former SDS members have taken refuge in communes on the East Coast. Authorities said Revolutionary Union recruiters received a good response from radicals in the Mother Jones collective in Baltimore, the Crazy Horse commune in New York City, and the K Street collective in Washington.[240]

The accuracy here is borne out by an RU member at the time who verified that in the case of the Mother Jones collective, "[j]ust about the whole group joined [the RU] with only one exception."[241]

In this, the FBI was actively trying to limit the gains the RU could make. Word was sent out to 14 different field offices to conduct interviews with people who had met with the RU representatives; the purpose "to make possible affiliates of the RU believe that the organization is infiltrated by informants on a high level;"[242] this tactic, portraying the RU and its leaders as government agents, was a recurring theme and tactic of the Bureau.

A full accounting of how successful this counter-intelligence effort was is unclear. What is clear is that the FBI in Yellow Springs, Ohio, was having trouble. Yellow Springs was home to Antioch College, which, along with Stanford and Berkeley, would serve as a key incubator for RU leaders and cadre. In 1971, 21 Antioch students "attended a meeting led by several RU national representatives." Those attending would go on to set up RU chapters in Springfield, Dayton, and Cincinnati, as well as some who remained at Antioch.[243]

According to the Cincinnati FBI field office, which oversaw Antioch, "a large organizing committee was set up for the purpose of developing collectives both in Yellow Springs and in large industrial cities such as Springfield, Dayton, Cincinnati, and Columbus."[244] However, they complained of "investigative difficulties," because the "college [Antioch] is operated under a system of total student control." As a result, the field office passed on the idea of interviews—a standard tactic of information gathering and intimidation by the FBI—saying, "Cincinnati does not believe interview in this division would be effective in disrupting the RU during its current drive to establish itself as a national organization."[245] While there is an inherent humor in the FBI being at loose ends in working in such an environment, the larger reality is that this was more the exception than the norm.

The government was also getting reports on the RU's efforts to consolidate and expand in the Bay Area. As a later report by the Congressional Committee on Internal Security titled *America's Maoists: The Revolutionary Union, the Venceremos Organization* explained, "a year after its existence was first publicized the Revolutionary Union had a dozen collectives in Palo Alto, Redwood City, San Jose, San Francisco, Berkeley, and Richmond."[246] Given the RU was headquartered in that area, the FBI at one point considered a scheme to penetrate the RU by setting up a "cover collective":

> ResFlet 5/19/70 captioned "Revolutionary Union (RU), IS -RU" suggesting a 'collective' be created in Marin County, California, with the long range objective of consolidating the notional group with the RU and thus obtaining informant

> coverage on the Central Committee or the Political Committee of the RU.[247]

The Bureau decided at the time not to go forward, however:

> [I]t is believed a cover collective of the nature proposed in Marin County could very likely be initially operated independently and targeted against other New Left, pro-Chicom, or black extremists and thereby increase your overall informant coverage. When the notional collective was developed and functioning, consideration again could be given to including the RU among its targets.[248]

The outcome of that plan is uncertain, but as we will see, the concept was something of a "tried and true" method going back to the Bureau's efforts against the CPUSA—and it was one they would use against the RU.

Such measures by the Bureau would seem to go beyond what could be reasonably expected by any organization confronting a hostile secret police—it is the stuff of spy thrillers. That said—and leaving aside what some in the RU may have known and were not talking about publicly—overall there seems to have been an under-appreciation for the sophistication of the Bureau's efforts.[249] This comes through in statements deflecting or minimizing such things. For example, Roxanne Dunbar-Ortiz, who was briefly part of the RU, in discussing the Goffs, offered the view that the RU was taken in because "[r]evolutionary organizations made up of mostly privileged whites tended to exoticize the working class and people of color."[250] From another angle, Bruce Franklin—commenting on the Goffs—told the press, "[w]e suspected they were pigs."[251] Given the FBI had an informant on the RU's Executive Committee from almost its inception and another entering that same body—at least in some capacity—soon after, and informants in the Chicago area they were drawing on in regard to the RU, such statements failed to confront the larger reality—people like the Goffs were only the tip of a larger FBI-driven iceberg and exemplary of the priority the Bureau was giving this.

All that taken into account, whatever the FBI was doing was largely *not* working. As the FBI's David Ryan, who was assigned to the Leibel Bergman "investigation", would later testify: "We found the Revolutionary Union rapidly spreading in terms of organization and contacts."[252] By February 1972, by the government's own account, there were RU collectives in existence in Chicago, RU representatives in Detroit, Reading, Pennsylvania and Trenton. On the campuses, the RU had a presence at Eugene, Antioch, and Fresno State College. There was also RU organizing going on in Los Angeles, New York City, at Pennsylvania State University, and in Philadelphia.[253] As positive as all this was, any further expansion was predicated on navigating an extremely important internal debate; one that would end in the Revolutionary Union's first major schism.

Chapter 4

Protracted Urban War or Protracted Struggle?

Revolutionary war in this country will also be protracted. Indeed, it already is.
— On Protracted Urban War (a Draft), Revolutionary Union (the Franklin Group), 1970.[254]

The Bureau believes Franklin's "Protracted Urban War" paper represents one of the most hard Marxist-Leninist-Maoist arguments for organized violence circulated to date in domestic communist circles. An exposure and penetrative interpretation of this document by a recognized private expert on Marxism-Leninism doctrine and tactics would alert the public to the continuing threat of organized domestic communism and also expose the semi-covert RU which is endeavoring to organize nationally.
— SAC San Francisco to Director FBI, 11/24/70.[255]

The year 1970 was a violent one. Instead of ending the anti-war movement with the invasion of Cambodia, it got a second wind. Domestically anti-war demonstrations popularized a new term, "trashing," with the object no longer being to make one's views known, but to do some property damage in the course of street demonstrations. Along with this, various groups, for various reasons, were planting bombs as symbolic protest or as actual assaults against the power structure. In 1970, political violence was the currency, and the Revolutionary Union confronted head on how it was going to stand in relation to it.

The Franklin Split

Bruce Franklin's residency in the RU appears to have always been tense. The informant on the Executive Committee noted early on that the Palo Alto group—which Franklin headed—were sound in terms of theory but "appear to be so enamored with revolution that they are impatient with the necessity of developing a broad political base."[256] Specifically there seemed to have been a problem where "BRUCE FRANKLIN has reached the point where he cannot carry on a normal conversation without injecting violent politics into it."[257] This became the basis for a good deal of conflict:

> FRANKLIN also reported on the Citizens Committee to Defend the Second Amendment, the anti-gun control law organization initiated by the Palo [A]lto group. The latter organization was the cause of a violent verbal clash between FRANKLIN and BERGMAN. FRANKLIN was obviously pleased with the groups [sic] progress and BERGMAN wanted them to "cool it." FRANKLIN really believes that the revolution should start tomorrow and his entire group are [sic] completely in accord with him. The group are [sic] sincerely interested in obtaining weapons and in using them. BERGMAN is too old, too wise and too practical to accept this viewpoint. He appears to appreciate and fear the harm precipitate action would cause. BERGMAN believes in the use of force and violence in theory and ideologically, but only when the time is right for this tactic.[258]

The terms of the final debate with Franklin, in one respect, were simple. Do you start military operations against the US government now, or is there a need to wait until different conditions are in place? The concluding event that ultimately resolved the matter was the circulation in the fall of 1970 of an internal RU position paper called "The Military Strategy for the United States: Protracted Urban War (A Draft)"—later identified by the US Congress as the "A Paper." That paper in turn gave rise to a response, a counter-position, in the form of a "B Paper," which rejected the A's basic assessment. The anonymous naming was initially to obscure the authors of the divergent positions, whom an FBI informant report in Steve Hamilton's files identifies as Bruce Franklin and Jeffrey Freed for the "A Paper" and Bob Avakian and Larry Harris for the "B Paper.")

The implications of the A Paper were sharp, and they sparked a major internal struggle in the RU. According to that paper, the current situation in the US was a desperate one of "developing fascism and armed struggle."[259] Given that, it cautioned that "the most insidious form of social pacifism agrees to armed struggle in principle but puts it off to some distant time in the future." In the paper's view, the time for revolutionary action, at least on some level, was at hand:

> Armed revolutionary acts, including the ambushing of dozens of pigs, all across the country seem to indicate that the Black nation is in a transition from the mass spontaneous uprisings of 1964-1968 to the first stages of organized guerrilla warfare.[260]

The paper further argued it would be possible to initiate and sustain guerrilla war because of advantageous conditions in "cities like New York or Chicago, with their high-rise apartments and multi-layered underground systems," calling them "three-dimensional jungles." Those conditions would constrain authorities because "[w]eapons and tactics that can be used against Hiroshima or Ben Tre can hardly be employed against the empire's centers of industry and government." In this view, it was not only necessary to begin protracted war; it was also possible to do so in a sustained way without immediately being overcome by US military and paramilitary forces.

The response to this argument by others in the RU was unequivocal. It characterized the position as a "more sophisticated version of the Weatherman line," noting that "any attempt to implement it would not only lead us away from our most pressing task at this time—building a real base in the working class," it would "lead to the early destruction of our organization."[261]

While this notion of the imminence of urban guerrilla warfare may read as fantastic today, urban guerrilla warfare in the early Seventies was a popular concept intimately bound up with movements and struggles of Black and other oppressed nationalities domestically and internationally. This was especially concentrated in what was happening within the Black Panther Party—which by 1970 was being pulled apart by two extremes—with no small amount of encouragement by the FBI and other police agencies.[262] At the dawn of the new decade, the Panthers had bifurcated into two basic positions: armed action championed by Eldridge Cleaver, and electoral politics and community service advocated by Huey P. Newton.

The Revolutionary Union, which revered the Panthers and often deferred to their vanguard status,[263] was thus impelled to jump through no small number of hoops in an effort to reconcile their ongoing support for the Panthers, with the growing disagreement with the actual positions of the Panthers' two contending factions. This was sharply drawn in the schism that became known as "the Franklin Struggle." In the polemics issued in that struggle's wake they wrote, "The Black Panthers are heroes of the people and that it is the duty of all genuine revolutionaries to defend them with their lives when necessary and to build mass support for the Black Panther Party." The polemic then attempted to distinguish the Franklin group from that of the Panthers:

> The Panthers had adopted some of the same positions as our former comrades—positions which we regard as fundamentally wrong—there is a much greater chance that

> the Panthers will correct their mistakes, because they have a base among sections of the Black people and the growing, if still beginning, movement among Black workers is about to have an effect on the outlook of the Panthers.[264]

This analysis, as events would soon show, contained no small amount of wishful thinking. The Panthers' peak power coincided with the urban insurrections that hit their apex in the years 1967 to 1968. By 1970, a new situation was emerging; one that could no longer sustain the harder edged insurrectionary posture of the more militant Panthers, though some in that grouping tried.

Some years later, when the fog of "urban guerrilla warfare" had cleared, Steve Hamilton was a bit more candid about the actual politics of the Panthers and the RU's need to come out from under their shadow:

> The politics of the Black Panthers had always contained an unsteady blend of Marxism, anarchism and Utopian idealism. Under Eldridge Cleaver's leadership in 1970, the Panthers developed an openly anti-working class and anarchist perspective that culminated in a sort of revolutionary nihilism.[265]

Hamilton's reflections are even more stark given the RU apparently saw the Panthers as an organization more or less in sync with their own, to the degree that the "RU had avoided recruiting Black members but instead encouraged them to join the Panthers"[266]—a position they would ultimately be forced to abandon. Given the ultimate development of the BPP, and its inability to maintain itself as a revolutionary organization, the RU would seem to have paid a certain price for this policy, not the least of which meant going forward as an overwhelmingly white organization.

During the Franklin controversy this itself was a touchstone;

as Hamilton writes, "criticism of a major Third World communist group was unthinkable to the Franklin faction."[267] In their view, "We support the Black Panther Party and recognize it as the vanguard of the American revolution."[268] For the RU's part, the struggle coincided with and reinforced their emphasis on working class organizing and began a shift away from emphasizing the struggles of national and ethnic minorities. This would soon pose its own crisis a couple of years later.

The FBI at Work

The FBI was well aware of the struggle consuming the Revolutionary Union and proposed and initiated measures that would make things worse. Importantly, they had a copy of Franklin's paper long before its existence or contents became public. First there was their informant, Lawrence Goff, who as chair of his collective "attended a meeting of the central committee of the RU, its highest administrative body, in San Francisco in October 1970."[269] This was a meeting that took up the Franklin paper. That meeting, it turns out, was subject to a detailed report written by the FBI a couple weeks later:

> At the Revolutionary Union (RU) Central Committee meeting 10/10-11/70 H. Bruce Franklin presented to the approximately 75 participating delegates a paper entitled "Protracted Urban War." This document urges immediate strategic application of the Marxist-Leninist-Maoist concept of protracted guerrilla warfare in the cities. Franklin urged the building of a well-trained RU guerrilla organization which would start actual attacks on the establishment with the objective of awakening the masses and overcoming any hesitancy of the membership to engage in armed revolutionary struggle. According to *informants* [emphasis added] present at the meeting, Franklin's vanguard revolutionary thesis highlights a split within the RU with the majority supporting

> immediate guerrilla warfare. It was decided a ruling on the matter would be deferred until an RU Central Committee meeting in December.[270]

The reference to "informants" rather than a single informant is significant. Who that might be is suggested within the papers of Donald G. Sanders, who had been Chief Counsel of the House Internal Security Committee, which authored *America's Maoists.* In those papers is a memo from Robert M. Horner, Sander's chief investigator. In it he discusses the procedure for meeting an RU informant: "I was informed officially on August 17th that a former high level informant in the RU will be made available to us." The memo, written in August 1972 after *America's Maoists* had been published and the Goffs exposed, contains all manner of restrictions; the informant would use an alias, would not testify publicly, and would need to have his FBI handler with him.[271] The appellation "high level informant" suggests this could be the person who had been on the Executive Committee from almost the start of the RU—even before the Goffs entered the picture.

The fact that the FBI knew about the Franklin struggle, and indeed had a copy of the precipitating paper, lead them to entertain certain ideas. Among them was a scheme to send the paper to *National Review* writer James Burnham, along with a forged letter from Franklin which would criticize Burnham's writing on the same subject:

> It is felt the note will stimulate Burnham to read and carefully analyze Franklin's document on "Protracted War" and very likely cause him to make inquiries and thereafter write critical commentaries exposing and discrediting the RU.[272]

It is not clear if the letter was sent, but the presence of the FBI in the midst of this struggle is unquestionable. This comes out even more fully in the debate in the organization on the paper. For example, as part of trying to win people to their position, the RU sent representatives to their emerging Chicago organization. What they were not aware of is that the FBI already had a high placed informant in Chicago, someone they put a premium on keeping secret. As the FBI report on the matter stipulated, *"Because the source is affiliated with a highly sensitive bureau run intelligence operation, information attributed to him must be carefully paraphrased."* [Emphasis added] This appears to be an extra caution, on the already cautious measures to protect the identities of their informants.

The ensuing report is detailed in describing how the RU members "were in Chicago essentially to relate their side of the unfolding RU split":

> They accuse REDACTED [Franklin] of "Weathermanism," of acting childishly by his toying with guns and of hurling epithets at them. In the source's opinion, the RU split is basically and essentially over personal animosity, however, it is shrouded in a revolutionary facade based on a difference in line.[273]

The last observation is best read as indication of the informant's assessment and outlook, rather than the nub of the issue. However, there do seem to have been personality conflicts involved. In that respect, an anecdote from Avakian is instructive. In his memoir, he recounts talking with a comrade who had just returned from Cuba being debriefed by Franklin and Avakian. At one point, the comrade referred to the "Sino-Soviet split," which prompted the following:

> [Avakian] Wait a minute, we don't talk about the Sino-Soviet split—you mean the struggle against Soviet revisionism that China is leading? And immediately Bruce Franklin jumped in and said to me, "I don't think you have the right attitude

> here, this is a bad method you are using. We sent these comrades down to Cuba and, now that they've come back, we should be trying to learn from them." I responded: "Well I'm very anxious to learn as much as I possibly can from them, one thing I don't want to learn from them is revisionism."[274]

While making more of this than the actual politics under debate would be misplaced, one does see a clash of personalities: the

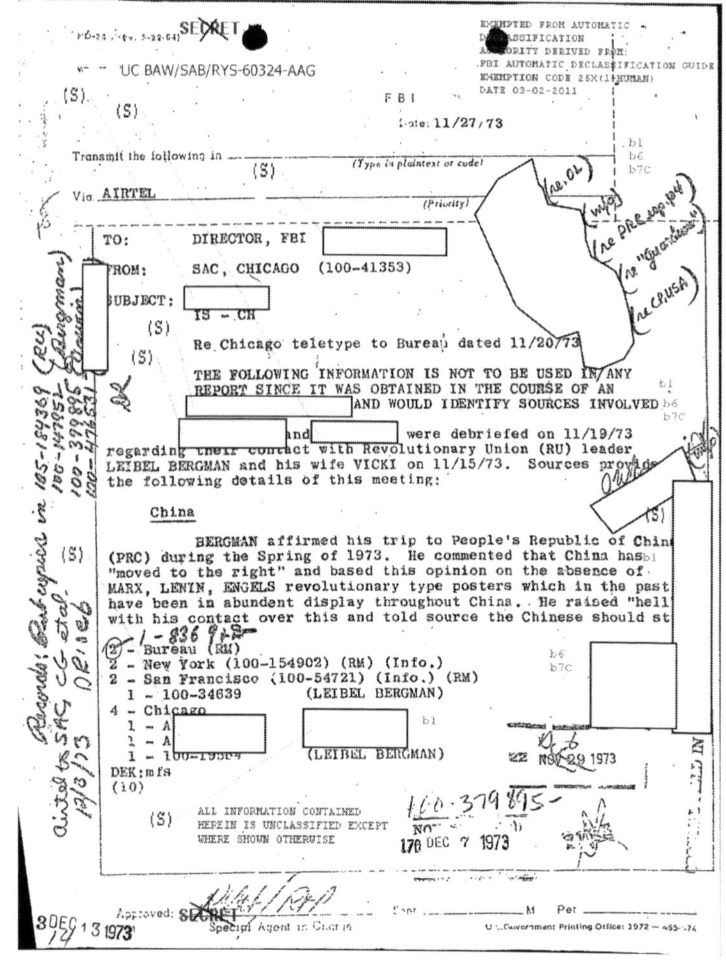

SECRET

UC BAW/SAB/RYS-60324-AAG

EXEMPTED FROM AUTOMATIC DECLASSIFICATION
AUTHORITY DERIVED FROM:
FBI AUTOMATIC DECLASSIFICATION GUIDE
EXEMPTION CODE 25X(1, HUMAN)
DATE 03-02-2011

FBI

Date: 11/27/73

Transmit the following in (Type in plaintext or code)

Via AIRTEL (Priority)

TO: DIRECTOR, FBI

FROM: SAC, CHICAGO (100-41353)

SUBJECT: IS - CH

Re Chicago teletype to Bureau dated 11/20/73

THE FOLLOWING INFORMATION IS NOT TO BE USED IN ANY REPORT SINCE IT WAS OBTAINED IN THE COURSE OF AN AND WOULD IDENTIFY SOURCES INVOLVED

and were debriefed on 11/19/73 regarding their contact with Revolutionary Union (RU) leader LEIBEL BERGMAN and his wife VICKI on 11/15/73. Sources provide the following details of this meeting:

China

BERGMAN affirmed his trip to People's Republic of China (PRC) during the Spring of 1973. He commented that China has "moved to the right" and based this opinion on the absence of MARX, LENIN, ENGELS revolutionary type posters which in the past have been in abundent display throughout China. He raised "hell" with his contact over this and told source the Chinese should st

2 - Bureau (RM)
2 - New York (100-154902) (RM) (Info.)
2 - San Francisco (100-54721) (Info.) (RM)
1 - 100-34639 (LEIBEL BERGMAN)
4 - Chicago
1 - A
1 - A
1 - 100-19564 (LEIBEL BERGMAN)
DEK:mfs
(10)

ALL INFORMATION CONTAINED HEREIN IS UNCLASSIFIED EXCEPT WHERE SHOWN OTHERWISE

100-379895-

22 NOV 29 1973

DEC 7 1973

Approved: SECRET Special Agent in Charge

FBI Informant report issued just before the Franklin split

doctrinaire tilt in Avakian's argument going up against the more academic disposition of Franklin.

That aside, the FBI's Chicago informant offers a specific—and sophisticated—accounting of the political questions involved, noting the key issues as being armed struggle, democratic centralism, and of whether to build a multi-national party or "an all-white organization to lend support to the Black Panther Party."[275] The report concludes with the assessment that "in about a month's time the victor, if such there will be, in the RU split will become known."[276] This was to be an accurate prediction.

Bergman v. Franklin

In the late 1960s the FBI saw Leibel Bergman as the key leader of the RU. Alternately they saw Bruce Franklin as the RU's most high profile member, one in their estimation who "represents one of the most militant radical extremists on American campuses."[277] It is no surprise then given a certain doctrine of trying to rend organizations that they attempted to set the two against each other. This was infused with a certain urgency; the RU appeared to be growing and there was a need to "take appropriate action to slow down the extent of its operations." To this end, the FBI "felt [it] appropriate at this time to attempt to cause more of a rift between REDACTED and BRUCE FRANKLIN."[278] As other documents relating to FBI schemes make clear, the redacted person they wanted to involve in the rift was Leibel Bergman.

One of the plans they devised was to try and make Franklin think Bergman was some type of agent:

> San Francisco proposal calls for alleged Chicom [Chinese Communist] agent to telephone Franklin in California from Canada to arrange for a later personal clandestine meeting in Vancouver. At Vancouver meeting the alleged Chicom

> agent would express distrust of RU leader Leibel Bergman, ask Franklin to investigate Bergman and furnish results to [REDACTED] and imply future funding of RU.[279]

Another plan had the FBI draft a letter, to be secretly sent to Franklin, again suggesting Bergman was working with the government. The memo suggests writing a letter from what is claimed to be an anonymous member of the Progressive Labor Party. That person would, in turn, raise suspicions about Bergman:

> In the CP he [Bergman] caused dissension, weakening the party[,] then dropped out. We were fooled by his so-called knowledge of Marxism-Leninism and got took in because he caused dissension and then dropped out. Then he suddenly gets into Red China. How did he get there[?] [W]ho but the CIA would give him the funds? Then he comes back and suddenly he is a big wheel in the RU, and when the establishment is worried to death about how to cope with it he uses the RU to split the SDS—a typical pig trick. He isn't working. Why didn't his name appear in Pig [Ed] Montgomery's article on you. Why hasn't he been active on the streets?[280]

Putting aside the crude accusations, it is highly audacious that the FBI, which actively tried to pit the RU against the PLP in SDS, in turn suggests a poison pen letter accusing Bergman of just such a "typical pig trick." Beyond that, as we will soon see, Ed Montgomery did quite a bit of work that favored the Bureau; invoking him in this context is a matter of skinning the ox twice.

With Franklin, they followed the same tactic with a slightly different skew, suggesting to raise questions about how an openly "militant extremist" is able to keep his professor position. In this, they suggest that:

> A rumor is brought to the attention of RU members that Franklin is able to keep his faculty position at Stanford because he is furnishing information to the government.[281]

After Franklin left the RU, the Bureau continued to pursue ideas that would raise suspicion about Bergman. Perhaps the most elaborate idea involved "a highly complicated technique" of publishing "a novel which would infer he is a Soviet agent working against the Chinese." The aim would be to not just to sully Bergman's reputation, but to "discredit" the organization and the pro-Chinese Communist movement. Given the bad relations between China and the Soviet Union, this particular idea—while a bit of stretch—was not without merit. It does not appear, however, the novel was ever written.[282]

Such efforts aimed at Bergman are especially important given his years of experience, and what one former comrade described as his inclination toward preserving unity.[283] In the Franklin struggle, he appears to have tried to reconcile those contradictions to the point where some years later this would be grist for criticism by his former RU comrades who accused him of trying "to play a mediating and conciliating role."[284] At the end of everything, the contradictions embodied in this debate would prove irreconcilable. The intervention of the FBI, however, could not have helped.

The immediate resolution of the controversy ended with Bruce Franklin, Jane Franklin, Janet Weiss and Jeff Freed expelled from the RU.[285] This was both unprecedented and precedent setting. As the RU put it, "Our organization has decided to do what we have never done before: publicly expel members and issue a public statement giving the reason for their expulsion."[286] The emphasis on this never having been "done before," in an organization barely two years old, would seem overstated; unfortunately it foreshadowed more to come.

Venceremos Organization

With the Franklin group expelled, the door was left open for those who agreed with them, but were willing to renounce that political strategy, to stay in the RU. Most of them did not; with Franklin's leaving, there was an accompanying exit of scores of RU members. That number, according to Betty Sue Goff, was 200 people. *America's Maoists,* in an un-cited estimate, puts the number at 150. The RU/RCP does not give an actual number but offers that it lost a third of its membership.[287] Regardless of the exact number, this was a serious schism for an organization barely out of its infancy.

In the wake of the split, Bruce Franklin published a book, *From the Movement Toward the Revolution,* a collection of revolutionary writings, including his own views. In it, he described what he saw as the choices for the road ahead:

> So American revolutionaries, as individuals and organizations, must decide which of two opposing courses they will follow on the question of armed struggle: whether to organize the people now for an eventual armed uprising at some point in the future or to use the present as the very first stage of a protracted revolutionary struggle in which developing urban guerrilla warfare will play an integral part in the organizing activity.[288]

Concretely, Franklin and the others who left merged with a smaller Chicano organization based in Redwood, California, called Venceremos, that revolved around a free two-year school (Venceremos College) with a mainly Chicano student body. The chairman of the new group, which would be called Venceremos, was a former member of the Chicano organization, Brown Berets, Aaron Manganiello. The actual numerical makeup of the new grouping is unclear, but the leadership was deliberately multinational, though indications are that Bruce Franklin remained the driving force in the new entity.[289]

The new organization continued some of the organizational elements and ties they previously had had in the RU. It continued to publish the *Free You* newspaper, making it bi-lingual. They also published the San Jose newspaper, the *Maverick.* It operated Venceremos College and the People's Medical Center, which were free alternatives to standing institutions. Along with this they "assumed recognized leadership" of a number of workers' caucuses, community organizations, and the local Young Partisans, which they described as having "chapters on all the local community college campuses and in many high schools and junior highs."[290]

They also took along at least one informant, Larry Goff, who went with Venceremos after having "sided with that faction and prepared and submitted a paper favoring the position held by Bruce Franklin."[291] His wife Betty Sue stayed in the RU—ostensibly keeping the door open for her husband's return if need be—telling the RU that "her husband was simply going through a stage and would eventually see the light and return to the RU."[292] Larry Goff only stayed with Venceremos a month before leaving to rejoin the RU. He was in turn "re-recruited," this time by his wife (who he himself had recruited).[293] Betty Sue by this time had been made chair of her collective, which in turn put her on the Local Executive Committee, which also meant she would attend a Central Committee meeting in January 1971.[294]

As things turned out, this would not last. Soon after, the Goffs would hang up their informant shoes for good, but not before presenting Congressional investigators with an assessment of the two sides in the split. In his testimony, Larry Goff told Congress that the discipline in Venceremos was "more lax and the organization itself much more disorganized." His feeling was that "many who went with Venceremos were those who had difficulty in accepting the strict discipline of the RU." The two informants' overall assessment was prescient:

> The Goffs offered the opinion that, of the two groups, the RU is the much more dangerous because of its long-range plans for revolution, the secrecy and subterfuge of its operations, and its concentration on building a "mass line" among the working classes. The Goffs feel that the Venceremos group is composed of individuals ready to engage in unorthodox and unwise activities and is more immediately dangerous in terms of terrorism and violence, but that Venceremos will divulge its planned activity and, as a result, its members will be arrested or killed before Venceremos can present a long-range threat.[295]

While the Goffs were later ridiculed by some as unsophisticated and obvious agents, their assessment here was largely on the mark.

For its part, Venceremos started falling apart almost as soon as it was constituted. No sooner had the former RU people joined with Venceremos College than in the summer of 1971, half—mainly based on the Stanford campus—quit to form the "Intercommunal Survival Committee to Combat Fascism" (a BPP auxiliary)."[296] They were in turn denounced by the Venceremos Central Committee as "racist sissies."[297] Venceremos remained, however, a substantial organization. According to the Congressional report, by February 1972 there were 225 members.

Meanwhile, the state kept up its efforts against Bruce Franklin. As the US continued to wage war in Southeast Asia, supporting attacks on Laos in 1971, Franklin continued to protest the war on the Stanford campus, giving speeches in defiance of the US moves. After one of these speeches in February 1971, Richard Lyman, who had taken over as president of Stanford, moved to fire him from his tenured position. A campus advisory board heard the case in which Franklin represented himself, though he did have a young ACLU attorney, Alan Dershowitz, offering advice.[298] The conclusion was not good for Franklin; in 1972 he was fired.[299] As the *New York Times* somberly noted, "[i]t was not only the first firing of a tenured professor in Stanford's history, but also the only such dismissal at a major university since the Joe McCarthy era."[300]

Venceremos, meanwhile, continued to work in the Palo Alto community, including running in elections, sponsoring community service programs, and helping run Venceremos College—a free two-year school in Redwood, California, with a mainly Chicano student body.

Things decisively came apart in the fall of 1972. The catalyst for this was Ronald Wayne Beaty, a prisoner, alleged Venceremos recruit, and the reported romantic interest of Jean Hobson, who had been on the Venceremos Central Committee.[301] In October of that year, Beatty, who had been jailed, was scheduled for a court appearance. On the way to court, to which he was being driven by two guards from California's Chino prison, the car was forced off the road by four people later said to be Venceremos members. Things from there moved quickly. After freeing Beaty, "23-year-old Venceremos member Robert Seabok shot both guards at point blank range killing 24-year-old Jesus Sanchez and wounding his partner George Fitzgerald."[302] The group, which included Seabok, Jean Hobson, Andrea Holman Burt, and Benton Burt, was able to flee the scene, but their remaining free time would not be long.

Two months later, Hobson and Beaty were arrested on the Bay Bridge, with Beaty quickly agreeing to be a state witness. He identified four people he said helped him escape, and specifically identified Robert Seabok as the gunman. He also claimed that other members of Venceremos helped hide him in a rural San Mateo County mountain cabin for close to a month. Beaty then pleaded guilty for his involvement in Sanchez's death and received a life sentence. The four people Beaty identified were brought to trial and found guilty. Hobson and then 19 year-old Andrea Holman Burt, along with 31-year-old Douglas Burt, were found guilty of second degree murder, while Seabok got life imprisonment after a first degree murder conviction.[303]

Attempting to leverage the incident to roll up other elements of the Venceremos organization, authorities arrested Bruce Franklin, along with eight others in December 1972, charging them with harboring the fugitive Ronald Beaty. The government later dropped charges on Franklin due to lack of evidence.[304] Two other members of Venceremos, Bruce Hobson and Morton Newman, however, were ultimately convicted and sentenced to four and five years in prison.[305]

In the wake of the incident Venceremos appears to have tried to tighten ship, but this was doomed to failure, as the following report suggests: "Franklin and Manganiello were to train other individuals who would also help in security checks for the group"—to avoid infiltration. Unfortunately, their efforts were duly reported by an informant.[306] Overall, however, the fallout from the incident was too much. By September 1973 Venceremos was no more.

In the aftermath of these events, Bruce Franklin no longer discussed his time in the RU or Venceremos. His 1975 memoir, which opens with his harrowing arrest for harboring a fugitive and the terrorizing of his family, never mentions the Chino incident. Instead, he describes how he "felt a mixture of relief and apprehension because this didn't even sound like a plausible charge."[307] A review of his book in the *Village Voice* noted the absence of such crucial episodes and asked him about this. Franklin claimed his book was a "historical essay about America since World War II, told as a political autobiography, not a book about himself."[308] By the time of that interview, he had resumed teaching, and was putting distance between himself and his persona as a revolutionary leader.

As for Aaron Manganiello (who died in 2009), he serves as something of a coda and cautionary figure for the Venceremos experience. When Larry Goff remarked on the indiscipline of

Venceremos, one thinks of Manganiello. He had been, initially, chairman of the organization, then an advisor to the Central Committee, and then a rank-and-file member of Venceremos. As a result of being in jail for an assault charge stemming from a demonstration soon after the Chino events, he was approached for an interview by FBI agents, Kent O. Brisby and Robert C. Wanamaker. Manganiello, breaking a basic rule of radicals in relation to the FBI, agreed to talk to the agents. According to the extensive FBI report of the conversation (it ran six single space typed pages) Manganiello told them he was:

> Not sure if the Venceremos is in fact, involved in the escape. Manganiello advised that the Venceremos Central Committee supports the action taken at Chino as does he personally. Manganiello repeated that he had no personal knowledge of the escape, but did state that as far as he knew, BURT and the DE LUNAs were not members of the Venceremos Organization. He doubted if the Venceremos Organization was in fact, involved in it, but that he said, was his own speculation.[309]

Less than two years later, after having become politically inactive, Manganiello would again talk to the FBI, this time after they approached him while he was in his front yard. They asked him about former Venceremos member, Joseph Remiro, who had become part of the Symbionese Liberation Army (SLA).[310] During the interview Manganiello told them that he was "sorry to see Jean Hobson, Andrea Holman Burt and Douglas Burt sentenced for the murder of a Chino guard" and that "[h]e personally believes that he is somewhat responsible for their facing long prison terms inasmuch as they followed his revolutionary rhetoric."[311]

The fact that Manganiello was willing to talk—albeit in a self-serving way—led the FBI to conclude that a "limited rapport has been established between him and Bureau agents."[312] That, combined with the fact that he was facing prosecution by authorities "for selling stolen auto parts and grand theft,"[313] put in the FBI's mind that Manganiello might be informant material:

> This source has excellent potential in uncovering clandestine terrorist groups and in furnishing valuable information concerning the bombing activities of the WU, NWLF, RGF, AFJ and CLF as well as penetration of WU. Therefore, it is believed the request for initial $2,000 to be paid to source at SAC discretion is warranted.[314]

The Bureau did not appear to have been successful in their approach, but rather ends on an ambiguous note:

> On 10/22/75, source [Manganiello] advised "It just won't work now." He was advised that in all probability that in the course of investigating Bureau cases, it was likely that he would be contacted again by the Agent. He displayed no resentment to that idea and it is felt that the vital element of rapport with this individual has not been lost or damaged at this time.[315]

This is the last report in the file.

Strategic Confusion

In hindsight, the notion of initiating revolutionary military action within the US ought to stand as misguided in the extreme. Yet at the time there was not only confusion, but a romantic allure. Leaving aside the moral element, to argue as the paper *On Protracted Urban War* did, that things were entering the phase of armed struggle, was a serious misreading of the actual situation. This confusion, in turn, had consequences. Such nascent "military" actions taken by radicals against the authorities and their institutions in such a context ultimately would be confronted as a law enforcement matter and would by and large stand isolated from broad support. They would largely be seen (and *were* largely seen) as illegitimate in the Weberian sense, of the state having a "monopoly on the legitimate use of physical force"[316]—and here we need to put aside the particularity of the urban insurrections among Black people in the US in the mid to late Sixties, and the relative legitimacy of that violence, among large quarters of the affected populations. That is not to say a large number of people, especially youth, did not champion such things, but that does not negate the overarching reality. In that regard, the RU struggle with Bruce Franklin *et al.*, is instructive. It likely saved them from going over a political cliff. It nonetheless left its marks, impelling the RU in its own problematic direction.

Political Line

The Franklin struggle seems to have been a touchstone in elevating the notion of political line—and democratic centralism—to a much more commanding position in the young Revolutionary Union. In summing up the Franklin matter they wrote, "[i]t becomes increasingly evident that what is at issue is not simply the question of the military aspect of struggle, not even just the question of the military strategy for the American revolution, but the whole question of political line."[317]

The concept of line the RU was adopting was taken from Mao and the Chinese Communists:

> If you want knowledge, you must take part in the practice of changing reality. If you want to know the taste of a pear, you must change the pear by eating it yourself.[318]

There was also, however, in Mao's outlook, a strong current of voluntarism (in the philosophical sense of the primacy of will).

A concentrated exposition can be seen in the following:

> The correctness or otherwise of the ideological and political line decides everything. When the Party's line is correct, then everything will come its way. If it has no followers, then it can have followers; if it has no guns, then it can have guns; if it has no political power, then it can have political power.[319]

Allowing for Mao's use of overstatement for emphasis, this nonetheless reads as highly problematic. It transforms the concept of having principles, strategic vision, and a core belief system into a dogmatic construct. And it was this concept of "line" that the RU and later the RCP would increasingly embrace.

The RU's views on this were articulated in an article published in their newspaper *Revolution* titled "Correct Line Achieved Through Study, Struggle, Criticism."[320] While the concept of "study" is the stepping off point, it is not study in the sense of research and investigation. Instead, it is the study of revolutionary theory, specifically the works of Marx, Engels, Lenin, Stalin, and Mao. For the RU, revolutionaries—especially leaders—need to be studying this: first, foremost, and mainly.

This concept was modified, to a degree, by the notion of the mass line, which Mao had popularized:

> We should go to the masses and learn from them, synthesize their experience into better, articulated principles and methods, then do propaganda among the masses, and call upon them to put these principles and methods into practice so as to solve their problems and help them achieve liberation and happiness.[321]

On one level this was quite unique among communists and offered a connection and entrée among groupings of people in a way many other organizations missed. Actually, listening to people, and to a degree, taking counsel from them was a powerful concept. However, the RU/RCP, like their Chinese comrades, were not relinquishing their authority; all this was firmly rooted in the Leninist vanguard model:

> The experience of the masses, especially the mass of workers, is the *raw material* for correct lines and policies. But it is not the finished product, the correct line itself. To develop this correct line requires the application of Marxism-Leninism to "process" the ideas gained by the masses through their experience. It is *this* that the Party must return to the masses and persevere in propagating and carrying out.[322]

In this way the notion of line was tethered to a wider mass imperative, but at the end of the day it was ultimately the Party, through their application of Marxism-Leninism, that was in a position to determine what was in the best interests of the masses.

This also had clear organizational implications. In this they invoked no less an authority than Josef Stalin: "After a conflict of opinion has been closed, after criticism has been exhausted and a decision has been arrived at, unity of will and unity of action of all Party members are the necessary conditions."[323] Stalin's particular track record on such matters aside, this indicated a certain shutting down of aspects of dialogue within the organization. As Steve Hamilton would later write:

> I think a great mistake was made at this point [in the wake of the Franklin struggle] in fostering in the RU some of the long-standing practices of the communist movement in regard to constricting the rights of membership and minority elements within leadership.[324]

What was arrived at was a further closing the door on the 1960s mindset of questioning everything and challenging authority. In its place was the entrenchment of a quasi-religious apprehending of Marxism—though the RU was hardly the worst in this in the new communist movement—coupled with a hierarchal / authoritarian organizational model, albeit one that self-consciously rejected such a characterization. This did not happen immediately or at a single moment, but it was the path they went down.

The Franklin rift was also a touchstone of sorts on how to sum-up schismatic internal struggles. Here, they argued that it allowed "[r]apid progress theoretically, politically and organizationally."[325] While this was not without truth, it was also the case that quite a bit was lost it would seem, from their perspective—not the least of which were a good number of young revolutionaries taken down a path that would in one way or another lead to them no longer being part of a revolutionary movement, to say nothing of some garnering significant prison time. It also needs to be pointed out that the FBI was not wholly unsuccessful—though it is hard to gauge their actual impact—in rending Bruce Franklin from Leibel Bergman; and here we must leave aside whether or not it could have been otherwise. There was also a problem with the RU's misplaced minimizing of the damage done, and the 'good riddance' attitude they assumed as regards those in sharp disagreement. This would continue as a problem going forward.

Allowing for all that, RU leaders guided a sizable section of the organization in not going down a road that too much of the movement—out of despair, rage, frustration, confusion, or some combination of these elements—was going down. In not doing so they were positioned to leap ahead as the new decade unfolded.[326] In this they had something going for them that no other organization around at the time did. The House Internal Security Committee itself understood this, and saw the RU in the context of what were shifting relations between China and the US:

> It is also noteworthy in this time of changing Sino-American relations that these are the two principal Maoist organizations in the United States [referring to the RU & the PLP]. Their members consider Mao Tse-tung's thought to hold all truth and the Chinese communist revolution is their model for the hoped-for revolution in the United States. Revolutionary Union members have already visited Peking. They thus hold the "American franchise" for Maoism abandoned last year by Progressive Labor Party.[327]

The material example of the People's Republic of China was likely the single most important thing the RU had going for it.

Chapter 5

People's China

What kind of spirit is this that makes a foreigner selflessly adopt the cause of the Chinese people's liberation as his own? It is the spirit of internationalism, the spirit of communism, from which every Chinese Communist must learn.
— Mao Tse-Tung, "In Memory of Norman Bethune," December 1939.[328]

The gist of the subject's speech was the praising of the current social and economic conditions in Communist China. The speech extolled the excellence of various facets of Red Chinese Life
— Report on Victoria Garvin speech to a meeting of US-China People's Friendship Association, August 1971.[329]

Returning from China in 1953, William Hinton had a lot in his luggage. Stuffed into his suitcase and footlocker was material collected from his five years in China. It included:

63 posters.
112 books and pamphlets printed in Chinese.
9 pounds of single-spaced, typewritten, carbon copy on very thin paper, including reports on activities in China.
Several hundred photos and snapshots of various scenes and gatherings in China.
45 books and pamphlets, printed in English concerning China.
2 notebooks.

If that audit seems a bit precise, there is a reason; this was how the FBI itemized the material in an internal memo typed up just after the US Customs agency seized the lot of it.[330] What

William Hinton with Chinese Farmer,
date unknown. Courtesy of Monthly Review Press

followed for Hinton was years of struggle to get the material back, culminating in one of the more influential books written in the Sixties. The story of William Hinton's book, and the work of other supporters and advocates for the People's Republic of China, is a critical element in understanding Sixties history, and particularly in understanding the Revolutionary Union and later the Revolutionary Communist Party.

What Hinton encountered on his return to the United States was only the beginning. The seizure of his material meant not only the sidelining of his book project, but a disruptive investigation by both the FBI and by the US Congress—despite the fact that the FBI early on determined:

> No evidence in subject's luggage to indicate he had been

> recruited by the Chinese Communist for subversive activities in the US or to act as an agent or propagandist for the Chinese Communist government.[331]

That conclusion aside, instead of closing the case and returning his files, his papers were sent to the Mississippi Senator James Eastland, who headed the Senate's Committee on Internal Security. Eastland in turn held nationally televised hearings in 1953. The Committee wanted information. They wanted to know not only about Hinton's time in China, but his political affiliations. They promised him that if he agreed to appear, he would have his materials returned. It was not a promise they kept.[332]

The Eastland hearings were a contentious affair. During one exchange, Hinton demanded, "When am I going to get these papers back, because this committee has been weaseling on that thing ever since 9 months ago when they were seized." The committee's Senator Welker responded by changing the subject: "Speaking of weaseling, will you not weasel now and tell me whether or not you are a member of the Communist Party as of this moment?" Hinton in turn refused to answer.[333] Things went downhill from there. In response to one of Hinton's answers, Senator Welker sarcastically asked, "Did you learn that in the tractor school in Red China?" To which Hinton responded, "I learned that from the Bill of Rights," which elicited the following exchange:

> Senator Welker: Oh. You are pretty proud of that Bill of Rights, the first and fourth and fifth amendments?
> Mr. Hinton: Yes. And I notice you aren't very proud of it. You said yesterday if it weren't for the fifth amendment—obviously, you would like to get rid of that fifth amendment, wouldn't you, and the fourth, and the whole Bill of Rights?
> Senator Welker: I would like to get rid of it when it came to witnesses like you.[334]

In the wake of these hearings, the Committee continued to hold his materials. It would be another five years before they finally returned them. When they were finally released, and Monthly Review Press published the book in 1966, the political landscape of the United States was in the midst of a fundamental change.[335] The timing could not have been better. After quickly selling out in hardcover, the paperback edition by Vintage Books would go on to sell 200,000 copies.[336]

Hinton's book was ostensibly about agrarian reform in China. Titled *Fanshen* (literally "to turn the body" or "to turn over"), he explained in the introduction that this particular focus was because, "[w]ithout understanding the land question one cannot understand the Revolution in China, and without understanding the Revolution in China one cannot understand today's world."[337]

What went on in China after 1949 when the Communists came to power was of keen interest to a new generation becoming radicalized and a section of the intelligentsia disillusioned with the Soviet model of socialism. What Hinton documented was at once that of a country emerging from a horrific poverty, but at the same time seeming to go beyond the more rigid and authoritarian Soviet social model. The first thing that strikes one in reading *Fanshen* is its description of the suffering during the years before the Communists came to power, particularly in relation to famine. It showed a China in which mass starvation was not a rare event, but a standing condition. Early in the work, he recounts some witness testimony:

> There were three famine years in a row. The whole family went out to beg things to eat. In Chinchang City conditions were very bad. Many mothers threw newborns into the river. Many children wandered about on the streets and couldn't find their parents. 'We had to sell our eldest daughter. During the famine we ate leaves and the remnants from vinegar

> makings. We were so weak and hungry we couldn't walk. I went out to the hills to get leaves and there the people were fighting each other over the leaves on the trees.'[338]

The book goes on to report on efforts by the Communist Party in the Chinese village of Long Bow, to lead in land reform aimed at eliminating such conditions. The story is one full of conflict as the various villagers wrestle with changing their basic living circumstances born of centuries of tradition. In the end, according to Hinton, "not only had the land system of imperial times at last been completely done away with, but the political and cultural superstructure and beyond that the very consciousness of men, had also been remade."[339] This was not, in his telling, limited to men: "Land reform had broke the patriarchal rigidity of the family by granting property rights to women. With property of their own they were able to struggle effectively for equal rights," though as he points out there remained "a great gap."[340]

On the whole, *Fanshen* presents an overwhelmingly positive narrative, one from which it draws global conclusions:

> Thus the peasants, under the guidance of the Communist Party, had moved step by step from partial knowledge to general knowledge, from spontaneous action to directed action, from limited success to over-all success. And through this process they had transformed themselves from passive victims of natural and social forces into active builders of a new world.[341]

Hinton documents events in the Communist base areas prior to their nationwide seizure of power and the socialist aftermath. Regardless, his emphasis and aim is in extolling the events he witnessed, and while it is not without negative events, there is overall an absence of a more critical scrutiny.

Hinton's was one of a wave of books and testimonies coming

from Western authors with experience in China that hit the shelves in the late Sixties and early Seventies.[342] Such works served not only as a counterpoint to what was being propagated about China within the US, they also suggested a workable alternative to the capitalist-materialistic West. For example, the physician Joshua Horn, in *Away With All Pests*, documents the contrast between pre-revolutionary Shanghai and what he found on a visit to the same city in 1965:

> I searched for scurvy-headed children. Lice-ridden children. Children with inflamed red eyes. Children with bleeding gums. Children with distended stomachs and spindly arms and legs. I searched the sidewalks day and night for children who had been purposely deformed by beggars. Beggars who would leech on to any well-dressed passer-by to blackmail sympathy and offerings, by pretending the hideous looking child was their own.
>
> I looked for children covered with horrible sores upon which flies feasted. I looked for children having a bowel movement, which, after much strain, would only eject tapeworms. [343]

The outcome, of course, was that in 1965 things that had once been everywhere were no longer on display, having been largely eradicated. Given the prevalence of such conditions existing still in larger parts of the world beyond China, this had no small impact.

Fanshen itself was uniquely successful, even seeping into the larger culture. An indication of the kind of impact it made can be seen in the fact that the 1975 play by David

Original cover of Fanshen. *Courtesy of Monthly Review Press*

Hare came to the stage in New York (in the early 1980s). On release Frank Rich, writing in the *New York Times,* observed: "Though the characters know they want freedom from poverty and repression they can't create a just system without answering such complex and previously unthinkable questions as, 'Who depends on whom for a living?'"[344] For the American theater, to say nothing of the larger US culture, this was unprecedented.

This was, however, highly contested, and the FBI proceeded on the basis that at its core, Hinton's work was subversive and needed to be monitored and suppressed. The FBI surveillance trail on Hinton comes through in documents released in response to a Freedom of Information Act request for this book. Hinton himself tried while he was alive to get access to the thousands of pages of FBI records on him, but the releases were so heavily redacted as to be useless. As he said in response to his frustrated efforts to get the records, "I'm paying 10 cents per page for blank pages."[345] The government records delivered for this book consist of files from 1953-1955, and 1982 and 1983. It appears that all FBI records involving Hinton's involvement with the RU and the USCPFA have been destroyed.[346]

Still, there are some records available buried in a background check of the US diplomat and former Vice Presidential candidate, R. Sargent Shriver.[347] In his youth, Shriver was a student assistant for a school run by Hinton's mother, Carmelita. Shriver, as part of the school, went on one of the trips it sponsored for students, traveling to Europe during the summer.[348] As a result, the FBI has information on William Hinton in Shriver's records. Included in this material is the result of an informant report that recounts Hinton's removal from leadership from the Communist Party in 1963:

> After a review of HINTON'S stand in which he sides with the Chinese Communist policies rather than those of Russia, [Gus] HALL [General Secretary, CPUSA] recommended that

> the CP, Eastern Pennsylvania and Delaware, hold one more discussion with him, and if he refuses to stop spreading "anti-Party poison" he would be expelled from the Party.[349]

The result was that in April 1963, Hinton was removed from his leading positions on the District Committee and the District Executive Committee in Philadelphia. Little more than a year later, in June 1964, he was expelled from the Party itself.

Hinton's break with the CPUSA did not mean he was retiring from political life. His exit came at the time of the formal split between China and the Soviet Union, after many years of souring relations and battling polemics. According to the CPUSA infiltrator's report, Hinton was attempting to win people to his position and was "holding meetings with the idea in mind of initiating a new organization which will promote the ideological point of view of the Red Chinese."[350] Of course, Hinton would go on to be part of the Revolutionary Union.

Just as Hinton never publicly identified himself as a Communist Party member, he never publicly identified himself as a member of the RU. This was, however, a moot point, given Larry Goff's 1972 Congressional testimony.

> Mr. Ferry: Did you know William Howard Hinton to be a member of the Revolutionary Union?
> Mr. Goff: Yes sir.
> Mr. Ferry: How did you know William Howard Hinton to be a member of the Revolutionary Union?
> Mr. Goff: He attended meetings where only RU members were allowed.[351]

This was all in line with the fact that Hinton was more than an abstract "friend of China." He was a politically partisan advocate of Maoist socialism.

In this, he appears to have played a key role in the early

years of RU organizing. Raymond Lotta, an RU veteran and theoretician for the Revolutionary Communist Party, recalls how Hinton visited his campus in 1970. He describes how Hinton "had a great effect on us. He illuminated the historical arc of the Chinese revolution—the stages it passed through—and the incredible breakthroughs of the Cultural Revolution."[352] Hinton's influence was not limited to those in and around the RU. Former SDS leader and later Weatherman, Mark Rudd, pointedly mentions Hinton in his memoir, noting that *Fanshen* "was required reading in all collectives."[353]

While Hinton had a certain following, especially among young radicals, conversely, the ruling elites were less smitten with him. In a revealing document K.M. Wilford, a British Foreign office official who had taken part in a forum with Hinton, offered the opinion of Hinton's talk that "it was, as you can imagine, something like an article from the *Peking Review*." While he allowed that he found Hinton "personally agreeable," he was also "naïve as they come and utterly impervious to argument.[354] One is left to imagine Hinton's impression of Wilford.

China Books and Periodicals

It was in 1959 that Henry Halsey Noyes—born in Guangzhou, China, son of Presbyterian missionaries—started the hugely influential book distributor, China Books and Periodicals. Initially, the operation was based in Chicago, but in 1963 moved to San Francisco.[355] During this time, the US legally prohibited trade with China because of the "Trading with the Enemy Act," specifically prohibiting capital to be exported to China. The law did not, however, prohibit the importing of books. It was through this loophole, and with the agreement of the Chinese publishers, that the funds generated by Noyes through his book sales were deposited in a blocked account, thus allowing Noyes to set up shop.[356] It was through such an arrangement that publications from the People's Republic of China were made available in the US. This proved, by the mid-1960s, to be no small matter—perhaps most famously leading to the supply of the nascent Black Panther Party with *Quotations from Chairman Mao Tse-tung,* a title they would in turn use for fundraising their armed patrols of the Oakland police as well as ideological sustenance.

China Books' metamorphosis, like William Hinton's, had its roots in the CPUSA. Noyes had started the operation at the prompting of an old friend, Paul Romaine, a self-described "communist and businessman."[357] According to the FBI, Noyes himself was a communist. As a result, the government acted aggressively toward him, having at one point the INS attempt to build a case for his deportation. As outlined in his FBI file:

> NOYES is currently an alien, as is his wife GERTRUDE NOYES, and both have been active in the Communist Party and related front groups in the past. INS is currently attempting to develop witnesses who can testify to the CP membership of either the subject or his wife at the time in order that deportation proceedings can be realized.[358]

Unfortunately for the Bureau, this turned out to be unrealizable. Failing that, the FBI kept him in their sights, viewing him as a hostile presence on the US scene. This comes through clearly in an FBI memo from 1965 by J. Edgar Hoover, addressing a query by US Congressman Clement J. Zablocki. The Representative was outraged upon learning that "Chinese Communist" literature was being sold in the US and had made his concerns known to the Bureau. In response, Hoover wrote:

> [I]t is not possible for me, as a matter of policy, to comment specifically on those agencies which distribute foreign publications, as information contained in the files of the FBI must be maintained as confidential in accordance with

> regulations of the Department of Justice. I want to assure your constituents, however, that this Bureau is fully aware of these activities and is discharging its responsibilities in the internal security field with thoroughness and dispatch.[359]

The Government's hostility to China Books was on particular display when in receiving literature from CB&P's mail-order catalog, a prominent stamp was displayed inside certain publications reading "A copy of this material has been filed with the Foreign Agents Registration Act" and that registration "does not indicate approval or disapproval of this material by the Government of the United States."[360]

China Books and the Revolutionary Union never had a formal relationship, but all indications are that the two had close and friendly relations. The FBI informant who had infiltrated the Executive Committee had apparently been close to Noyes, to the degree that in 1968, Noyes invited him to go to China in 1969, in connection with the 20th anniversary of the seizure of power. Similarly, when Noyes was away on a selling trip, an RU member, also on the Executive Committee, was asked to fill in at the bookstore in his absence.[361]

Perhaps more importantly, the activities of the two entities were mutually reinforcing; with the former routinely allowing RU cadre and supporters to take literature on consignment[362] and the RU in turn running ads for the store in its newspaper *Revolution* (a by and large ad-free publication). One such advertisement in *Revolution* from 1974 highlighted what the bookstore had available. Not only were there Red Books (*Quotations from Chairman Mao Tse-tung* (vest pocket 35 cents, regular 60 cents), but also the *Selected Works of Mao Tse-tung,* Karl Marx's *Critique of the Gotha Program*, Lenin's *Materialism and Empirio-Criticism,* as well as current issues of *Peking Review, China Reconstructs,* and popular pamphlets from China such as *Philosophy is No Mystery* and *Scaling Peaks in Medical Science*.[363] Given China's policy of popularizing the spread and study of "Marxism-Leninism, Mao Tse-tung Thought" in the days before the internet, these were portable, inexpensive, and available in bulk.

The overall effect of China Books is hard to gauge—the influence of such literature being hard to quantify. However, given the impact on the Black Panthers, the New Left, and the wider radical intelligentsia, it can safely be said that it was a much bigger influence than has heretofore been acknowledged.

Leibel Bergman's Plan?

In discussing China, it is important to note the way US authorities looked at the person they felt was the founder and key leader of the Revolutionary Union, Leibel Bergman. In the FBI's thinking, the RU was not a product of the domestic turmoil within the United States at the time, but rather the product of conspiratorial interaction between Bergman and the leadership of the Chinese Communist Party. In a report prepared for President Richard M. Nixon, Nixon's former associate counsel and staff assistant Tom Huston wrote of Bergman, specifically outlining how in 1965 he:

> Clandestinely travelled to Communist China where he resided for approximately two years utilizing a pseudonym. Shortly after his return to the US in August, 1967, Bergman advised reliable sources of the FBI that he had returned "to do a job" for the Chinese Communists.[364]

According to Huston, Bergman had a threefold mission to form a national union of pro-Maoist radicals, to forward information to the Chinese Communists, and to recruit agents to be trained in China, "after which they would return to this country and operate on behalf of Communist China in a nonpublic or submerged fashion."[365] The information in the Huston report corresponds closely to the FBI's assessment that Bergman "had promised his friends (Chinese) that he would do a job for them."[366] The similarity in tone of both reports suggests that Huston and Nixon were getting their information from the FBI. In their view, "Bergman is an identified Chicom Intelligence Agent."[367] This was a highly dangerous label to be put on a US citizen, but it was a large part of the basis for justifying the FBI's campaign not only against Bergman but the larger RU.

The Bergman Surveillance

As a result of the secret allegations, however, the government—at the highest levels—undertook an intensive campaign of watching Bergman's activity, not only by monitoring publicly available information and through informant reports but also by establishing telephone taps, breaking into his apartment and placing microphones into his living quarters, and contemplating—and quite possibly acting on—deploying closed circuit television cameras in or outside his residence.

In the 1980 trial of FBI agents W. Mark Felt and Edward S. Miller, for their illegal activity against the Weathermen, a good deal of information on the FBI's effort against Bergman was revealed.[368] Felt, the former Deputy Associate Director of the FBI who would later gain notoriety as Watergate's "Deep Throat," had a lot of responsibility in the early Seventies for the FBI's efforts against radicals, especially the Weathermen. Among the myriad efforts he and Miller oversaw were illegal break-ins and other extra-legal measures, which in turn led to their being brought up on charges (they were convicted in 1980 and pardoned soon after by the incoming President Ronald Reagan)[369]. In the course of the Felt-Miller trial—and largely escaping scrutiny—the Bureau's massive effort against Leibel Bergman was revealed publicly. The campaign against Bergman comes through clearly in the testimony of the FBI agent, who oversaw the Bergman investigation:

[Prosecutor Frank Dunham]: Were you using surreptitious

> entry against Leibel Bergman in 1969?
> The Court: That's the Question.
> [David Ryan]: The answer is yes.[370]

According to Ryan, this was "probably done in connection with the installation of sensitive coverage"[371]—sensitive coverage being a euphemism for "microphone coverage."[372]

The Bureau also obtained a floor plan of Bergman's San Francisco apartment:

> Q: And what is the purpose of the floor plan attached to the document?
> A: According to the document, it appears to be a paraphrased, or redacted area. It says, copies of the floor plan are submitted, to augment the San Francisco office's suggestion for potential photographic coverage of Bergman's apartment.[373]

This did not appear to be enough. Ryan later explained the purpose of a memo he had written: "to secure authority for two FBI laboratory experts to travel to San Francisco to conduct a survey of installation of closed-circuit television."[374]

All of these measures were reviewed and approved by top FBI officials. For example, when Bergman moved to a different San Francisco neighborhood in the fall of 1969, and Ryan was trying to set up commensurate surveillance, first Mark Felt came to oversee things, and then approvals went up the Bureau chain of command:

> Q: Does that recommend Mr. Felt undertake a survey of the situation?
> A: Yes, it reads, "It is recommended Mr. Felt travel to San Francisco for on the scene discussions along the above lines."
> Q: And does Mr. Hoover have a comment on that document?

A: Mr. Hoover states in his handwriting. "I concur."[375]

All this was being done under the justification that Bergman, and by extension it would seem, the RU, were acting as agents of a foreign power. Yet throughout this time, Bergman was never charged with espionage or otherwise acting as a foreign agent. Which suggests the larger concern on the part of the government. Unlike other radicals in the field, Bergman held to a more long term view. As an FBI stipulation (an account entered into the court record) at the Felt-Miller trial noted, Bergman "demonstrated his dedication and patience when he said he would overthrow the U.S. government if it took five or fifty years..."[376] Bergman's was a more long range view, and the various government reports project a certain anxiety, a worried look over the shoulders if you will, vis à vis domestic revolutionaries adhering to Maoism. Whether or not Bergman ever "promised friends" that he was "going to do a job for them" would seem beside the point—though as will be seen, this is not necessarily a whole-cloth construct. Fundamentally, though, there was a large interest by those who were in the midst of going through 'the Sixties' in what was taking place in China, particularly the Cultural Revolution. In that respect, it was not so much a matter of *if* that would take a concrete organizational form but *when*, and on what scale.

The RU Visits China

In the fall of 1971, a half dozen members of the Revolutionary Union traveled to China "on invitation" of the Chinese government for six weeks. As part of the tour, as Xinhua English-language news broadcast from October 5, 1971 noted, they met with Zhou Enlai. The RU delegation was part of a larger group of Americans visiting the country that included, among others, members of the American Friends Service Committee and the Black Panther Party, including its leader Huey Newton.

According to official Chinese reports, the RU meeting with Zhou was "cordial" and "friendly."[377] The full content of what the RU delegation—Bob Avakian, Leibel Bergman, Mary Lou Greenberg, Doug Monica, Joanne Psihountas, and Donald H. Wright, along with Pablo Guzman, of the Young Lords Party[378]—discussed with Zhou is not known. What is known is that an informant was embedded within the larger American delegation of 70 plus people, and he or she reported quite specifically on what they learned.

For example, among the visitors meeting Zhou was Bill Epton, a Black American formerly with Progressive Labor. Epton had left the PLP in the wake of its position that "all nationalism is reactionary." Since that time the PLP had become increasingly hostile to China's politics and by 1970 went so far as to proclaim that "Mao Tse-tung's leadership [is] pursuing right-wing policies with a vengeance" and that the country was on the "path of capitalism."[379] This was apparently on Zhou's mind when he met Epton:

> CHOU asked EPTON about the strength of PLP and the latter said that it seemed to be as strong as ever. CHOU asked if there were some dissidents in the PLP and EPTON said there were not many. CHOU asked whether EPTON felt he would be able to draw many people out of the PLP and EPTON said, "No." EPTON'S answer seemed to disappoint CHOU and I sensed a chill of sorts enter the hall and affect CHOU and the audience.[380]

Such an exchange, if accurate, shows a good deal of interest on the part of the Chinese as to what was happening in US radical circles. It also adds certain weight to the oblique references of FBI reports that Leibel Bergman was "doing a favor" for his Chinese friends. Such speculation aside, it does show that the PLP's time as being seen by the Chinese as the force that they would officially sanction was, for all intents and purposes, over.

The politics of PLP aside, the RU visit to China was happening at a pivotal moment for that country. China had set a course on an opening to the West, and US President Nixon would meet with Mao a few months later. This visit by radical and progressive Americans, in that context, appears as sending something of a mixed message by the Chinese to the US power structure.

When the RU delegation landed on September 20, 1971, in Shanghai, the country was in the midst of the "Lin Biao Affair." Lin had been head of the People's Liberation Army. He was also credited with the creation of *Quotations of Chairman Mao Tse-tung*, the book that would become synonymous with China's Cultural Revolution even though Lin was only "marginally involved in determining in the book's specific form and content."[381] Early in the Cultural Revolution, Liu Shaoqi, Mao's former handpicked successor, was the primary target. Once knocked down, Lin was made Mao's successor. However, in a baffling turn of events, Lin was said to have attempted a counter-revolutionary coup, and failing that, on September 13, 1971, attempted to flee the country to the Soviet Union. His plane crashed, killing all aboard. While a complete explanation of that incident is in many ways still forthcoming, in the end it was intertwined with a number of critical events—the US finding a way out of Vietnam, China finding a way out of the prospect of war with its Soviet neighbor, and the Chinese leadership attempting to navigate intense struggles at the top of their power structure. This was a highly fraught time, and it is no exaggeration to say it would set the terms of the world going forward.

The RU delegation waded into the room with all these disparate factors in play, and, while not oblivious to the complexity of things, was incapable of understanding the situation fully. For example, they were well aware of the canceling of the official celebration in Tiananmen for more local celebrations. As Bob Avakian recounted, they were told, "Well, this year we're going to do things a little differently. We're not going to have one big celebration in the central square, Tiananmen, we're going to spread out the celebration in parks all over the city to get more people involved." Avakian tells of how Leibel Bergman offered the explanation that the Chinese did this to avoid having a noticeable absence of Lin at the celebration. He also remembered Bergman's response to the Lin Affair as being along the lines of, "Oh that Mao—anybody gets close to him and down they go."[382] Avakian took issue with this, thinking such criticism was evidence of Bergman abandoning Marxism in favor of a "psychological analysis."[383] For his part, Avakian was more inclined to accept and analyze things based on official statements and published articles—especially by those of the radicals in China. This would become more of an issue between the two in the not too distant future.

All that taken into account, the RU's first-hand experience of what they saw in China on this trip was keenly influential in their later development. From their perspective, in contrast to the currency today that allows for little, if anything, positive in that period, the RU delegation saw things that impressed them. They talked to Iron Women's Teams who had been instrumental in dynamiting through mountains in order to divert a river through it. They met with "three-in-one leadership committees," and revolutionary committees in which Party cadre, administrators and workers collaborated on managing factories. They visited hospitals undertaking what they felt was cutting edge surgery for various cancers that implemented acupuncture as a less drastic anesthesia. They also met with cultural teams going into the much poorer areas to propagate socialist movies and plays.[384]

The RU drew on this first-hand experience as they worked to build their organization. For example, at a public meeting in Los Angeles in 1972, RU member Mary Lou Greenberg—who an informant described as "a young mod with [a] gentle even manner"—related an anecdote from her time in China. She described how

> She and other Americans were billeted in unheated drafty accommodations, and they were also ill. The Chinese people of the area ignored the climatic conditions and went out and harvested the last kernel, not that they needed it, because they were very well off respectively speaking, and much surplus [sic], but in so doing they were thinking only of their fellow Communists all over the world, and therefore the unity of spirit.[385]

This particular informant seems to have been committed to not being taken in by Greenberg, asserting that her "dedication and gentle manner gave the feeling of an iron fist in a velvet glove."[386]

A fuller account of the RU's sense of conditions in Maoist China comes through in a piece written a couple years later, by former SDS National Secretary and RU partisan, C. Clark Kissinger. Kissinger visited China in late 1972 and on his return submitted an article to the *Chicago Tribune*.[387] The piece opens by explaining that his hosts "bent over backwards to take me to see anything I requested and opened the doors of factories, schools, and people's homes for my inspection." From his standpoint, he had unfettered access.

Visiting China at a point when the US domestically was undergoing the twin phenomena of stagnation and inflation, Kissinger noted that "[i]n China there is no inflation. There have been no price increases in China's state-controlled economy for years, and the prices of some important consumer goods have even gone down." Admittedly, most of those goods were the "necessities of life" such as food, household implements, ready-made clothing, and dry goods. He did, however, see what he called "an impressive array of simple 'luxuries' like radios, bicycles, electric fans, sewing machines, cameras, musical instruments, children's toys, and books, books, and more books." Higher end luxury items, however, were more or less out of reach. "[T]he one item on display that most families could not afford was a black-and-white TV set." Still, much of people's entertainment was more social and interactive:

> It seems every village, factory, school, and neighborhood has a basketball court. There are some spectator sports, such as table tennis and soccer matches, but the great emphasis is on participation. Swimming and gymnastics are also very popular. The Chinese seem to go to the movies a lot, and live concerts and plays are more popular than in the U.S. Most big factories have their own amateur theatrical groups. China also has many beautiful parks and museums where families stroll and picnic.[388]

As for housing, he describes a scene as one in which "[n]ew housing is going up everywhere, both in the cities and in the countryside" with the priority being given to "families with the worst old housing," getting served first. He also describes the strong role of the family, relative to what was happening in the US in the Seventies, "[u]nmarried children almost always live at home and retired grandparents live with their children." In Kissinger's estimation:

> [o]lder people are seen as an asset to society not as something to be shut away. Retired workers are urged to take an active part in their neighborhood committees. And elderly people frequently visit the schools to talk to the children about what life was like before the revolution.[389]

This was not just for nostalgia, but for a particular propaganda purpose: "the children of today have never experienced the famine, starvation, and misery of the old China, but for the old people it is still a living and bitter memory."[390] This seems a bit overstated, given that China had seen famine in the early Sixties under the Communists, but it is consistent with a certain myopia in his report.

Among the more striking things in Kissinger's accounts is the day-to-day life for women in China. He describes the breaking with the notion of women as appendages to their husbands—which in the early Seventies was only beginning to be shattered in the US. He tells of how "[t]here is no way to tell whether a woman is married except by asking her. There is no form of address like 'Mrs.'. There are no wedding rings." Women, as a matter of course, kept their own family name and "[f]or all practical purposes, there are no 'housewives' among the younger generation." Along with this was the ready availability of divorce, where a woman "is free to walk out at any time." At the same time, the sexual mores seem to have been steeped in a kind of socialist puritanism. Birth control was not available for unmarried women; the justification was that the social standard was there was to be no pre-marital sex.

Kissinger also described the matter of safety in the places he visited, noting that crime was virtually nonexistent: "one can walk the streets of the great cities at any hour in complete safety, and many hotels do not bother with room keys." In Kissinger's view, "[t]he absence of crime is due to the elimination of poverty and drug addiction and to the new social values."[391]

This and other such accounts are clearly one-sided, failing to critically explore opposite elements of what they discovered, instead taking things more or less at face value. Regardless, the experience of people like Kissinger, Avakian, Greenberg, Hinton, Bergman, and others was of keen interest to a section of the US population that had just come out of the turmoil of the Sixties. What they presented was a living alternate model of a society of hundreds of millions that seemed to have tackled some of the most pressing problems humanity faced. In this respect, the RU's visits to China, with their element of seeing things firsthand, gave them a legitimacy, platform, and an audience. It would be hard to underestimate its effect in allowing the RU to go forward and expand.

Chapter 6

Coalitions, Infiltrators, and Schisms

"We have two purposes in calling this meeting tonight," said Guardian writer Renee Blakkan, who served as moderator. "The first is to arrive at greater clarity on the question involved–the building of a new party. The second is to arrive at a higher level of unity among the new Marxist-Leninist forces."
— The *Guardian*, April 1973.

The major purpose of my assignment from 1972 to 1974 was to develop a position of contact and trust within other left-wing political groups in this country, to prevent their cooperative action, specifically the merger of the Revolutionary Union (RU) and the October League (OL).
— Former FBI Informant, James Burton, July 1980.[392]

With the exit of Bruce Franklin in late 1970, the Revolutionary Union was free to pursue a course that would allow it to significantly expand its organization and influence throughout the United States. That expansion, however, would take place amid a thicket of shifting conditions and circumstances. The polemical battle with Franklin had infected the emerging organization with a lower tolerance for internal dissent and inclined it toward a more sectarian point of view. Meanwhile, the abandonment of Maoism by the nominally Maoist Progressive Labor Party left the field wide-open for the RU to be adopted by the Chinese as its representative within the US; yet this was so at a time when the Chinese were moving toward a geopolitical alliance with the US. Amid all this was the FBI, bruised and battered by exposures of its nefarious work in the previous decade, but committed to counter what it saw as the emerging threat the RU posed. The road ahead would not be an easy one.

The years since Franklin's departure had seen a significant shift in the group's organizational model and areas of concentration. By 1972, the RU had moved its national headquarters from San Francisco to Chicago. Bob Avakian had moved to Chicago in the spring of 1972,[393] as had Barry and Mary Lou Greenberg. Leibel Bergman too would move to Chicago after living in the New York/New Jersey area.[394] Also in 1973, the group started a national newspaper, *Revolution*; this would be its official voice in the years to follow, outlining its key positions, giving a snapshot of its organizational presence throughout various sectors of US society, and serving as a forum for polemics against a widening array of forces they felt they were competing with for the position of revolutionary vanguard of the working class.

From its strongest base in the Bay Area, the RU continued deploying cadre into industry. Former students of UC Berkeley, Stanford and other schools in the Bay Area now found themselves working in places such as the San Francisco Municipal Railway, the Pacific Telephone and Telegraph Company, and the US Postal Service.[395] This would be a scene replicated nationwide in all the places where collectives and individuals joined the RU. These mainly former students would be directly entering the working class by getting manufacturing and other working-class jobs.

The RU also sent cadre to El Paso, Texas in October 1972, to investigate a strike by 4000 Chicano workers, mainly women, against the Farah textile company—then the largest manufacturer of men and boys' pants in the US. [396] What followed was an effective strike-support effort on the part of the RU that included establishing committees in 19 cities nationwide. These committees sponsored support programs, distributed leaflets, and spread the word of what the Farah workers were engaged in. There was also, at times, a more militant edge where people also went into department stores and removed slacks from the racks, or even spilled paint on them.[397] The RU's effort in this case coincided with a successful outcome. The strike, which ended in early 1974, concluded with union recognition.[398] The activity around the Farah strike—much like the earlier Standard Oil Strike—would serve as a type of model for the new communist movement.

FBI: New Rules, Same Mission

By 1972, Richard Nixon had been to China and J. Edgar Hoover was no longer among the living. The FBI, now under the leadership of L. Patrick Gray, showed considerable enthusiasm in targeting the RU. His view was that this was an organization that "I want to go after HARD and with innovation."[399] Gray amplified his marching orders in a July 1972 airtel marked "personal attention," sent to the Special Agents in Charge in fourteen cities:

> There has been good informant penetration of the RU, but coverage is not by any means sufficient in either quality or quantity. In a number of instances, investigations relating to the RU and its membership have been delayed and reporting has been delinquent. Some offices have not afforded investigation of the RU *sufficient imaginative attention.* Special Agents in Charge ... must insure sufficient manpower is afforded to the investigation of this organization, its membership and activities as well as to developing well-placed informant coverage. Insufficient investigation and delays in reporting will not be tolerated.[400]

Gray was largely following in Hoover's footsteps, but because of the increasingly tarnished image of the FBI, through exposures of its COINTELPRO, and the crisis of Watergate, he had to modify the way he did business. For example, he implemented a different filing system that, theoretically, would fly under the radar of investigators, marking memos dealing with illegal break-ins as "do not file" and another set to be marked as "June Mail" for information obtained from illegal sources.[401] In this way, he led the Bureau in attempting to minimize the paper trail of illegal activities. Things, however, had a way of getting out, the work of Sheila Louise O'Connor-Rees being a case in point.

The Informant File of Sheila O'Connor-Rees

In 1972, Sheila Louise O'Connor was a busy woman. She had a job in the Washington, DC office of the National Lawyers Guild;[402] in her off time, she attended demonstrations organized by the Youth International Party (YIPPIES!), she went to meetings of the Vietnam Veterans Against the War/Winter Soldier Organization, and was a committed member of a study group of the Revolutionary Union. She had one other job, that of a paid informant for the Federal Bureau of Investigation code-named "Reverend."

O'Connor-Rees was one half of a duo of freelance spies. In the parlance of FBI coding, she was initially WF [Washington Field Office] 5728-PSI [Potential Security Informant] along with her husband, the British national/journalist/spy John Herbert Rees, who was WF 3796-PSI. John Rees produced a journal called *Information Digest.* That journal served as a clearinghouse for information on the anti-war movement and radicals and was made available to local police agencies. While Rees was not a paid FBI informant at the time his wife was, he was a paid informant for the DC Metro Police, and among other things was subsidized to set up the "Red House" bookstore in Washington, DC in 1971. The thinking being this would bring Rees in touch with activists the police wanted to target.

For her part, Sheila Rees adopted her maiden name of O'Connor and used her ties in the DC activist community to become an FBI informant. An FBI document notes, O'Connor "is knowledgeable about and is in a position to supply information concerning the Revolutionary Union, United States China Friendship [sic], National Lawyers Guild, YSA/Socialist Workers Party, Youth International Party" and numerous subjects of investigative interest.[403] In other words, she was strategically positioned.

As events developed, John Rees' work on the *Information Digest* would lead to the termination of Sheila's work as a paid FBI informant, but that was in the future. First, she would spend considerable time and effort as a member of a collective of the Revolutionary Union in Washington, DC.

O'Connor's efforts coincided with the RU's work to expand and create a chapter in DC. What her informant file reveals is that by 1973 the Bureau had an established doctrine of doing just that:

> HQ experience has determined that the best possible time to target sources and informants for penetration of the RU is during the initial stage of development of new study groups and collectives. An effort should be made by WFO [Washington Field Office] to capitalize upon any logical means to place sources in contact with these groups.[404]

On one level, the O'Connor file is a compilation of bureaucratic and bookkeeping items. There are the various memos authorizing and justifying her pay, which averaged $150 a month (equivalent to $900 in 2022 dollars). It documents the personal background check conducted on her before she could be brought on as a paid informant and contains a photocopy of a hand-written affidavit testifying to her willingness to be an informer. Removing any ambiguity about what she was doing, she wrote out the following: "I voluntarily agree to cooperate with the Federal Bureau of Investigation in a matter affecting national security."[405]

The heart of the file, though, is the short descriptive notes—

typed up by her handlers—of what she was learning and of her goals:

> Source has become a full member of the DCRU, and besides providing weekly summaries of the activities of the DCRU, source has set as one of her goals to find any information regards "secret members" of the RU.[406]

It outlines specifically *how* she should go about the business of informing, stipulating she "[n]ot retain copies of informant reports, to submit these reports written in the third person, not to personally contact the office and to use a pay telephone, when making phone contacts with the office."[407]

While the FBI was mindful of its own security, there is a particular focus dealing with unearthing (and assumedly being able to undermine) the security of the RU. One report describes how the group "devised a telephone code to prevent police or anyone else from bugging members' (DCRU) phones or from obtaining members' phone numbers."[408] Another describes how one member talked about the need for security by "encouraging different locations for meetings." Yet another claims to describe a member talking about the three different types of RU members: open members who are known to be RU members by people both inside and outside the RU; closed members who are known to be RU members only by other RU members; and secret members who are known to be RU members only by select RU members.

While allowances need to be made for the informant and her FBI handler's interpretation of what they were hearing in the study group, it is clear that the bulk of the measures the group took to operate outside the purview of the FBI were well compromised before they were ever implemented. The paradox is that the grouping was more than justified in wanting to avoid the FBI and other agencies "watching them." There is, however, a further irony. These discussions were held in the presence of not one, but *two* government agents. In an informant report of May 1974, in the context of itemizing the status of various study group members, the following fact is revealed:

> Ted Falk: Source advised TED FALK is a code name used by a Maryland State Police undercover agent who has penetrated the Military Law Project (MLP) and VVAW/WSO.[410]

Little is revealed in the report about "Falk" or his role outside of O'Connor's earlier reports, which describe him generously having meetings take place in his apartment.

Beyond that, reports trace a July 1974 visit to the DC area of Bob Avakian, then a national spokesperson of the RU, and other leaders of the group on a national tour as part of efforts to build the Party.[411] One entry recounts how Avakian spoke before 90 people at American University and talked about the RU's success in going into the working class and the limitations of the October League (another Maoist grouping) "for being undependable and not following the Marxist-Leninist-Maoist line correctly."[412] This is striking in its attention to detail and consistent, as we will see, with the FBI's effort in keeping the RU and the OL at odds.

In the wake of Avakian's visit, the work of the DC collective seems to have tapered off. As a result, O'Connor went fishing elsewhere, to keep her value for the FBI current: "When source noticed a lack of activity in the DCRU, she took upon her own initiative to take an active role in the RU dominated organization, the Baltimore Newsreel."[413] Alas, it would be short-lived. O'Connor's undoing was ultimately bound up with the number of pots she had her hand in. Her file ends abruptly in 1976 when the FBI learned the New York State Legislature was investigating John Rees' *Information Digest*, and was intending to subpoena his wife to testify. The FBI concluded:

> This exposure of informant, although not identifying her as a Bureau informant, renders the Bureau susceptible to numerous inquiries. It will also nullify her value as an informant. WFO advised in referenced Bureau telephone call that this informant is not invaluable.[414]

In the parlance of the FBI the "captioned case should be closed." O'Connor was dropped as an informant.

The National Liaison Committee Unravels

In March 1973, a forum titled "What Road to Building a New Communist Party?" was held in New York City. The event drew so many people that it had to be moved from New York University to the Manhattan Center to accommodate the 1,200 in attendance.[415] This would be the largest of six forums sponsored by the *Guardian* newspaper.[416] The forum was a snapshot of the new communist movement at the time, attempting to go forward and unite disparate organizations that were embracing Marxism, and generally looking to China as a model of socialism. Among the speakers at the March forum was Mike Hamlin of the Black Workers Congress, Mike Klonsky of the October League, and Donald H. Wright of the Revolutionary Union. According to the *Guardian*, Wright, who was Black and himself inclined toward a more nationalist position, stressed the RU's stand of the need for "[t]he correct handling of the national question." A vital component of this, according to Wright, was that "revolutionaries had to support both national and multinational forms of organization at this time." The tone of the meeting was generally congenial and the *Guardian* optimistically noted that the unity "was evident from the common effort and participation of the organizations represented." Subsequent forums took up the "Question of the

Black Nation," "Women and the Class Struggle," and "Roads to Building a Workers' Movement."[417]

These forums, along with an organizational entity, the National Liaison Committee, were part of a process of integrating several organizations into a single new communist party, all of which seems to have been proceeding well. Then—behind the scenes—things took a bad turn. When the new political terms emerged, the results were a sharp political shift. As informant Sheila O'Connor would report:

> [t]he RU now views the national question (blacks, Chicanos, Indians), as no longer being primary. The changes in the U.S. are now being made by the working class black and white. This change in position cost the RU two allies. The Black Workers Congress and [the Puerto Rican Revolutionary Workers Organization].[418]

O'Connor's version—or whoever transcribed her reports—of the struggle is at once an oversimplification and a capsulation. The two allies O'Connor refers to had been part of the National Liaison Committee (NLC). Begun in 1973, the NLC initially consisted of four groups: I Wor Kuen the Puerto Rican Revolutionary Workers Organization (formerly the Young Lords), the Black Workers Congress, and the Revolutionary Union.

Of all the struggles the RU engaged in in its seven years of existence, this is one of the most baffling. On the surface, it is the story of an effort at uniting the mainly white students of the RU who had turned to Maoism, with the Black, Asian American, and Latino organizations that had followed a similar path that tragically ended in a failure to achieve unity. Officially, the RU explained this as being a major debate over the "national question" and a failure to come to agreement on the role of non-white revolutionaries in a new party formation. While that explanation may have been at the political core of contention and indeed the overwhelming issue, a closer look shows other things in play that have never been dissected. First though, it is necessary to examine the two key players, beyond the RU, in this effort.

The Black Workers Congress

The Black Workers Congress (officially the International Black Workers Congress) grew out of the actions of Black autoworkers in Detroit, specifically a wildcat strike at the Dodge Main unit of Chrysler in 1968 against harsh working conditions. The organizational entity that was formed, the Dodge Revolutionary Union Movement (DRUM), later became a model extended to other plants in the area such as the Ford Revolutionary Union Movement (FRUM) and the Eldon Avenue Revolutionary Union Movement (ELRUM) at Chrysler. This, in turn, was aggregated into the League of Revolutionary Black Workers. Unlike the Black Panthers, whose famous Ten-Point Program had as a focus the rights and dignity of Black people, the BWC stated a more communist vision, as witnessed in Point One of their program:

> Workers' control of the means of work and production, transportation services and communication facilities so that the exploitation of labor will cease and no person or corporation will get rich off the labor of another person but all people will work for the collective benefit of humanity.[419]

Like much of the rest of the radical movement of the day the League confronted a sharply changed situation as the anti-war movement diminished and the Black rebellions that rocked the cities especially in the period of 1963-1968 subsided, and the limits of legitimate protest and dissent were reached. In this context, there was a deeper embrace of Marxism-Leninism, though the exact interpretation of it was a matter of controversy.

One consequence of this was that by 1971, internal conflict had split the League into two formations, one section going with the Communist League, the other becoming the International Black Workers Congress (BWC). BWC was largely a construct of Student Non-Violent Coordinating Committee (SNCC) veteran James Forman, who would be its head in its first two years of existence. It also included, among others, Mike Hamlin, Ken Cockrel and John Watson. BWC's founding in Gary, Indiana, in the fall of 1971, was likely its high point. This was an event attended by just over 400 people—though the group claimed to have reached a membership of 500.[420]

The Puerto Rican Revolutionary Workers Organization

Like the BWC, the Puerto Rican Revolutionary Workers Organization (PRRWO) had evolved from other groups and was attempting to cross the bridge of the Seventies by embracing Maoism. The group's roots lay in the Chicago street organization the Young Lords Organization that was transformed into the Young Lords Party, whose membership was based mainly in New York and Chicago, though they had a presence in other cities such as Philadelphia, Boston and in Connecticut. The group in New York grew mainly out of the efforts of students at SUNY Old Westbury and Columbia University, and through ties in East Harlem and the Lower East Side. Through actions such as intervention in trash pickup, doing what the city would not do, then joining with people as they built barricades and set trash on fire, and an occupation at the Bronx's Lincoln Hospital around health care in the Puerto Rican community, the group had a reputation and name-recognition nationally.[421]

The PRRWO's relations with the RU appear to have been more integral than the RU's with the BWC. Not only did they attend the *Guardian* forums on Party Building, they also attended meetings of the RU's student-based Attica Brigade. While exact numbers are unclear, given the PRRWO's limited geographic reach, they seem to have been a smaller organization of less than 100 members.[422]

One other organization, I Wor Kuen, an Asian-American organization based in New York (and later San Francisco),[423] was brought onto the NLC at the prompting of the PRRWO, but eventually found itself in disagreement, and left soon after.[424] Combined, however, the RU, the PRRWO and the BWC held out the promise of a much more multi-national new communist party emerging out of the myriad struggles that had broken out in the course of the previous decade.

To get an idea of the political struggle in the NLC it is worth looking at two key papers. In 1972 the RU published *Red Papers 5: National Liberation and Proletarian Revolution in the U.S.* Less than two years later they published *Red Papers 6: Build the Leadership of the Proletariat and its Party*. The differences in position are exemplified in their titles, the latter bearing no mention of the specific struggles of Black, Latin, Asian, and other oppressed peoples. Steve Hamilton later noted that in *Red Papers 5,* the RU "[s]till maintained that the Black struggle was also an important revolutionary struggle in its own right," but by *Red Papers 6,* "[t]he RU leadership decided that bourgeois nationalism was a bigger problem than white chauvinism within the communist movement."[425] Hamilton's assessment is borne out by Bob Avakian, who was at the heart of articulating the evolving position. In answer to a question at a program in 1974 he defended the RU's new outlook saying that within the revolutionary movement "[w]e have to recognize, that what has been the main danger for the reasons that I outlined, has been narrow nationalism."[426]

What had happened in the interim was that a struggle had gripped the RU, and the larger movement—one with longstanding implications. Much of the debate that animated the new communist movement in the 1972-74 period—inscrutable as it might appear today—argued for the primacy of a separate nation for African-Americans in what was known in some circles as the Black Belt South. As Hamilton noted, this coincided with a tendency in "the anti-revisionist movement to reaffirm antiquated COMINTERN positions."[427] What followed was a specialized debate on the matter of a "new democratic Republic in the Black Belt," and whether or not secession was a right or a demand and how the new communist movement would stand in regard to this.[428] This was all pointedly debated in the National Liaison Committee.

The other question pressing on efforts toward unity was what role would these national struggles play in a larger party—would non-white organizations as part of a multinational party have a separate identity or not? The official RCP summation put things as follows:

> There were two questions around which the three organizations were divided into two camps: First, is the slogan "Black Workers Take the Lead" a correct slogan for the working class movement or for the Black liberation struggle in particular? And second, the issue of revolutionary nationalism—is revolutionary nationalism the same thing as Marxism-Leninism, is there an equal sign between them?[429]

The RU, in its *Red Papers 6*, with a defensive look over its shoulder to its earlier indictment of Progressive Labor and their stand on the question of Black people's struggle, wrote:

> So, are we reversing ourselves and saying with Progressive Labor that "all nationalism is reactionary?" No. But, in the final analysis, all nationalism is—nationalism. And all nationalism, even the most progressive, is, in the final analysis, bourgeois ideology. It is the ideology of "my nationality first" which reflects and serves the interests of the bourgeoisie of the particular nationality.[430]

Such were, in broad strokes, the political terms. But there was an internal organizational dimension that seemed to have exerted an important influence in bringing the RU to this peculiar place. Specifically, in the midst of this tense and complex struggle—one involving the highly volatile matter of 'race' and nationality—the behavior of RU Central Committee member Donald H. Wright became a problem.

The Strange Case of Donald H. Wright

One of the most curious—and politically disruptive—characters to pass through the RU was Donald Herbert Wright. Most comrades who came in touch with him have a lasting impression, either not quite knowing what to make of him or being downright suspicious. His most contentious period as a leading RU cadre coincided with the life of the NLC.

Wright joined the RU during its national tour in 1970. According to Bob Avakian, he had come to the RU through Leibel Bergman, who knew his father from his time in the Communist Party. As Avakian recalls, Wright was said to have been part of "some sort of a caucus, or a sort of a semi-secret group" within the CPUSA that "was supposed to be more radical than the CP itself"—while at the same time Wright was part of the Chicago area Black Panthers.[431] That CPUSA affiliation is a matter of controversy.

The "secret CP" grouping Wright came out of appears to have been something called the "Ad Hoc Committee," or AHC. AHC was an entity of dubious beginnings, being wholly sprung from the imagination of FBI Special Agent Herbert K. Stallings. The description of the program is one of those hall-of-mirrors one often hears of, but rarely encounters outside of fantastic film or fiction, let alone having it so meticulously documented. The following, from the FBI personnel file of Stallings, recommending him for a bonus for his good work, explains the program.

> It will be recalled that in November, 1962, this agent created from his own imagination based upon developments within the communist movement in the Chicago area a non-existent Ad Hoc Committee (AHC) for a Scientific Socialist Line as the publishers of an anonymously circulated "Ad Hoc Bulletin." This bulletin, in direct line with the Bureau's over-all objective, is designed to disrupt and fragmentize the communist movement in the Chicago area, and nationally if possible. It has taken a pro-Chinese, Marxist-Leninist line, and the general over-all purpose of the bulletin is to create in the eyes of the CP the existence of a factional grouping within the Illinois District and nationally if possible which adheres to the Chinese interpretation of Marxism-Leninism, as against the pro-Soviet line of the CPUSA and the Illinois District.[432]

The independent role AHC played within the CPUSA as it evolved past the bulletins is a matter ripe for research, though the evidence suggests it became an actual organizational entity.[433] For its part, the full government file on AHC (FBI File 100-HQ-442715) consists "of eight federal records center boxes," and is approximately 17,000 pages long. Unfortunately, because of the backlog at the National Archives, the authors of this work were told "it will be a number of years" before the file will be fully available.[434] It is, however, clear that the AHC's origins were a wholesale construct of the FBI, aimed at undermining the CPUSA.

However, it seems AHC also was deployed against the New Left. AHC shows up specifically in relation to the Revolutionary Union and its work in Chicago from the RU's very beginnings. The memo referred to in Chapter 4 dealing with a Chicago meeting centered on the Franklin split, is pointedly copied to "AHC 100-47215"—meaning copies of the Franklin bulletin went into the AHC file.[435] Likewise, a memo on an RU meeting in Washington, DC, submitted from the FBI's Chicago office is also copied to "100-442715 (AHC)."[436]

It is also noteworthy that evidence shows the Chicago RU had an informant in place from its origin. A Bureau report on an inspection of the Chicago office pointedly documents the state of the RU in that City in the period 1970 to 1971. It records that there were seven members positively identified as being in the RU, it names the two people it felt were in leadership, and then lists under "Identity of SI [security informants] and PSI [potential security informants] affording coverage to file as, 'B.4'. Under the heading is a redacted section, larger than anything else on the document table, with only the notation B.4.[437] Chicago was thus a much more problematic place for the RU than they likely realized.

Leibel Bergman seems to have been familiar with the AHC from early on, and to have taken it at face value. Notes in David Sullivan's file—the former RU/RCP member who donated his papers to NYU—appear to be of an interview he did with Bergman about AHC and Donald H. Wright. According to those notes, Bergman encountered this entity in its gestating period: "AHC put out a bulletin condemning CPSU politics as revisionist say[ing] what was going on in China—[was] mostly pretty good." Bergman also felt that "for a while [it] had some influence in [the] CP." Also, according to the notes, "Bergman was only one who had contact with them–they were very security conscious."[438] There is one other thing in Sullivan's notes: "DH was in AHC when he joined the RU." While it cannot be established with certainty these notes were indeed an interview with Bergman (both Bergman and Sullivan have since passed away), they are consistent with Avakian's remarks on Wright's background, and the FBI's description of the program.[439]

For his part, Bob Avakian's account of Wright raises as many questions as it answers. He describes an early meeting with Wright—who he refers to only as "D.H."—where the matter of the oppression of Black people was debated. Wright took the position that a white person could not truly understand such oppression. One gets a sense in this telling of someone who would not be comfortable in the mainly white RU, yet as Avakian writes, "for whatever reasons"— and he does not speculate on what those reasons might be—Wright joined the RU.[440] Not only did he join, he became a high profile member of the Central Committee. [441] He was also the RU point person on the NLC, at what appears to have been his own initiative:

> [Wright] was more and more asserting that he should be playing a leadership role in relation to the Black members within the RU in particular, and he was pushing that he should be the RU representative on the Liaison Committee. Leibel [Bergman], interestingly enough, was opposed to this.[442]

Avakian explains this in terms of only whether a white or Black person could represent the RU's line, and does not venture anything further about Bergman's hesitations beyond the political questions—though it is clear in Sullivan's notes that Bergman had serious misgivings about Wright, beyond politics.

Regardless, at first things seemed to have gone well, with the RU noting that reports of joint work received from comrades around the country showed "growing ideological unity in the liaison committee," and deemed this encouraging. In fact, the RU's Secretariat, "with Wright concurring, moved to step up the work of the liaison and, together with other organizations, to develop the [ILLEGIBLE] for building the Marxist-Leninist Party in a systematic way."[443] The notes from the Bergman interview are similarly optimistic: "Liaison [Committee] made + approved a Party-unity motion."[444]

In this period Wright had even married the new leader of the PRRWO, Gloria Fontanez—though that too had its own controversy, apparently involving the break-up of Fontanez's existing relationship.[445] Regardless, this included a "movement" wedding celebration that stood as a symbol of the soon-to-be marriage of the organizations.[446] However, things would soon take a bad turn. A report by the RU gives a sense of the problems:

> We cannot understand why members of these organizations [in the NLC] have been telling our comrades on a number of different occasions, that <u>part</u> of your leadership is trying to negate the national question, that <u>part</u> is no good and should be struggled against [i.e., the leadership of Bergman and Avakian]. Why, if Wright really upheld democratic centralism, didn't the comrades in these other organizations just say that your leadership and not <u>part of your leadership</u> is guilty of this."[447]

Wright, rather than putting forward the position of the RU, was putting forward his own position and suggesting that within the RU there was dissension. Given his critical role as the RU point person on the National Liaison Committee, this was highly divisive; rather than working toward unity, it encouraged rupture.

Internally, there was concern beyond the divergent politics. An FBI report recounts an exchange between Leibel Bergman, his wife Vicki Garvin, and two guests—who were in fact FBI informants—visiting them in New Jersey from Chicago. The report makes clear that Bergman was having difficulty with a highly placed Black comrade in the RU, to the degree that he suspects the comrade might be working for the government:

> Bergman said he is having trouble with REDACTED and although he doesn't quite know how yet RU plans to REDACTED. This will create REDACTED as REDACTED and the Black Workers Congress. He described REDACTED as having become a Black militant ... Later, when they were

> alone, Bergman asked REDACTED could be an "agent?" Source did not think so because the role of an agent is to be cooperative and conciliatory with his target where as REDACTED. Also, having known REDACTED doubted his REDACTED could become an informant for the opposition. Bergman replied. "I guess you are right."[448]

The redactions include the informant's name, the RU person under discussion, and people and organizations in the NLC. Given everything involved, the RU person under discussion would likely be Wright. It is striking that the informant, who knew the person under discussion, defends him. This could be simply a matter of reflex, defending someone who might or might not be a fellow informant, or it could have been an effort to consciously protect someone they knew was an informant.

Here a couple of things need to be noted. First, Bergman's suspicions of a high level agent were in keeping with the FBI's stated objectives:

> At the FBI conference relating to the Revolutionary Union (RU) and pro-Chinese communist matters, held in San Francisco, 1/22-23/73, it was recommended the study paper "Summary of Radical, Political Thought" be updated, revised as necessary, and thereafter be disseminated to all offices involved in this investigation. The paper will be used to indoctrinate Special Agents in the fundamentals of Marxism/Leninism/Maoism looking to development of quality informants who may be targeted to penetrate domestic pro-Chicom groups at a leadership level.[449]

The paper this was drawn from, "Summary of Radical Political Thought," was not authored by Herbert K. Stallings.[450] Stallings had apparently been brought in to help with the emerging Maoist threat, one apparently deemed worthy of its own conferences. Second, as regards getting the informant up to "a leadership level," the Bureau had already accomplished this, as has been shown with its Executive Committee penetration. The following, however—a report from the RU's National Central Committee meeting that took place from March 12-14, 1971—reveals the infiltration continued as the group became a national organization.

> STEVE HAMILTON gave a mumbled, rambling account of the RU's relationship with the BPP. HAMILTON noted that the RU in eastern Pennsylvania was holding joint workshops with the BPP and doing support work for the Panthers. HAMILTON criticized this practice because BPP was not Marxist Leninist. Delegates from eastern Pennsylvania took umbrage at HAMILTON's remarks because they said he was implying that no black organization can be Marxist-Leninist.[451]

The level of detail in this synopsis was made possible because of a Bureau informant at the meeting; "REDACTED attended the NCC and related the comments herein to SA JOHN W. MCCAFFREY on 3/16/71."[452] At the time McCaffrey was based in the Chicago Field Office.[453]

Identifying the informant short of a confession or Bureau gaffe is an uphill slog. The Bureau early on stipulated that reports be "prepared in a manner to protect informants, sensitive techniques, and operations."[454] However, the *presence* of multiple informants was revealed as early as August 1968 (pre-dating the Goffs), i.e., there were at least two people in the Bay Area serving as informants, *plus* the Bureau had informants it was enlisting in Chicago:

> Pertinent information developed through REDACTED, REDACTED and *Chicago informants* [emphasis added]

> should be incorporated, paraphrased as necessary, into the RU report and reports on RU members.[455]

While the identity of the specific informants is a matter for future disclosure, the fact that the FBI had two high level informants in the RU from its beginnings is established, as is the fact that they had an informant in the Chicago RU, this too from its very beginnings. And now it is also clear that by the early Seventies, they had an informant—whose identity might overlap with the above—on the Central Committee.

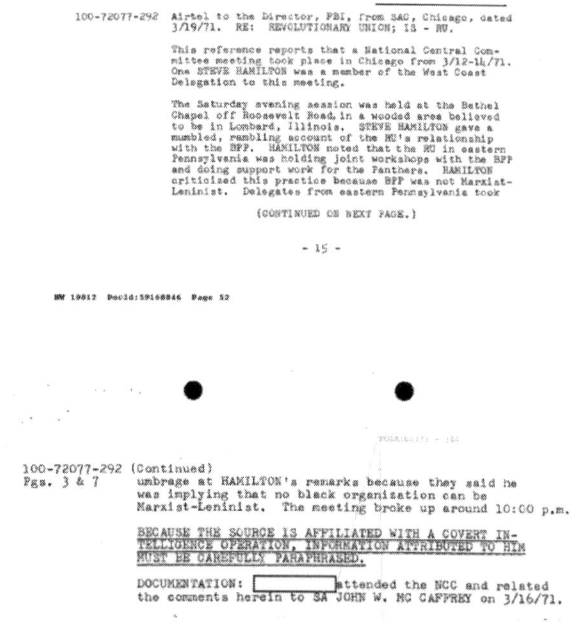

100-72077-292 Airtel to the Director, FBI, from SAC, Chicago, dated 3/19/71. RE: REVOLUTIONARY UNION; IS - RU.

This reference reports that a National Central Committee meeting took place in Chicago from 3/12-14/71. One STEVE HAMILTON was a member of the West Coast Delegation to this meeting.

The Saturday evening session was held at the Bethel Chapel off Roosevelt Road, in a wooded area believed to be in Lombard, Illinois. STEVE HAMILTON gave a mumbled, rambling account of the RU's relationship with the BPP. HAMILTON noted that the RU in eastern Pennsylvania was holding joint workshops with the BPP and doing support work for the Panthers. HAMILTON criticized this practice because BPP was not Marxist-Leninist. Delegates from eastern Pennsylvania took

(CONTINUED ON NEXT PAGE.)

- 15 -

NW 19812 DocId:59168846 Page 52

100-72077-292 (Continued)
Pgs. 3 & 7

umbrage at HAMILTON's remarks because they said he was implying that no black organization can be Marxist-Leninist. The meeting broke up around 10:00 p.m.

BECAUSE THE SOURCE IS AFFILIATED WITH A COVERT INTELLIGENCE OPERATION, INFORMATION ATTRIBUTED TO HIM MUST BE CAREFULLY PARAPHRASED.

DOCUMENTATION: [redacted] attended the NCC and related the comments herein to SA JOHN W. MC CAFFREY on 3/16/71.

Informant report in Steve Hamilton's Bureau file revealing an informant in the RU National Central Committee.
US Government document

As for Wright, he would soon leave the RU, but not before one last incident. With the NLC disintegrating, Wright was called to account by the RU for his behavior. The results were startling:

> At the next meeting of the Secretariat the question of deterioration of the relations between the organizations was at Wright's insistence put first on the agenda, but as soon as the meeting started and the question of Wright's responsibility for the deterioration in relations began to be raised he refused to discuss it and met it with physical attacks on the comrades of the Secretariat. After a couple of attempts at restoring order and principled struggle, the meeting broke up.[456]

According to one former RU comrade, Wright physically attacked a leading comrade who was also in VVAW, breaking a couple of his fingers.[457] This would be Wright's last meeting as a member of the RU.

The political disagreements, exacerbated by Wright's actions, created an intractable situation. Approximately two weeks after the Party Unity motion had been signed, the NLC fell apart.[458] While the RU recognized the collapse "as a severe setback,"[459] they publicly cast this only as a difference of line on the matter of Black and other oppressed people, and portrayed Wright as an "opportunist"—a catchall phrase with the benefit of many meanings. Wright, who was expelled from the RU, seems to have thereafter dropped off the political radar. He passed away in 2009.

Meanwhile, the shift in how the RU saw the role of Black, Latino and other ethnicities in the revolutionary struggle also seems to have led Steve Hamilton and "at least a fair number in the Bay Area" to leave the RU.[460] For its part, the RU was later able to attract some individual cadre from the former BWC and PRRWO, but they were small in number, and carried less of the political prestige and heightened legitimacy a merger would have offered.[461]

As for the Bureau, the creation of a new, more fully multi-

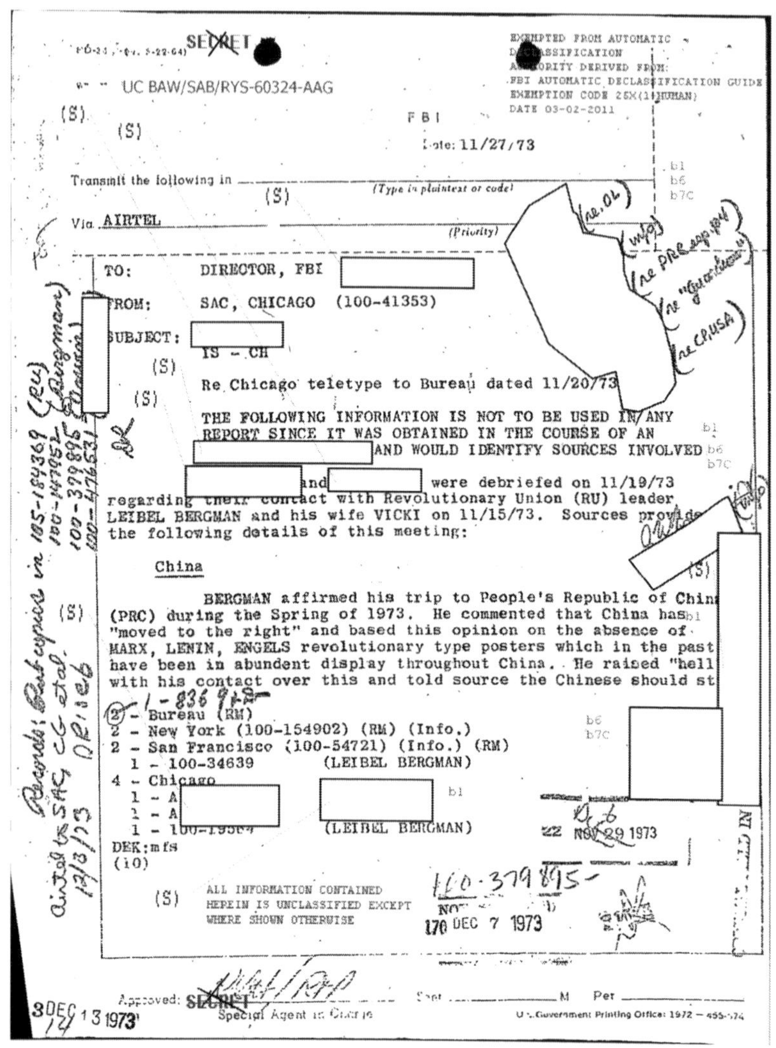
SECRET

UC BAW/SAB/RYS-60324-AAG

EXEMPTED FROM AUTOMATIC DECLASSIFICATION
AUTHORITY DERIVED FROM:
FBI AUTOMATIC DECLASSIFICATION GUIDE
EXEMPTION CODE 25X(1)(HUMAN)
DATE 03-02-2011

FBI

Date: 11/27/73

Transmit the following in (Type in plaintext or code)

Via AIRTEL (Priority)

TO: DIRECTOR, FBI

FROM: SAC, CHICAGO (100-41353)

SUBJECT: IS - CH

Re Chicago teletype to Bureau dated 11/20/73

THE FOLLOWING INFORMATION IS NOT TO BE USED IN ANY REPORT SINCE IT WAS OBTAINED IN THE COURSE OF AN AND WOULD IDENTIFY SOURCES INVOLVED

and were debriefed on 11/19/73 regarding their contact with Revolutionary Union (RU) leader LEIBEL BERGMAN and his wife VICKI on 11/15/73. Sources provide the following details of this meeting:

China

BERGMAN affirmed his trip to People's Republic of China (PRC) during the Spring of 1973. He commented that China has "moved to the right" and based this opinion on the absence of MARX, LENIN, ENGELS revolutionary type posters which in the past have been in abundent display throughout China. He raised "hell" with his contact over this and told source the Chinese should st

2 - Bureau (RM)
2 - New York (100-154902) (RM) (Info.)
2 - San Francisco (100-54721) (Info.) (RM)
1 - 100-34639 (LEIBEL BERGMAN)
4 - Chicago
1 - A
1 - A
1 - 100- (LEIBEL BERGMAN)
DEK:mfs
(10)

ALL INFORMATION CONTAINED HEREIN IS UNCLASSIFIED EXCEPT WHERE SHOWN OTHERWISE

NOV 29 1973

DEC 7 1973

Approved: SECRET Special Agent in Charge

U.S. Government Printing Office: 1972

Informant report on Leibel Bergman, 1973.
US Government document

national communist Party had derailed. If it had been serendipity, they were likely thanking the universe for this favorable turn. If it had been their planned objective, with more pro-active efforts on their part, there must have been champagne toasts.

James Burton's Purpose

James Burton was a former janitor and swap-shop operator based in Tampa, Florida.[462] He was also an early Seventies implementation of the Ad Hoc Committee / notional collective model the FBI had deployed to such good effect against the Communist Party USA.

In the early 1970s, "at the direction of the bureau,"[463] Burton founded something called the "Red Star Cadre," a fake new communist organization set up to further the FBI's efforts. Red Star Cadre benefited from the dynamic in the new communist movement in the mid-Seventies, wherein anyone who claimed the mantle of "anti-revisionism" was on a mission to create a new communist party. The result was a frenzy of activity by organizations both sizable and minuscule. This was ample raw material for the Bureau to deploy its notional collective concept, with subsequent jargon—buffeted by the insights of people like SA Herb Stallings.

Among Burton's efforts was joining together with several other new communist groups for a conference in Canada with the aim of creating a new party. Of the seven groups participating, five were from the US: American Communist Workers Movement (M-L), Association of Communist Workers, the Red Collective, the Communist League and Red Star Cadre.[464] Two of those groups, Burton's Red Star Cadre and the Red Collective, were FBI manifestations.[465]

The Schafers

The Red Collective was a construct of Harry E. "Gi" Schafer—who had been an FBI informant in SDS—and his wife, Jill Schafer. After the Red Collective's break down of relations with two new communist groupings, the Central Organization of US Marxist-Leninist (COUSML) and the American Communist Workers Movement (ACWM), the Bureau appears to have tried to link them up with either the RU or the October League (OL) in New Orleans:

> Currently, both the October League and the Revolutionary Union are making overtures to a group of independent New Orleans activists, including JILL SCHAFER[466]

The New Orleans SAC felt that because of the trouble the RU was having with their radical contact in the area, there might be an opening for the Bureau, though he underscored that it could not be done under the Red Star name, because it had been associated with the "objectionable" (to the RU and OL) COUSML. So, the name would need to be retired, but if "the need arises for a label for the local activists, one will be chosen by those activists;"[467] in other words, a new phony collective name. The director, in turn, responded alluding to an unnamed informant (Jill Schafer?) pursuing this:

> It is suggested you direct REDACTED to continue close contact with local revolutionary activists particularly those who seek association with the RU, in anticipation that REDACTED will be able to become a member and possibly a leader in the event the organization eventually establishes in New Orleans.[468]

This effort appears to have been interrupted by the Schafers refocusing on the 1972 takeover at Wounded Knee, where they set up one last phony collective, i.e., the "Crazy Horse Collective." In the course of their Wounded Knee activity, their provocative efforts continued, increasing skepticism by activists and making further work untenable. By 1975, the FBI was publicly admitting they had been paid informants.[469]

* * *

A sense of the disruptive ability in such constructions comes through in Burton's sworn statement. In December 1973, while visiting Chicago with the leader of the Communist League, Nelson Peery, he said, "Under the FBI's direction, I discouraged this group from working with the Revolutionary Union by characterizing the RU as being populated by old line members of the Communist Party who were working for the FBI."[470]

According to Burton, the Bureau supplied him and his group with everything from operating funds to T-shirts with a large red star and the legend "Fight Back."[471] In addition to Burton, the Tampa "cadre" included "several former intelligence officers from the military and area students being paid by the FBI." It also had ties with police agents who had infiltrated Vietnam Veterans Against the War, "who broke up the local chapter and promoted a split with the national organization."[472]

While Burton and his group trolled around various new communist entities between 1972 and 1974, his key objective was to prevent "the merger of the Revolutionary Union (RU) and the October League (OL)."[473] Next to the Revolutionary Union, the second largest new communist Maoist group—leaving aside the problematic Progressive Labor Party—was the October League. As far back as the struggle with Marv Treiger, who left the RU and joined with the October League's Mike Klonsky (for a time), the RCP and the OL had a contentious and competitive relationship. There was, however, a short-lived moment where it seemed relations between the two groups were thawing. In the words of RU, the "OL had at this point abandoned some of its initial ultra-left criticisms of the RU."[474] This was the context in which Burton carried out his work for the FBI.

A sample of his efforts comes through in an affidavit from a class action lawsuit the ACLU brought against the Chicago police intelligence division. In it Burton stated:

At a 1972 meeting in Atlanta, which was held to discuss a

> possible national merger between the Revolutionary Union and the October League and other domestic political groups, I made statements, under the FBI's direction, that individuals in the Revolutionary Union were dishonest and could not be relied upon.[475]

Burton's efforts took place in the heightened sectarian atmosphere within the new communist movement in general, and the RU in particular. By the mid-Seventies, the RU was displaying willingness; indeed, an eagerness to launch polemics against any organization it felt was claiming *its* rightful mantle as the new vanguard. Throughout 1974 *Revolution* ran extensive polemics against the *Guardian* newspaper, the October League, the Black Workers Congress, the Puerto Rican Revolutionary Workers Organization, and the Communist League.[476] The RU sought to distinguish itself from all others, as the true vanguard that would soon be manifested in a new communist Party. The irony is that they, like those they polemicized against, were in a race to a finish line that would soon vanish—as events in China took their decisive turn.

Boston Busing

Meantime, the fallout from the political terms set by the National Liaison Committee controversy had direct consequences. This was best exemplified in Boston in the fall of 1974. At the end of the 1973-74 school year, a Federal judge in Massachusetts, Wendell Arthur Garrity, issued a ruling that Boston school authorities had "knowingly carried out a systematic program of segregation." The remedy, the court said, was to implement a busing program to integrate the schools. What came about as a result was a plan to transfer students between primarily Black and white neighborhoods, including the old Irish-American neighborhood of South Boston, notorious for its racial intolerance.[477] In this way, the RU attempted to implement its newly found position of putting the unity of the working class front and center. What they came up with was a scheme where working class unity could trump the brutal contradictions of race. Taking things to an extreme, a headline in *Revolution* in October 1974 proclaimed, "People Must Unite to Smash the Boston Busing Plan."[478] For the RU, this was a matter of the ruling class dividing "the workers and [attempting] to drive a wedge between the struggles of the working class and the struggles of oppressed nationalities."[479] A follow-up article elaborated the RU's view:

> Those who think that the only way to stand with Black people and other oppressed nationalities is to attack white workers as simply a bunch of racists, who think that the ruling class is the friend of the oppressed, can at best only drag at the tail of the struggle, and, if they continue in this path, can only end up falling over backwards completely into the camp of the ruling class.[480]

This astonished quite a few people, including the *Boston Globe,* who noted, "Unlike most radical leftist groups such as the Progressive Labor Party, the group [RU] opposes busing." This in the context of ugly demonstrations—with white mobs bombarding buses carrying Black students, with rocks, bottles, and eggs.[481] The RU's position was ridiculed widely on the left, and inside its own ranks it created serious dissension. Regardless, they held firm. Years later—after the group had repudiated this position—Bob Avakian would reflect on the episode saying, "We missed the essence of what was going on," and that he was personally "horrified at the initial [*Revolution*] headline."[482] The damage, however, was done. The political fallout would have lasting consequences for the RU in terms of loss of prestige if not legitimacy in certain quarters.

Chapter 7

Sinking Roots and Making the Papers

I said: "I'm going to go down to Keystone [West Virginia], to that pool hall, with anyone who will go with me. We will warn the people there and stand with them." Anyone who wanted to attack Cinder Bottom's beer joint would have to come through us. With that, the moment passed. The strike leaders stepped up, and started loudly organizing pickets. There was no more talk that night of raiding the Black community.
— Mike Ely, RU cadre based in West Virginia circa 1974-79.[483]

In December 1974 he left with a female aide and turned up in the West Virginia coal fields in early 1975. By August he had a committee going. With him were two other young RU men. By early September [Lewis "Skip"] Delano and his cadres had provoked 80,000 coal diggers into a long illegal strike.
— "Revolutionary Union Building Activist Marxists Cadres." Victor Riesel, column, May 1976.[484]

The RU's trouble in the Boston Busing crisis and the National Liaison Committee aside, they continued to expand their organizational reach, both among students and veterans, but perhaps most significantly within the working class. As they did so, they confronted not just the limits of doing radical political work among a population largely non-receptive to radical politics, but also the consistent attention of the FBI and its proxy agents, particularly the Bureau's friendly media.

West Virginia / The Miners' Right to Strike

The RU's work in industry was always an uphill climb, albeit one with shimmering moments. Here perhaps, the quintessential experience was their initiative to create a communist political presence in the West Virginia coalfields. They had in mind to go "among the masses" and build a base, and dig in for the long haul of struggle. From their standpoint, here was the working class in concentrated form. Yet it was the working class in the context of the volatile situation in the mid-Seventies: the energy crisis, neoliberal economic shifts, an attempt to re-cohere the US homeland on a much more conservative basis than that of the previous decade.

Regardless, the organization began stealthily moving select cadre into the area, especially in the period of 1973-1974. Mike Ely, a former RU/RCP Party cadre who worked in the coalfields, would later write vivid memoirs of his experience, which lasted from early 1973 until he "was fired and blacklisted at the end of 1979."[485] In his telling, this was a challenge even before it began.

The first problem confronting RU cadre was to be able to erect a screen between their former political selves and where they were going, in order to gain a foothold in this sharply different section of the population. To that end, "What we did was move off the grid for a while"—not only not being politically active but being extremely circumspect in establishing themselves in West Virginia. This was not for no reason, as Ely later learned authorities had "contacted people in at least three states trying to uncover where we [his partner Gina Fall and he] had gone."[486]

The ability to make such queries was based in no small part on the radical histories of those moving to the coalfields; a "typical" example being Oliver "OV" Hirsch—who came to the coalfields somewhat later than the first wave of RU cadre. Hirsch had come under the purview of the authorities in 1968 for being one of the Nine for Peace, as a 22-year-old enlistee from Bethesda, Maryland. Hirsch initially had been a radar instructor, with the rank of sergeant, until he, along with eight other military men from four different branches of the services, publicly refused to go to Vietnam.[487] Hirsch's released FBI file—which focuses on whether or not to add him to the Administrative Index (which it declined)—reports that he "was identified as a member of the Tacoma chapter of RU since June 1973." His identification as being part of the RU likely came from an informant within the Tacoma RU. This particular record-release ends because ostensibly the FBI decided, "Subject does not meet Adex [Administrative Index] criteria"(formerly the Security Index). Hirsch's file was however "[m]aintained in a pending status due to a San Francisco Division presently reviewing subject's INS file."[488]

As for Ely, he had hardly gotten settled before he and Gina Fall were confronted with their first major challenge. In 1974 there was a wildcat strike in sections of West Virginia in the wake of the state's governor, Arch Moore, instituting gas rationing. Moore's measures, in response to the ongoing energy crisis, limited gas consumption to such a degree that it impinged miners' ability to get back and forth to work—a circumstance unacceptable for many who traveled to get to the mines.[489] The result was an unsanctioned, or "wildcat" strike. Ely describes his own experience of an incident where he initially was the only picketer, and how "[t]his story of my one-man picketing made the rounds. There was some good-natured teasing, but also the beginnings of a certain acceptance among the other pickets."[490] He also describes the racial polarization in operation in this section of the country, which came as a bit of a surprise: "It was the first inkling we had that the most militantly active miners were not necessarily the same as the most politically advanced miners."[491]

This realization coincided with something else. One of the earliest matters confronting these newly settled cadre was a controversy around a social conservative issue. In the fall of 1974 right-wing forces, led by some clergy in the area, but with the hand of the John Birch Society lurking in the background, sought to ban textbooks quoting such figures as George

Jackson, Eldridge Cleaver and Alan Ginsberg, from school shelves.[492] Beyond their verbal protests, the forces behind these moves sparked wildcat strikes in support of their efforts. As Ely recalled, "it was a paradox that one of our first serious tasks was to use those connections to help suppress and constrain a reactionary right-wing strike—and convince the militants not to take it up."[493] They did this by working with some militant anti-racist Black Vietnam veterans based in Beckley, West Virginia—producing literature in opposition to the protesters. In this way, some of the steam was taken out of these reactionary efforts. The volatility in the textbook strike was, however, two-fold; on the one hand, this was an attempt to incite people around highly conservative issues—where there existed no small basis for it—on the other, it utilized the historic solidarity to enlist people in this unjust cause.

That solidarity was especially pronounced in opposing measures that were perceived as an unjust labor discipline, in the form of denying the right to strike and issuing draconian legal measures, in the form of injunctions, in order to stop them. The result was that in the mid-Seventies there were numerous wide-ranging, militant wildcat strikes. In this, the RU's organization, the Miners' Right to Strike Committee, was at the heart of things. This would become, at points, quite large. In 1975, there was an eight week wildcat strike over grievance procedures that at its peak involved nearly 50,000 miners.[494] In the course of this, a federal judge sent Lewis "Skip" Delano and fellow miner Bruce Miller to jail. The judge, K.K. Hall, said "they were a danger to the industry and the UMW."[495] Delano, a Vietnam Veteran and RU partisan, would become a particular target both of reactionary forces in West Virginia, but also, as we will see, in the newspapers.

Over the next couple years there would be other strikes where the RU-initiated Miners' Right to Strike Committee was involved. As their influence grew, so did the attacks against them, including in the press. For example, the *New York Times* in the fall of 1977 ran a major profile of the Miners' Right to Strike Committee and its links to the Revolutionary Communist Party. The article profiled the re-emergence of "red-baiting," "on the strength of the discovery of a handful of Maoists in the mines."[496] The *Times'* claim of "discovering" this, however, is contradicted by Curtis Setzer, in his 1985 book on the struggle in the mines. As he writes, "the presence of a few avowed revolutionaries in the mines was not news in the coalfields. RCP members had never concealed their ideology from either the press or their fellow workers."[497] While Setzer's assessment strikes some former RU cadre as overstated,[498] the bigger problem was the impact these communists were having, and the media attention was working to undercut that influence.

The RU/RCP's work in the coalfields is worthy of a volume of its own, but one last thing needs to be noted, and here Mike Ely's reminiscences are instructive:

> In the West Virginia coalfields, life was strictly divided by sex roles. Only men worked in the mines. The women here sometimes found jobs in the schools, the hospitals or stores. Really, most women were confined to domestic chores and raising children in small ingrown coal camps. Even at parties in people's homes, men and women would often separate off—each grouped in their own room—having very different conversations, based on very different experiences.[499]

Not only was the overall patriarchal tradition part of the topography of people living in the area, it held implications for the RU/RCP people as well, i.e., cadre had a clear division of labor—the men went to work and the women carried out other political tasks. While all of them shared the same risks and sacrifices, the divide added a level of stress, and was contrary to the sense of shared commonality in the movements they had come out of.

The RU's work in the coalfields was at once exceptional and typical of what the group's cadre were confronting as they moved into steel, meatpacking, auto, and other major industries—a certain receptivity toward bread and butter issues, but less attraction by most, to their communist politics. One could argue that the limits they met were similar to those argued for by such groups as the Weathermen who railed against "white workers who just want more privilege from imperialism."[500] However, this was always a moving target, and the space between 1968 and 1977 was considerable. Put another way, the coalfields in the mid-Seventies were not Standard Oil in the late Sixties. The US was no longer locked in a losing war in Vietnam, nor did it have the twin challenge of the Soviet Union and China internationally. It was also not confronted with unrelenting turmoil within its cities and on its college campuses. Instead, it was in the midst of a neoliberal transformation that was reshaping industry within the US itself. The RU's communist work in industry was always going to be difficult, but as the decade went on, it became more so.

The Bureau and the Journalists

While the *New York Times* shone a certain light on the RU's work in the coalfields in its role as "the paper of record," other elements of the press had a more overt partisan agenda. This can be seen to an extreme degree in the writings of Victor Riesel. For example, in 1975, Riesel reported "the RU has been active in the coalfields for several years." He particularly singled out Skip Delano: "it took Delano only four or five months to get settled in the bituminous fields, and whip up a following and get them to continue the wildcat to such a point that US marshals subpoenaed him and an ally last week."[501] Riesel's columns about Delano and the RU—the journalistic equivalent of painting a huge red target on their backs—were part of a larger role he played for the Bureau.

* * *

During the nearly fifty years that J. Edgar Hoover occupied the top position in the FBI, he had assembled a list of contacts in the press, to be called on when he needed to get the FBI's position out, or in other ways needed their assistance. In 1975-76 the United States Senate Select Committee to Study Governmental Operations with Respect to Intelligence Activities, known as the Church Committee, issued several reports. One of those detailed how the FBI went about using the press in targeting radicals:

> Typically, a local FBI agent would provide information to a "friendly news source" on the condition "that the Bureau's interest in these matters is to be kept in the strictest confidence." Thomas E. Bishop, former Director of the Crime Records Division, testified that he kept a list of the Bureau's "press friends" in his desk.[502]

Victor Riesel was one of those "friends."

Riesel was a New York journalist who covered the labor beat as a syndicated columnist from the 1940s till the early 1980s. At the height of his career he was carried in nearly 350 newspapers, giving him a direct voice to the mainstream in the US. He is perhaps best known for an incident in 1956, when he was attacked on a Manhattan street by a man who threw sulfuric acid in his face, blinding him—this in response to a column he wrote in regard to a Long Island union and the mob. While Riesel's 1995 *New York Times* obituary dutifully mentions that incident, it makes no mention of his work for the FBI. Instead, they describe how, "Mr. Riesel never stopped inveighing against gangster infiltration and other corruption in labor unions that had stirred his emotions since his youth."[503] Absent also is his role in promoting the blacklist during the McCarthy era,[504] his personal friendships with Richard Nixon and Ronald Reagan,[505] and his close association with the FBI and J. Edgar Hoover. The exact contours of his relationship to the FBI were not public, documented only in his personal papers and the FBI file on him.

Among Riesel's papers, amid the numerous correspondences, appointment diaries, notes and drafts of columns, are three file folders of correspondence with various FBI officials from the Sixties well into the Seventies. The correspondence in the file started as the FBI began to confront the growing unrest on the university campuses in the Sixties. In 1965, the number three man in the FBI, Deputy Director Cartha DeLoach, wrote to Riesel: "As is well known, the communists are attempting to influence the minds of college students and are eager to do anything possible to promote their own selfish aims on our campuses."[506] That same year Hoover himself wrote to Riesel, thanking him for a column dealing with the mob and vending machines: "I feel you have performed a real public service by bringing this information to the attention of your readers." Written on the Director's letterhead it was signed with the familiar, "Edgar."[507] Another correspondence explains how Hoover had agreed to write a guest column for Riesel.[508]

The documents make clear that Riesel's relationship with the FBI continued after Hoover's death in 1972. There is a note in 1973 from the new director Clarence Kelly that says: "Your staunch support and kind comments regarding our accomplishments in 1973 certainly mean a great deal to all of us in the FBI."[509] Such relationships continued right up through the administration of William Webster—who Riesel lunched with in 1978, soon after Webster took over the Director's job.[510]

These were not just friendly correspondence among acquaintances. Riesel was playing a direct role for the FBI on a number of fronts. For example, in 1970 he wrote an article against the Black Panther Party and its newspaper. According to the Church Committee:

> In November 1970, seeking to create a boycott by union members handling the newspapers shipment, Mr. Hoover directed 39 field offices to mail copies of a column about the Panthers by Victor Riesel to "unions such as the Teamsters and others involved in handling shipment of B.P.P. newspapers." The column was also to be sent anonymously to "officials of police associations who might be in a position to encourage a boycott."[511]

The FBI was not just circulating his completed columns, but feeding him the raw material to construct the columns in the first place. As a correspondence from the FBI's Bishop to Riesel in 1972 shows clearly:

> In connection with your request this morning about the publication "Right On," I am enclosing a copy of the undated issue distributed in October, 1971. You will note the article in which you are interested is set forth on page 19 entitled "Black Cops."[512]

The note goes on with further background—and the FBI's assessment of the status of publication:

> "Right On" is the official publication of the Cleaver faction of the Black Panther Party. Although advertised as a bi-weekly newspaper, financial difficulties apparently have plagued the paper since its first issue in April, 1971. Since that time 11 issues have been printed and distributed on a nationwide basis.[513]

What stands out in Riesel's case is the ongoing attention he gave the RU from its first public appearance in the late spring of 1969. It was at that point that Riesel received a packet of material from the FBI's Bishop, with a cover note:

> I thought you might be interested in the attached material concerning the Revolutionary Union (RU) and the activities of one of its leaders, Robert Avakian, in support of recent strike activity by the Oil, Chemical and Atomic Workers Union. A memorandum, also attached, sets forth Avakian's connection with the RU, a militant pro-Chinese communist organization and shows attempts to take advantage of labor problems.[514]

The letter ends with the explicit instruction that "[n]o attribution, of course, should be made in connection with any use you can make of this material."[515] This was not the Bureau canvassing journalists, the FBI explicitly decided to approach Riesel:

> Labor columnist Victor Riesel, who has been very cooperative with the Bureau, recently wrote an article on the New Left movement and its advances into labor. The activities of Avakian in recent oil strike, together with his connection with RU, could be of interest to Riesel in a follow-up article as an example of communist attempts to take advantage of labor problems.[516]

The memo continues noting that if approved, "attached newspaper articles relating to Avakian's activities in the oil strike will be confidentially furnished by the Crime Records Division"—of which Thomas Bishop was head. This, of course, is exactly what happened, as Bishop's subsequent letter to Riesel confirms. As a result of the information he was receiving, he began to incorporate very specific political information about the RU into his columns:

> RU's objectives are a United Front, development of a working class unity and leadership in the struggles to organize a new national Communist Party, based on Marxism-Leninism-Mao-Tse-tung thought which would lead to the overthrow of the US government by force and violence.[517]

In another, he obliquely refers to Leibel Bergman describing the RU as being "directed by an American Maoist who had just returned from Peking."[518]

Throughout the Seventies, Riesel wrote numerous columns zeroing in on the RU's work in industry. He particularly singled out Skip Delano:

> For several years now the Revolutionary Union through a faction which calls itself "The Outlaws" has attempted to seize power in the New York Metro Area Postal Union (AFL-CIO)… And there is the saga of the big, tough, fist-thumping RU man, roving activist Lewis (Skip) Delano who though educated and skilled got a job as a part-time "Sub" on the midnight shift in the New York General Post Office. Soon he was a union shop steward.[519]

In 1978, Riesel even indexed his targeting of Delano: "Delano—as I reported in 1975 and 1976 and 1977—has been in the storm center of the illegal wildcat coalfield walkouts for over three years during each of the past three summers."[520] Riesel was on a mission to make trouble for Delano and the larger organization he was part of.

J. Edgar Hoover, Ed Montgomery, and Congress

Riesel, based in New York, had his opposite number on the West Coast in the person of Ed Montgomery. Montgomery was an award-winning reporter for the *San Francisco Examiner* and a long-time friend of the Bureau. He had dutifully reported on the anti-HUAC protests of 1960, putting forward a version of events coinciding with the Bureau's, that the student protest there had caused a "full blown riot"[521]—contrary to the more complex swirl of facts which had the police opening fire hoses to expel demonstrators from San Francisco's City Hall. Montgomery himself had testified as a witness in front of HUAC in 1967, pointedly putting Bob Avakian's name into the record, quoting him as saying we must, "come to the aid of the Black revolution."[522] He was one of the first reporters to put the RU into the newspapers in an article titled "Leftists Lift Lid on Revolutionary Plans,"[523] an article for which he sought out Bruce Franklin for an interview. The journalist Herb Borock would later describe the Bureau's role behind that piece:

> In February 1969 Hoover suggested a "cooperative news media source" interview Franklin about his relationship with "his close associate who lived in China and a 'young friend' who had served in the Red Guard.[524]

The subsequent Montgomery article dutifully named RU members Chris Milton and William Hinton, both of whom had been to China. The FBI in turn suggested that the article be the basis for subpoenaing Franklin and Avakian to appear before the House Internal Security Committee, adding,

> [t]he HCIS may also consider granting Avakian, [Michael] Vawter, and Franklin immunity in their testimony, thereby making them subject to contempt of Congress proceedings should they refuse to testify.[525]

Then there is the matter of how Congress came to have these hearings in the first place. Not surprisingly, the Bureau had furnished them extensive—albeit selective—material from their already burgeoning file. The following cover letter from Hoover to the San Francisco office accompanied copies of the material he'd already forwarded:

> Enclosed is one copy of a 10 page blind memorandum dated 4/28/69 captioned "revolutionary Union (RU), aka," which has been confidentially furnished to the House Internal Security Committee (HISC). It is not known at this time what action, if any, HISC will take based on this information.[526]

The "action" Congress took would be an extensive investigation culminating in the publication of a 224 page report titled *America's Maoists: The Revolutionary Union, the Venceremos Organization*—the most comprehensive accounting of the Revolutionary Union published, and for the most part the only non-Party, comprehensive history of the group.

In his book *Subversives,* documenting the Berkeley Free Speech Movement, journalist Seth Rosenfeld repeatedly came across Montgomery's work. At one point, Rosenfeld asked Montgomery about his relationship with the Bureau, to which Montgomery angrily responded:

> There's this myth ... that what it was, that Montgomery was a parrot for the FBI, or a funnel through which the FBI was putting this information out to the public. That's a lot of horse manure. [527]

Montgomery's FBI files seem to have gone by the wayside, with his records reportedly "destroyed on June 19, 1990, and June 5, 1993, pursuant to routine records retention schedules."[528] Regardless, Montgomery's relationship with the Bureau is beyond doubt, as can be seen in the following from J. Edgar Hoover:

> You should consider referring additional public source-type information to your source Ed Montgomery, Staff Writer, "San Francisco Examiner and Chronicle," which he might

use as a follow up to his article dated 3/23/69, to expose and disrupt the RU.[529]

All of Montgomery's protestations aside, his work speaks for itself.

From the Attica Brigade to the Revolutionary Student Brigade

Despite such efforts in the media, the RU in this period continued to benefit from the residual effect of the Sixties/early Seventies upsurge, especially on the campuses. Despite its focus on getting cadre into strategic industries, the RU had not abandoned efforts to fill the vacuum left by the collapse of SDS. In a pamphlet issued in 1972 they laid out their aim to build a student movement based on the politics of anti-imperialism, this in the face of claims

The Attica Brigade at a Throw the Bum Out! demonstration, Washington, DC, April 27, 1974. Courtesy of Reading/Simpson

that "the student movement was dead and buried."[530] The RU's experience would bear out this assessment to a degree—while things had markedly declined from the peak years of 1968-70, it still had a considerable vitality—albeit one quickly waning.

The initial organization the RU helped develop was the Attica Brigade—named after the uprising in Attica State Prison in September 1971. The Brigade got its start on November 6, 1971, at an anti-war demonstration in New York's Central Park, proclaiming its politics as "anti-imperialist, that the struggles at the Attica Prison and in Vietnam were part of the same fight."[531] By March 1973, it had expanded membership to 45 campuses across the US, including twelve chapters in New York City alone. At a conference held at Columbia University that year, 200 people attended to take stock of what the group had accomplished and where it was headed. One of the participants, Columbia student Bruce Bernstein, told the *Columbia Spectator:* "I think I can safely say that the Attica Brigade has the best possibility of becoming the largest and most active student organization in the country." Another Brigade member, Richie Chavet, of City College, described the group's purpose as "support for national liberation struggles abroad" and "support for oppressed groups at home"[532]—a view consistent with the anti-imperialist predicate of the group the RU was working to create.

In July 1974, the Brigade met again, this time in Iowa City, Iowa. The RU's newspaper, *Revolution,* ran laudatory coverage: "the student movement is indeed being rebuilt—stronger, more unified, and more politically conscious of its role to bring down US imperialism." In all 450 people from 25 different states attended. Speaking at the conference was Peter Zastrow, of Vietnam Veterans Against the War. Zastrow, in keeping with recent transformations in that organization, spoke about "the developing veterans' movement being oriented toward revolution and not reformism." C. Clark Kissinger, the former national secretary of SDS, also spoke, saying the new group needed to go beyond what SDS was able to do in its time. Bob Avakian, from the Central Committee of the RU, expanded on Kissinger's remarks saying the Brigade should be part of efforts to bring forward "a revolutionary student movement."[533]

The evolving group, however, was also informed by the struggle that had broken out around the National Liaison Committee. Kissinger's speech emphasized that one of SDS's most serious errors was "seeing SDS as a white students' organization" which would play only a supporting role in the struggle against national oppression. Conversely the Black student movement didn't take up the struggle against the Vietnam War. His point was that one group ought to do both. The convention even debated—and quickly dispensed with—the matter of whether or not to have minority caucuses within the organization. Consistent with the position the RU had established in the wake of the struggle with the BWC and the PRRWO, they ruled it unnecessary and, in fact, counterproductive.[534]

While there was discussion of the difficulties the group was having, such as the cynicism people were finding on the campuses, what was striking was how the convention saw a movement waiting to be brought to life—even though with the conclusion of the Vietnam War near at hand, a major shift was under way in US society. Despite this, with the Attica Brigade, which the Iowa convention resolved to rename the Revolutionary Student Brigade,[535] the RU now had an established vehicle for expanding its influence on campuses across the US.

Vietnam Veterans Against the War

A critical element of the expanding RU was its relationship with Vietnam Veterans Against the War (VVAW). This relationship was one which, given the overall revolutionary aims of the RU, and VVAW's radicalism *and* military training, would amplify the government's already high level of concern about both entities.

At the end of 1971 Vietnam Veterans Against the War offered a snapshot of itself—it was striking in expressing the group's overall makeup and reach. According to its official history, membership of VVAW was then at 20,000, with chapters existing or forming in all fifty states, and pointedly, in Vietnam itself. This all had come about in the four years since its founding in the spring of 1967; an event accomplished by six veterans living in New York City.[536] Reading this particular history, one gets the impression of an organization always a breath away from fading from the scene, only to be buoyed back to life by the redoubled efforts of the US ruling structure towards elusive victory in its war in Vietnam. Of course, VVAW's efforts dynamically interacted with this, and in this there was an impetus toward a more and more radical direction. This can be seen in the major initiatives the group undertook. On Labor Day Weekend in 1970 they conducted operation Rapid American Withdrawal, a four day, 86-mile simulated search-and-destroy mission from Morristown, New Jersey to Valley Forge, Pennsylvania. This was an agitational exercise, in the form of guerrilla theater, to display for people in the US how the war was being fought. This was followed in the winter of 1971 with the "Winter Soldier Investigation." That event, held in Detroit—and publicized in a free full-page ad in the February issue of *Playboy*—was a forum for veterans to deliver firsthand their experience in Vietnam. The testimony was harrowing and stark. The following from veteran Scott Camil is exemplary:

> I was a Sgt. attached to Charley 1/1. I was a forward observer in Vietnam. I went in right after high school and I'm a student now. My testimony involves burning of villages with civilians in them, the cutting off of ears, cutting off of heads, torturing of prisoners, calling in of artillery on villages for games, corpsmen killing wounded prisoners, napalm dropped on villages, women being raped, women

> and children being massacred, CS gas used on people, animals slaughtered, Chieu Hoi [safe conduct] passes rejected and the people holding them shot, bodies shoved out of helicopters, tear-gassing people for fun and running civilian vehicles off the road.[537]

This, and other testimony, was relentless, riveting, and shocking.

"Operation Dewey Canyon III," an action that rattled the national consciousness, followed the Winter Soldier investigation. Held over five days in April in 1971 in Washington DC, it included the prominent participation of the future politician and diplomat John Kerry[538]—the demonstration culminated with a symbolic throwing of medals earned in Vietnam back at the US Capitol.

It was through such actions VVAW asserted an absolutely unique position in the wider US history, as they wrote "[n]ever in the history of American warfare, have veterans of that war protested it while the war they participated in was still in progress"—and this included members still on active duty in Vietnam.[539]

As the Seventies continued, increasingly VVAW faced an existential crisis: how to continue as an organization whose foundational base was opposition to the Vietnam War in the absence of that war? Here, different paths presented themselves, and this manifested itself in the sparring of different political trends within the organization. This was in operation at the national meeting in Placitas, New Mexico in 1972. It was in Placitas that the group formerly changed its name to Vietnam Veterans Against the War-Winter Soldier Organization, allowing the group to include non-vets (and women) and broaden its focus to other issues. The Revolutionary Union, which had ties with VVAW/WSO, particularly through cadre who were veterans and were part of the organization, did not agree with this. It was their view that the shift to VVAW-WSO had the effect of "liquidating the vets movement and making it into an overall united front organization with the main task being 'education.'"[540] Such issues, including a good deal of sparring among different forces within the organization who did not have the same radical agenda as the RU, was a source of internal pressure that was pushing for some kind of resolution. In this instance, the RU did not let things follow their own course.

The result was the RU moved decisively. The FBI, which had infiltrators throughout VVAW-WSO, followed this closely:

> The NO [National Office] proposed that VVAW/WS [sic] become affiliated with the RU. Discussions were heard on this proposal and a heated argument took place pro and con. RU backers were well prepared and any persons arguing against RU were called "red baiters." Several people advocating affiliation with RU including P ___ REDACTED Milwaukee, who stated that there would be a revolution in the U. S. regardless of how many years it takes.[541]

VVAW-WSO and supporters at Military Appeals, Washington, DC, July 2, 1974. Courtesy of Reading/Simpson

In the end, the vote was no contest. The RU members and supporters had a clear majority and were able to carry the day by a more than two to one margin.[542] In this way, a several year period ensued in which VVAW-WSO, for all intents and purposes, was under the political control of the RU and soon to be RCP.

The government's concern about this development comes through tellingly in the following: "One of the stated objectives of the RU aid [sic, and] VVAW/WSO coalition is revolutionary education and recruitment of GIs so that in the event of war, the military will have no men."[543] This, among other things, helps explain the following FBI missive on the status of VVAW leadership on its list of those to be rounded up in the event of a national emergency:

> All VVAW/WSO National Officers, with the exception of B. ROMO, are on the ADEX. Los Angeles is Office of Origin in the case of BARRY LOUIS ROMO and Chicago is unaware of his ADEX status.[544] To date, Chicago has been unable to verify the presence of ROMO in Chicago.[545]

Unlike the RU/RCP, VVAW has been written about extensively both in academic works and in popular publications, and the RU/RCP's presence is mentioned, to a degree, in that context. There is in this, however, a standard narrative, one in which Maoists and hard-core radicals wrecked the organization. For example Andrew Hunt in *The Turning* describes the RCP's "ruinous influence over the national office."[546] Similarly, Gerald Nicosia in *Home to War* writes, "[t]he danger was that every member of the RU was pledged to carry out the will of its monomaniacal chairman, former Berkeley activist Bob Avakian."[547] The latter statement would seem more an insight into that author's assessment rather than the actual situation, given Avakian did not wholly dominate the RCP until the bulk of VVAW parted company with the RCP in 1977. That aside, there was something more fundamental in play, which Nicosia himself acknowledges:

> Existing VVAW leaders had simply been recruited into the RU because their enormous anger was pitched to a similar frequency as the RU's raging frenzy against the capitalist system.[548]

This would seem more the nub of the issue; the national leadership of VVAW-WSO came under RU influence because a hard core of its membership at that moment had no interest in coming back into the American fold. In short, the RU convinced a large section of VVAW-WSO's leadership that Maoism, and the RU, were the path forward for tearing down the US empire. Understood in this way, it is not so much that the RU *took over* VVAW in the mid-Seventies—though there was an element of that—it was more the case that *VVAW took itself into* the RU.

The Progressive Labor Party vs. the Revolutionary Union

While the RU was expanding, the Progressive Labor Party was hitting a wall. By 1971, the PLP saw its position as the only US Maoist organization recognized by the People's Republic of China slipping away; its positions repudiating the national liberation struggle in Vietnam and condemning the Black Panthers as reactionary nationalists had taken their toll. While it ostensibly controlled the SDS name, it was control over an organization that no longer existed as it once had, i.e., it was essentially the student group of the PLP. In April 1971, an investigator for the House Committee on Internal Security testified before Congress that "[w]e estimate the membership fluctuates in the area of 300 nationally."[549] The organization's main bases were in New York and Boston, with some presence in the Bay Area. However, in tandem with their controversial positions, they were beset with desertions, as Congressional investigator Robert Horner testified to Congress:

"They are an extremely dogmatic group and find it difficult to get along with anyone else."[550] Given their combative relations with others on the Left, this was not an inaccurate synopsis.

The FBI, for a time, saw the RU and the PLP as the twin hydra of US Maoism. However, they were increasingly identifying the RU as a rising force to be watched. In an article written for the *Veterans of Foreign Wars* magazine in 1971, FBI Director Hoover described the PLP and the RU as "the two main pro-Maoist groups."[551] The piece estimated the size of the PLP at 300, but held back from estimating the RU's size ("membership is not large, perhaps several hundred.")[552] However, even as Hoover was writing that column, things were shifting. The leadership of the PLP was adopting a position that China's leadership was "revisionist," a stand that would end their status as the main Chinese-backed organization in the US.[553] Meanwhile in Congress, Robert F. Horner predicted, "I think if any party replaces the Progressive Labor Party it will be the Revolutionary Union,"[554] an accurate prediction. Little more than a year later, the FBI would report, with a certain alarm, that "the Revolutionary Union, a coalition of Maoist groups, [is] now operating in 10 states."[555]

Hoover's *VFW* piece, which was a window into how the Bureau was viewing domestic Maoists, itself existed in a shifting geopolitical situation. The *Boston Globe,* in reprinting the piece, pointedly noted that:

> Hoover had planned a reprinting and wider distribution of the article, but decided against it, in his words, "for budgetary reasons." However, some feel his decision was based on President Nixon's announcement of this coming visit to Red China.[556]

China's opening to the West, which led to the deterioration and severing of relations with the PLP, and buoyed the RU, also seemed to have set certain limits on the FBI. It was an odd historic moment, one that would not last.

Chapter 8

The Short Leap From the RU to the RCP

The Revolutionary Communist Party of the U.S. working class has been founded with a correct line and Program.
— Main Political Report, adopted at the founding of RCP, USA, 1975.

The RCP, RSB, and its front groups, identified as the VVAW, UWOC, and USCPFA, represent a threat to the internal security of the United States of the first magnitude.
— FBI report on the RCP, September 1976.

The Founding of the RCP

In the wake of the wreckage of the National Liaison Committee, the tarnished prestige from its position on Boston Busing, the ongoing low-intensity conflict with the FBI, and with China on the precipice of a major reversal, the RU pushed ahead with its

The RU, RSB, VVAW marching to the White House on July 4, 1974.
Courtesy of Reading/Simpson

plans to form a new communist party. So it was that in October 1975 it announced the founding of the Revolutionary Communist Party. Given its numerical strength, relative influence, and organizational sophistication, set against its intransigent political methodology, hardening hierarchal leadership, and leaden sectarianism—the event stands in hindsight as the group's high and low point.

The gauge of what this new entity was is best expressed in its 1975 *Programme and Constitution*. The program was both a synthesis of everything that had brought it to that point and a product of the moment. It spoke to the economic dislocations of the Seventies: "prices towering over wages, massive layoffs and millions out of work, debt piling up...."[557] However, given the old left framework it invoked in analyzing economic crisis, it mistook a retrenching of capitalism through a neoliberal turn to instead be symptomatic of intractable crisis and decline. As such, they failed to see that at a time when they were sending cadre into the stalwarts of industry, such as steel, auto, and other manufacturing, these same industries were evaporating from the US industrial scene.

The program also laid out positions on such things as the united front, that incorporated views from the just finished National Liaison Committee struggle, making the focus of all things the working class. As it stated, "[t]he united front against imperialism is not a 'grand coalition' of 'different constituencies,' nor is it built by piecing together different 'united fronts' of separate groups – 'Black United Front,' 'Women's United Front,' 'United Front of the Trade Unions,' etc."[558] This was stating, once again, the preeminence of the multi-national Party of the working class and minimizing the importance of national struggles.

Given this logic, it felt compelled to state that while, "the women's liberation movement of recent years has overall advanced the struggle against the bourgeoisie," it warned of efforts by the "bourgeoisie to misdirect this movement, with ideas like 'men are the enemy' and 'equality' is an end in itself." Concretely, it opposed the Equal Rights Amendment, because it granted only "token opportunity to women, especially executives and professionals, while actually robbing working women of protective legislation won through many hard-fought battles in the late 19th and early 20th centuries."[559] Such reductionism, which unfolded everything from the struggle of the working class, opened a gaping chasm between themselves and the larger women's movement.

A Vision of Socialism

The RCP presented a picture of socialism in the United States that combined elements of what they had learned in China with their focus of the time, the US working class. It had at its core the Marxist dictate of seizing the means of production, including taking control of "credit and trade, stripping the capitalist bankers and corporation heads of the economic basis of their power." It would then set about undoing what capitalism had wrought.

Unemployment would be ended to make "use of the labor of everyone in society." With this new machinery and scientific methods would be developed to "expand output," but "as machines can replace workers, workers will not be thrown into the streets, but transferred to other jobs–according to an overall plan–and gradually the work day for all workers will be reduced."

The socialist society would take on the problem of homelessness and bad housing by "the building of well-constructed housing for the masses of people." Likewise with healthcare, it would no longer be a vehicle for generating profit, "but a means for the working class to prevent disease and to preserve the health of the people."

It talked of a model of education highly informed by the Cultural Revolution in China, transforming education to "serve the interests of the working class in building socialism, suppressing the forces of capitalism and continuing the revolutionary struggle to transform all of society and achieve communism." At the same time, education would "put reality back on its feet and expose" bourgeois propaganda. For its part, religion would not be allowed to "exploit and oppress the people" and the Party would lead the masses of people to understanding that they are the true force that changes the world and that they can conquer nature.

As for culture, also as in China, "[c]ultural workers will join in productive labor together with the masses of people," and "culture will truly become the weapon of the whole working class."

Finally, crime would be dealt with by the dual tactic of finding work at "a living wage" for those reduced to crime to live, while for professional criminals and organizations like the Mafia, the Party stipulated that they "will be ruthlessly punished" and their organizations "smashed by the armed power of the working class."[560]

A startling point toward the end of this section, one that would dog the Party for the rest of its days, dealt with how they would do away with the "decadence of capitalism":

> The prostitutes, drug addicts, homosexuals, and others who are caught up in these things will be re-educated to become productive members of society, with working class consciousness. The shame connected with these practices will be taken from the shoulders of these victims and the guilt will be placed where it belongs-on the bourgeoisie.[561]

In regards to homosexuality, this was codification of a position that had incubated and been adopted by the RU. For the RU, homosexuality was "an individual response to male supremacy and male chauvinism," but one that "turns its back on the struggle between men and women." While their position conceded a particle of agreement with lesbianism, "[w]e think that Lesbianism is more understandable, as an escape from male chauvinism," for gay men, the feeling was that it "reinforces male chauvinism in its refusal to deal with relationships with women."[562] In the RU/RCP's view, homosexuality was akin to religion; it was a belief system and a conscious choice. As for how it fit into the struggle, they were firm that the larger movement toward gay liberation "is counter-revolutionary and anti-working class," because it sought to find a place for gay people in the established society. The same document did allow that individual "gay people can be anti-imperialist" but was clear they could not be communists.[563]

Stripping off the Marxist pretensions, for what was supposed to be a forward looking and visionary Party, their position was striking in its conservative, even puritanical, sensibility. It was further problematized by the fact that an upsurge of gay men and women in the United States was already underway and was about to hit critical mass—something this newly proclaimed vanguard would deliberately stand apart from. This was all made worse by its intransigence; once adopted as "line," it was set in stone, and would not be abandoned until decades after the RCP's peak strength and influence had come and gone.

The irony here is that the Party and the RU before it, like the rest of society, included gay men and women—though only in a closeted capacity. Perhaps most notable in this regard, but hardly unique, was Steve Hamilton, who was privately gay before coming out in 1980. This only *after* leaving the group.[564]

Even with all the cultural and moral conservatism, the new RCP continued to exude a certain revolutionary edge—perhaps its most lasting legacy from the Sixties period, even though it was embedded in an illusory working class romanticism. As they wrote, "[t]his program is both a declaration of war on the ruling class and a battle plan for the working class of this country." It was this bedrock radicalism that continued to be a pole of attraction for a certain type of the more radically inclined in US society, and a subject of concern for agents of the government tasked with controlling such things.

Amid the triumphalism and invocation of Thirties-style worker-ism remained the reality that the formation of the Party was more nominal than substantial. The positions it had forged in the years before were the same, though now codified into a new program and constitution. As Steve Hamilton noted after having left the RU, "we should avoid mystifying what 'party building' actually meant. The RU already functioned effectively as a party."

The FBI had a similar view. In a report obtained by two Chicago informants two years before the actual founding, they outlined Leibel Bergman's assessment:

> Bergman's comments indicate he sees difficulty in merging with any pro-PRC group and apparently plans for RU to go it alone with respect to Party building. He seemed to place emphasis on Party building as opposed to United Front work and made no mention of consolidating "Collectives" throughout the United States. Indeed, it would appear that "BERGMAN's Party" will simply be RU with a different name.[565]

The FBI and informants' view—aside from their characterization that it was "Bergman's Party"—was relatively on the mark, corresponding to Hamilton's view that "the only real significance of 'party building' would have been its willingness to carry out struggle with other forces toward a more unified movement-wide organization."[566] That, of course, did not happen, but the RU, like the rest of the new communist movement, had put so much emphasis on "Party Building" in the mid-Seventies that it is hard to conceive of any stepping back from this.

In the end, all the RU was able to do was to bring in the much smaller Revolutionary Workers Congress—a splinter of BWC—various individuals who had been in the PRRWO, assorted individuals who had been working with the RU. There was, however, one exception: the Asian-American group Wei Min She.

Wei Min She

Based in San Francisco's Chinatown, Wei Min She—"Organization for the People"—members had cut their political teeth in the struggle for ethnic studies at San Francisco State and Berkeley.[567] The group itself came out of the Asian Community Center, which had been created by the Berkeley Asian American Political Alliance in March 1970. In 1972, the Alliance moved to become an anti-imperialist, Marxist-Leninist organization, adopting the name Wei Min She.[568] Their bookstore, Everybody's Books, a storefront in the larger International Hotel, was a center and magnet for Asian-American activists in the Bay Area—and included ample amounts of Marxist, Leninist, and Maoist literature.[569] According to Wei Min She member Steve Yip, by 1974, "most of us in WMS had come to the conclusion that imperialism/capitalism was the problem which required revolution to resolve."[570] As a result of the "close and comradely working relationship with the Revolutionary Union,"[571] many had in turn joined that organization.

The group's relations, however, were subject to the RU's shift in position that was the fallout from the collapse of the NLC—or what was now being referred to in its dismissive shorthand as the struggle against "Bundism"—a name chosen to compare the current debate with that of the Bolsheviks and a Russian Jewish socialist organization from 1903. The RCP's rush toward a worker-centric orientation and turning away from accommodation (or even compromise) with more nationalist tendencies lead them to instruct WMS to disband, abandon its community service work, and join with or work directly under the leadership of the RCP. A bulletin setting out the policy described how:

> Already work is being done in the right direction: people taking on jobs in the class, doing UWOC [Unemployed Workers Organizing Committee] work, etc. Also a number of people in the past have been doing work among youth and students. We see these former members of WMS continuing this work, not as members of WMS though, but under the leadership of the RCP.[572]

In this way, the organization was no more. Though the RCP held that "all members of WMS who do not join the Party can still work with it."[573] Writing in 2008 Harvey Dong, who had been part of Wei Min She, looked back bitterly on the experience:

> Even though Wei Min She had roots as an Asian American organization, it aligned itself in 1975 with one of the national left organizations that sought to build a vanguard party and WMS disbanded. The self destructive direction took its toll on the bookstore and the grassroots organizational work that had begun earlier.[574]

For the time, however, the Party's ties with WMS allowed it to play a critical role in the Asian American community in the Bay Area. In 1977, it was at the center of a mass struggle over the eviction of elderly Chinese and Filipino men housed in the International Hotel in downtown San Francisco. The hotel was slated for destruction, and the city had moved aggressively to clear the remaining residents. This in turn was taken up as a cause of opposition, and at one point a demonstration of five thousand surrounded the Hotel. It was a struggle that resounded throughout the City and beyond. In the end, the eviction went forward and the building was destroyed, but this had become an important example of political struggle in the relatively sedate mid-Seventies.[575]

The US-China Peoples Friendship Association

Another major RU/RCP success in this period—a result of the Party's unique relationship with China—was its influence in the rapidly expanding organization, the US-China Peoples Friendship Association (USCPFA). For several years in the early Seventies, there had been a number of regional Friendship Associations with the mandate of education and travel to China. This was widely popular for those who had come to see China as a certain alternative model, were curious about what was taking place, and wanted to see first-hand what was happening. Due to its popularity, in 1974, the various groupings cohered into a national organization.[576] The founding congress of the USCPFA explained the group's foundation in response to interest "by more and more Americans in the momentous transformations of life and work in the People's Republic of China." At the core of the national USCPFA were two people with long ties to the RU, C. Clark Kissinger and William Hinton. As well as being founders of the group, Kissinger was its Vice President in 1974, and Hinton, its National Chairman from 1974 to 1976.[577]

While the purpose of the group was ostensibly "to promote friendship, [and] understanding" that was "mutually beneficial" between the American and Chinese peoples, there was a larger agenda. Beyond the *implicit* politics of friendly cultural relations, there was an *explicit* politics. This is best seen in the Friendship Association's 1971 constitution, which called specifically for the withdrawal of "all US forces from China's Taiwan Province and the Taiwan Strait and the dismantling of all US military bases there." It also put forward that China be seated in the United Nations as "the only legal government representing all the people of China."[578] In this way the RU, to the degree it worked in the USCPFA, found itself not only generally supporting what was taking place in China and popularizing the socialist experience as a model within the US, but was also working specifically for the diplomatic and geopolitical interests of China. It would not be long before this became deeply problematic for the Party.

As for the FBI, they saw the USCPFA as a front organization pure and simple:

> On August 2, 1972, a source, who has furnished reliable information in the past, advised that the U.S. China Peoples Friendship Association (USCPFA) was formed by members of the Revolutionary Union (RU), as a front group for the RU. The objectives were to generate propaganda through the USCPFA and eventually develop an organization based solely on MAO Tse-tung thought. The organization does not intend to appear as an obvious front for the RU.[579]

The USCPFA certainly had a good number of active RU and later RCP cadre, including at its leading levels, working within it. However, it was far from a wholly controlled front of the RU, or any other group in the US, as the following report tacitly shows:

> No formal headquarters has been established; however, a 16-member National Steering Committee, of whom approximately one-half are also RU members, is responsible for all policy matters concerning the USCPFA and publication of the organization's magazine "New China," with offices at 41 Union Square West, New York, New York. The national organization has now assumed responsibility for maintaining relationships with the appropriate PRC agencies regarding future travel delegations to the PRC. Some chapters of the USCPFA have been identified as being completely controlled or dominated by the RU.[580]

If any external force ultimately controlled the US-China Peoples Friendship Association, and this would soon become abundantly clear, it was China itself.

Allowing for all that, the Bureau was keenly interested in

what was happening in the USCPFA. Their interest was to such a degree that they circumvented US law, breaking into the USCPFA offices, apparently in San Francisco. A critical reason, according to the FBI's SA Ryan, was to

> Identify some of the individuals who were associated with US-China Friendship Association in anticipation of we might be able to tie them in to other individuals with whom we either had a photograph or we had only a first name or we had limited identifying information.[581]

In other words, they were not content to just send informants to public meetings; what they could not get openly, they would steal.

The Conference on the International Situation

The RCP's association with the politics of China, however, was proving to be a sticky matter, especially as that country forged a different geopolitical doctrine. By 1976 the Chinese Communist Party was forcefully projecting a position internationally that held that not only was the Soviet Union a country in which capitalism had been restored but, to invoke a quote by Mao, used at the time: "The Soviet Union today is under the dictatorship of the bourgeoisie, a dictatorship of the big bourgeoisie, a dictatorship of the German fascist type, a dictatorship of the Hitler type."[582]

This was not a position totally foreign to the RU/RCP. In its *Red Papers 7: How Capitalism Has Been Restored in the Soviet Union and What this Means for the World Struggle,* it too had argued:

> [w]ith the seizure of power by the Khrushchev clique ... the centralized state apparatus was taken from the people and placed in the hands of the people's enemies. The Soviet bourgeoisie was thus able to move toward a fascist

> dictatorship without many of the difficulties associated with the transition from a "democratic" bourgeois republic.'[583]

That same *Red Papers* it should be noted, held that Stalin's achievements "far outweighed" his errors,[584] but that "the Soviet social imperialists" in imposing fascist rule "have imprisoned thousands of Soviet citizens."[585] Such were the political and ideological hoops the RU/RCP went through to maintain continuity with the Chinese position. Regardless, their position would soon diverge from that of the Chinese.

At it its most base level, the Chinese position held that the Soviet Union was the main danger toward a new world war and anyone who would stand with them against the Soviets was a potential ally. This position, and the controversy it evoked, in turn occupied no small attention by the community of the new communist movement, who looked to China as both a compass and barometer on the international situation.

To speak to the questions circulating and contending, the RCP, in November 1976, held a conference on the international situation which over 2,000 people attended from an array of organizations. For its part, the RCP attempted to strike a position in unity with Chinese socialism, against Soviet revisionism, but also—in contrast to the Chinese—hold that both the US and the USSR were the main dangers toward a new world war.[586] All this in keeping with the Chinese analysis that such a war was most certainly on the horizon.[587]

The Chinese argument, which the various political trends were wrangling with, was contained in something known as the Three Worlds Theory. Rather than the more popular understanding of the three worlds (underdeveloped countries being the third world, socialist countries being the second, and developed capitalist countries being the first), this theory saw the world categorized as the underdeveloped world, more developed capitalist/imperialist countries, and the two superpowers. For the Chinese, the aim was to build a coalition against the most dangerous superpower, the Soviet Union.[588] This view in turn led to no small amount of grief for those attempting to stay close to their Chinese comrades, as this strategy included China adopting friendly relations with dictators such as Mobutu Sese Seko of Zaire (now DR Congo), Augusto Pinochet of Chile, and the Shah of Iran.[589] Perhaps most awkwardly, this was on display in the Philippines where China aligned itself with the US-supported dictator Ferdinand Marcos, while the Communist Party of the Philippines was in the midst of a Maoist-inspired people's war.[590]

All of which led to stress within the RU/RCP, as can be seen in the fact that William Hinton—apparently no longer aligned with the RU—argued the Chinese position at the conference.[591] This was all complicated by the fact that the CCP itself was implementing a contradictory position. On the one hand, they were seeking an alliance with the US in opposition to the Soviets. On the other, they were striving to maintain solidarity with revolutionary efforts of Maoist organizations throughout the world. Such conflict could not coexist for long.

In that respect, the conference—with its nuanced debate over the standing positions of the day—today seems a jumble, an arcane exercise debating positions that lay atop mounds of geopolitical machinations and internal state struggles. However, it also serves as a certain bellwether of the ground shifting underneath the feet of not just the RCP, but the entire new communist movement. China was about to undergo a major transformation, and there would soon be no middle ground on which to stand.

A Political Battle in Philadelphia

In advance of the International Situation conference, and the percolating conflicts with China, the RCP had undertaken what would stand as among its most successful undertakings—a high point and end point for the newly minted Revolutionary

Communist Party. The occasion was the July 4, 1976 demonstrations to counter the US commemoration of the 200th anniversary of the signing of the Declaration of Independence.

In advance of the Bicentennial, the Party had initiated a call for people to demonstrate in Philadelphia under the slogan, "We've Carried the Rich for 200 Years, Let's Get them Off Our Backs." They formed a "coalition" which included Vietnam Veterans Against the War, the Unemployed Workers Organizing Committee, and the Revolutionary Student Brigade, i.e., groups wholly or mainly controlled by the Party. Plans for that demonstration, along with those of another coalition also planning to demonstrate, moved Philadelphia Mayor Frank Rizzo to attempt a war footing. With support of a young US attorney named Rudolph Giuliani,[592] he called for 15,000 federal troops to be on hand for what he suggested would be violent demonstrations.

The other coalition, which included the Puerto Rican Socialist Party, the Prairie Fire Organizing Committee (an above-ground support group of the Weathermen) and a number of other left organizations, had as a focus a "Bicentennial Without Colonies." The presence of the Prairie Fire organization and other groups that Congress suggested had ties to terrorists, prompted the House Internal Security Committee to hold hearings on the demonstrations. In their view, the protest

> bears the most careful watching because of (a) the links between the influential Prairie Fire Organizing Committee and the Weather Underground; and (b) the links between the Puerto Rican Socialist Party and the FALN [Fuerzas Armadas de Liberación Nacional]—both linked, in turn, to the Cuban DGI (which is believed by most intelligence specialists to be controlled by the KGB).[593]

The hearings also pointedly noted the presence of, "[a] rival radical group, the Revolutionary Communist Party (formerly the Revolutionary Union)." While most of the questioning in Congress revolved around the July 4th Coalition, local Philadelphia authorities seemed keenly interested in the presence of the RCP. Philadelphia Police inspector, George Fencl, head of the Civil Disobedience Unit (CD or Red Squad), especially focused on the Rich Off Our Backs (ROOB) coalition telling the Congressmen, "Based on the Rich Off Our Backs July 4th Coalition statements and participating group statements, this group is looking for and expecting direct confrontation with police and Bicentennial speakers, groups, et cetera."[594] Fencl's statement is confusing, seeming to at once single out ROOB, but also casting it with the other demonstration. Regardless, the ratcheting up of rhetoric was aimed at winning support for federal troops, but as we will see, reflected a longstanding attention the Philadelphia authorities had given the RU/RCP.

* * *

The Philadelphia police had been aware of and active against the RU/RCP for some time, a fact that comes through in the case of Bill and Judy Biggin. They had earned the ire of the Philadelphia police through their work on the underground newspaper the *Philadelphia Free Press*, begun in 1968. The *Press'* support of the Black Panthers and the anti-war movement was a particular sore spot for city authorities headed up by the brash and violent police commissioner Frank Rizzo. Rizzo had waged an ugly war against Philadelphia's Black Panthers, perhaps best exemplified in a raid on Black Panther headquarters where the arrested men had their picture taken and splashed across newspapers in various stages of undress. Rizzo (then police commissioner) later taunted them in the press: "Imagine the big Black Panthers with their pants down."[595] In Biggin's case, Rizzo went in for a certain—though not without substance—hyperbole on a 1970 TV broadcast, saying that "Bill Biggin and the *Free Press* are even more dangerous than the Panthers."[596]

Biggin not only had to contend with Rizzo and the CD, but as he became involved with the Revolutionary Union, he soon found himself under scrutiny of immigration authorities. Biggin, who had been a graduate biology student at Temple University, had been refused reinstatement of his enrollment—thus clearing the way for his deportation. This was something he argued "was capricious, arbitrary, and politically motivated."[597] He in turn brought suit against Temple in an effort to get reinstated, but was refused.[598] After exhausting all appeals, he was deported,[599] ending his relationship with the RU in Philadelphia.

As for the July 4 demonstration, Rizzo's call for 15,000 troops was ultimately turned down, but not before making major news, and chilling the atmosphere for anyone inclined to demonstrate but not up for a confrontation.[600] At the same time, the city refused a march permit for the Rich Off Our Backs Coalition in Center City where the focus of Bicentennial celebrations was going to be. The ROOB coalition was instead relegated to a march through the Kensington neighborhood, a working-class section north east of Center City. The authorities also engaged in various harassing techniques, such as impounding lumber the Rich Off Our Backs organizers had obtained to build a workers history pavilion a few days before the demonstration.[601] While such efforts frustrated preparations, they did not deter the demonstrations from going forward. In the end, there were two major counter-bicentennial marches in Philadelphia. The larger July 4th coalition drew in the range of 30,000 people. By comparison, the RCP event was considerably smaller, with press reports ranging between 3,500 and 4,000.[602] The numbers, however, do not convey the qualitative element in play. The Rich Off Our Backs action, with its guiding slogan, did carry a certain revolutionary charge. Further, more than just a single demonstration, the Party's campaign was spread over several days, beginning with a demonstration by its Unemployed Workers Organizing Committee in Washington,

DC on June 30. It then moved up to Philadelphia for roving demonstrations with various focuses: support of striking rubber workers, Philadelphia city workers, and a VVAW-led march at the US John Dewey docked in Philadelphia. The demonstrators, traveling via open-air flat bed trucks, worked to engage and connect with the people of Philadelphia, especially in the largely Black neighborhoods where they were generally warmly welcomed.

The Philadelphia demonstration was also a high point for the Party-initiated Unemployed Workers Organizing Committee. The UWOC seizing on the recessionary conditions of the mid-Seventies, had as its organizing slogan "Jobs or Income Now," accompanied by the (overstated) slogan, "Fight Don't Starve."[603] The latter slogan was a carryover from the Communist Party in the Thirties—perhaps not surprising given the UWOC work was led by the former Young Communist League member, Gertrude Alexander (who had passed away only a few months earlier).[604] The UWOC had spread quickly throughout the country, where it found a relatively receptive audience among the more angry unemployed, with its tactics of leafleting local unemployment offices and confronting various politicians to extend and increase unemployment benefits.

The Bicentennial also coincided with the release of an album by the musical duo Prairie Fire, made up of Mat and Sandy Callahan. Their album "Break the Chains" highlighted songs meant to promote working-class struggle.[605] As Mat Callahan explained, "we were full-time revolutionaries; music was a weapon." In that respect, the Prairie Fire album captured the RCP's view of culture. It should serve class struggle.

The culmination of July 4th itself was a rally in a park in the Kensington neighborhood—replete with Philadelphia police sharp shooters standing guard on the roofs of buildings surrounding the park. Here the radical edge was on display as the main speaker, Bob Avakian, after rhetorically posing the notion of defending the country, drove home his point:

> Well, we got something to say to them about that, 'Yeah, we're going to defend the country, we're going to defend it when it belongs to us. That's when we're going to defend it.' ... First of all we, the working class, got to take over the country. Then we'll set about defending it–against you. And against any other slave driver that might come over and try to take advantage of the situation.[606]

This was the Bicentennial message of what had become a sophisticated national communist organization. It was something the FBI was paying keen attention to.

Red Squads and Feds

Two months after the Philadelphia demonstrations, the FBI produced an overview of the Revolutionary Communist Party. It was something of a culminating statement of how they saw the organization. On one level, the document is a justification for the Bureau's extensive campaign against the group, setting down the legal groundwork needed to establish a justification to investigate. It is also, however, a document in tone that is wary of the decade just past and ominous about the one that recently commenced. The concern comes through pointedly multiple times, "The RCP and RSB" it states "could possibly influence national events far beyond that thought possible by their small membership." Additionally

> [i]t is felt that the magnitude of the threat by RCP and its front groups to accomplish its aims or [sic] organizing and leading a communist revolutionary force with the purpose of overthrowing the United States Government by force and violence warrants constant vigil so that we fulfill our

responsibilities for domestic security.[607]

And the "RCP, RSB, and its front groups, identified as the VVAW, UWOC, and USCPFA, represent a threat to the internal security of the United States of the first magnitude."[608]

These were consequential statements. By 1977 the FBI would have open investigations on the RCP in 22 cities, exceeded in number only by the Weathermen who at the time occupied positions at the top of the Bureau's most wanted list—though, in contrast, the RU/RCP leaders and cadre were neither fugitives nor suspects in criminal investigations.[609] By 1976, the RCP had become what the Bureau had sought to avoid seven years earlier. At that time, in undertaking efforts against SDS, they sought to head off the PLP control for fear it would "transform a shapeless and fractionalized group into a militant and disciplined organization."[610] The RCP by the mid-Seventies was a disciplined and militant organization beyond what the PLP had ever been, and it seemed to be thriving.

"Throw the Bum Out! Organize to Fight!" Washington, DC, April 27, 1974. Courtesy of Reading/Simpsons

The NUWO and the RCYB

In the wake of the Bicentennial demonstration, the advances in work in the coalfields, the strength of the Party's work in auto, steel, meatpacking and other industries, the group pushed for a leap in its organizing in the working class through the formation of a National United Workers Organization.[611]

On Labor Day weekend 1977, 1,500 people, mainly RCP cadre and supporters, based in industry came together in Chicago's Pick Congress Hotel to form the National United Workers Organization.[612] In the parlance of the RCP, this was an "intermediate workers" organization, a place for the Party to work with rank and file around day-to-day issues, but to also expose them to the broader radical program of the Party, up to and including recruiting them into the organization.[613]

Along with the higher profile steelworkers and miners, the array of those in attendance provided a window into the inroads the Party had made in industry. There were pineapple and hotel workers from Hawaii, agricultural workers from the Salinas Valley, electronics workers from San Jose, garment, hospital, and auto workers from the East Coast, textile, electrical, petrochemical workers from the South.[614] While showcasing the RU/RCP's in the previous eight years to establish a base in industry, it also attempted a continuity with the communist labor movement of the past. The speaker for the RCP was Vern Bown, a veteran of the Abraham Lincoln Brigade, an old comrade of Leibel Bergman's from their days in the Northern California CPUSA (he was also called before HUAC in 1960),[615] and an early member of the RU.[616] Bown, emphasizing the role of communists in struggle, told the audience: "All my life I have been a worker and most of my working life I have been a communist. And I have never seen these two as being in any way separate, or contradictory."

The convention consisted of key plenaries and workshops hammering out the positions of the new organization. This in turn culminated in a proclamation: "The working class and the employing class have nothing in common!" The statement emphasized the stand of the working class against discrimination, for unity of different nationalities, against unemployment, against war for empire—all in the face of "growing crisis and increased" attacks on the working class.[617] Such high sounding rhetoric was seen as a first step in what would be a highly influential organization advancing the overall work of the Party. As things turned out, this would be the last such convention.

In similar fashion, on November 19 and 20, 1977, on the University of Illinois campus in Urbana, students across the country gathered in a convention; in all, some six hundred came together to proclaim the formation of the Revolutionary Communist Youth Brigade. Along with the students was a smaller number of Party cadres assigned to work with working class youth, and some of the youth they had attracted. This was the Party's realization of a long sought effort toward establishing a "young communist league," i.e., a student-working class youth organization.

The convention heard of a member from the Iranian Students Association, Dave Clark, a former Black Panther from Trenton, New Jersey, C. Clark Kissinger, the former national secretary of SDS, now working in the US-China Peoples Friendship Association, and the RCP's Chairman, Bob Avakian, who gave the keynote speech.[618] Avakian spoke about not only the role of youth at the forefront of any revolutionary movement, but also the nature of communism that the new organization had at the core of its name.

A speaker at the close of the convention strove to end things on a high note: "We are determined to be the generation that grows up to establish socialism in this country. The future is ours, because we have shown this weekend that we do dare to take it."[619] Events just over the horizon would prove the statement, and the prospects for the newly formed organization, as illusory.

Chapter 9

The Final Split

BERGMAN affirmed his trip to People's Republic of China (PRC) during the Spring of 1973. He commented that China has "moved to the right" and based this opinion on the absence of Marx, Lenin, Engels revolutionary type posters which in the past have been in abundant display throughout China. He raised "hell" with his contact over this and told source the Chinese should stick to their line.

— FBI Informant report on Leibel Bergman, November 1973.[620]

To sum up the struggle there and its culmination in a certain stage with the arrest of the [Gang of] Four, one phrase can put it simply—"The wrong side won."

— Bob Avakian, 1977.[621]

By November 1977 the RCP had grown from less than two dozen Bay Area activists with members concentrated on several campuses and in a handful of factories, into a nationwide organization, with 900 to 1,100 members, thousands more supporters, and pride of place near the top of the charts in the FBI's threat analysis. While the bulk of organizations and individuals who had attained notoriety in the Sixties had largely come and gone, taking with them a certain brand of radicalism, the RCP by contrast, had traversed that terrain and expanded, and seemed poised to continue—and if not grow dramatically, continue as a sizable and significant radical force. Then Mao Zedong died, and it all started coming apart.

Mao's death in September 1976 sparked a crisis worldwide for a certain kind of revolutionary force. Maoist organizations and groupings had proliferated and thrived during the previous twenty years. Mao's death would set loose a flood of confusion and disorientation, leading once vibrant organizations to disappear, implode, or disband. At issue was the direction of the new leaders of China, who were renouncing the Cultural Revolution—the progeny of Mao himself—and striking a path leading toward unchecked commodity production and the race to reap the fruits of surplus value. All this foreshadowed the ultimate dismantling of huge parts of the socialist state apparatus, such as it was in China. Within the RCP, the death of Mao had pointedly raised the question of what stand to take on the changes rapidly unfolding in China. The matter of endorsing China's new leader, Hua Guofeng, Mao's sanctioned "chosen successor," or siding with four leading Politburo members (soon tagged "The Gang of Four") who had been arrested a month after Mao's funeral, including Mao's widow Jiang Qing, was being feverishly debated.[622]

In hindsight it is more than clear that these events were a watershed, signaling a major historical shift. At the time, however, there was plenty of room for debate (and confusion), especially given the Chinese Party was purposefully trying to obscure that shift, and emphasizing the continuity with Mao and socialism. Mainly though, events in China were bigger than what any organization could tolerate without major internal changes and soul-searching—though they did try. In this respect, one can say the RCP did about as badly as could be expected.

* * *

The organizational framework is of some note here. By 1976, the RCP was in a certain sense the inverse of what it had been during the struggle with Bruce Franklin. No longer was it an entity in which contending papers could circulate throughout the entire ranks, be debated out, with the inputs then coming back to the leading level of the organization for the ultimate decision based on what its membership was thinking. The party now had a hard democratic centralist organization, with each descending level subservient to the higher. In the words of their *Programme*: "The individual is subordinate to the Party, the minority is subordinate to the majority, the lower level is subordinate to the higher level, and the entire Party is subordinate to the Central Committee."[623]

This characterization, however, obscures the determinant power concentrated in the standing bodies *above* the Central Committee. In 1976 the real political decision-making body appears to have been a standing body of four people, followed by the Political Committee of the Central Committee, which was perhaps a dozen members, and then the Central Committee larger still.[624] Avakian himself gives a picture of the small number of people who ultimately decided the issue:

> There was another comrade in the very top leadership of the Party who had the same understanding of this [China situation] that I did. This was very important for me, both personally as well as in my ability to lead the Party as a whole, because in the top leadership core things were sharply divided: in addition to this comrade who was solidly with me on this, there were Leibel Bergman and Mickey Jarvis, who were supporting the revisionist coup with increasing vehemence.[625]

In this regard, Jarvis and Bergman argued for waiting and maintaining the status quo. Conversely, Avakian and Bill Klingel (the other leading member) advocated taking a stand more or less immediately. As a by Leibel Bergman later recounted, "[T]he day the Gang [of Four was] arrested A[vakian] and Klingle [sic] wanted to send [a] telegram condemning the arrest"—this from notes taken from a presentation Bergman made in the aftermath of the RCP's split.[626] While the notes are not definitive, they line up with

Avakian's view that, "[t]he initial reaction of myself and some other leaders of the Party was that this was a revisionist coup, a terrible thing."[627]

For Avakian things were already clear, the arrest of the Gang of Four "represented a right-wing coup and a serious blow against the proletariat in China and its revolutionary leadership."[628] In this view, the Four were the inheritors of the legacy of Mao Zedong, and their arrest represented a sharply repressive broadside against all he stood for. The Bergman-Jarvis position, which initially argued for further study within the Party, quickly found itself crafting their own firm stand: "The Gang [of Four] were not revolutionary heroes. They were counter-revolutionary traitors and enemies, and their fall is a workers' victory."[629] In this way, both sides staked out mutually exclusive positions on a quintessential issue within the largest Maoist organization in the US.

It had not always been so, at least for Bergman. In this, two things stand out. First is that he was not oblivious to the right-ward direction in China, as can be seen by the quote at the front of this chapter. This is amplified in an informant report—though decidedly not a neutral source:

> In the same context source [informant] mentioned the *Peking Review* has wished NATO well and even expressed hope that NIXON would survive Watergate. BERGMAN expressed incredulity, indicating he would research this himself and then said it was these rightist activities of REDACTED which caused the Cultural Revolution.[630]

The redaction is most likely a reference to Deng Xiaoping, who had been a key focus of the Cultural Revolution, along with his close ally and former President of the People's Republic, Liu Shaoqi. Even after events in China led to Bergman leaving the RCP, he appears to have continued to explain events in China in a way that suggested deeper questions:

> B[ergman] failed to convince A[vakian]. He tried to point out that while in essence the Cultural Revolution was good, it was not uniformly good. Till '66 good, but a failure to consolidate led to increasing opportunism. Further that Lin Piao incident was a great shock to the Chinese people—led to G4 [Gang of Four] attacks on Chou [Enlai], dogmatism, invoking the name of Mao to bring shame on Mao rather than the development of Mao thought.[631]

While the accuracy of the notes—Bergman's views interpreted through another person—need to be allowed for, they nonetheless suggest a more conflicted, and to a degree nuanced, view. While Bergman's analysis was ultimately lacking—it was more complex than the RCP would later represent.

In contrast to Bergman, Avakian's lengthy paper on the topic is striking in its certitude of what had transpired. In the following, he discusses why both Mao and the Gang of Four had been closely associated with the former top-leader, Lin Piao.

> [B]oth the genuine left and 'ultra-leftists' were temporarily united in fighting the main enemy at that time—the right (during this period, many of Lin Piao's actions and much of his line was "left" in form; as he reached the pinnacle of his power, however, his line became more and more openly right in form as well as essence). Therefore, naturally the genuine left, including the Four as leaders of it—and certainly including Mao—were linked with Lin Piao at that time.[632]

While Avakian cannot be faulted for not knowing things understood only in the rarified circles of China's elite, and his overall conclusions of a coup were accurate, his analysis of a Manichacan construct of good revolutionaries, battling bad capitalist roaders—or ultra-leftists, that were really rightist—

is overly simplistic (and paradoxically byzantine). Things were far more complicated in the final years of Mao's dominance over Chinese politics than his paper was willing to acknowledge, and the larger implications and conclusions to be drawn were not so immediately clear.[633]

Regardless, things in China were changing quickly. In that respect, the polemics passed back and forth by the two sides within the RCP—and they were not alone in this, the entire new communist movement was likewise engaged—had a ring of desperation. China was set on a dramatically different course, one that would move it far away from Mao's vision of revolutionary socialism. In that respect, the contending polemics aiming to stake out salvageable positions on Chinese socialism come across today as an effort to hold on to a piece of something that was quickly melting away.

* * *

Organizationally, however, there was a deadlock; "the two highest standing bodies of the Central Committee were evenly split on this matter," necessitating a decision on the level of the Central Committee.[634]

Since the arrest of the Gang of Four, the Party had counseled not coming to a decision, the idea being everyone review the situation with patient scrutiny[635]—objectively postponing serious discussion or debate or putting anything forward other than a unified position to lower-level cadre. This ended up backfiring. In the absence of broad, considered, and consequential debate, the small number in the top leadership of the organization, who had fully developed theses and increasingly vested interests in their respective positions, would set the terms in the debate that would inevitably come.

In this case, it meant that the Party in the eastern US and large parts of the Midwest would dig in on their position opposing

Avakian's assessment, arguing instead that the debate be taken to the larger Party. Short of that being accepted, they would array themselves in rebellion to the larger Party formation:

> At the Friday meeting, some of the CC members began to do self criticism and called for real rectification of the Party's work. This needs to be continued and deepened by all comrades. By contrast Avakian has rashly pushed our Party to the brink of a split and still arrogantly refuses to repeal his China bulletin as our Party's line.[636]

For its part, those grouped around Avakian claimed the authority of the Party and were pushing for a quick resolution. For those that held the name RCP, these oppositional views were "literally criminal and unconcealed attacks" that would "not be tolerated."[637] This was rending language soon brought to fruition. Avakian's recollections bear this out: "This is the Party, and you're either in this Party, or you're not. You're either in or you're out." To that end, there was a process wherein comrades who wanted to remain had to re-enroll in the Party and "to re-establish their dedication."[638] The window on this was not wide: "Members who have engaged in 'factional anti-party activity.' [sic] These people must re-enlist to assigned comrades or bodies within one week as of Thursday, January 12, 1978 or they will be dropped from the membership rolls of the Party."[639]

The results were immediate. Bergman and Jarvis left the organization, taking a third of the membership with them, mainly cadre in the New York, New Jersey, Philadelphia, Baltimore, Pittsburgh and Milwaukee areas, while splitting cadre in the Chicago and Boston area.[640] Here a point needs to be made, that for all the essentializing of "line" in this struggle, and this was also true in the Franklin schism, people tended (though this was not absolute) to break along familiar lines, i.e., they went with people and leaders they knew.[641] As for those leaving the RCP, they would go on to form a new group, which was named the Revolutionary Workers Headquarters (RWH).

In this, both sides behaved badly. Former comrades now ridiculed one another in the most unkind terms. There were death threats and violent confrontations, some quite serious, particularly on the East Coast and in the Midwest.[642] The vitriol was mean-spirited, from caricatures of Avakian dressed up as a pimp, amid the Gang of Four dressed as pimps, hipsters and hustlers, to attacking Avakian's then wife by writing her telephone number on a bathroom wall in the "for a good time" adolescent mode (leading to obscene phone calls).[643] On the opposite end there were *ad hominem* insults: "there'll be people like Jarvis around, even if Jarvis himself has choked on his Twinkie's [sic] and died (laughter)"[644] and name-calling leveled at former comrades, such as "the herky-jerky theoretician," and quite a few others,[645] all while railing against "unprincipled methods."

As bad as this was, things went even further into the realm of airing personal information (in a stigmatizing manner) and political secrets. On the anti-Avakian side was this:

> The pressure catapulted this self-proclaimed "high roader" into an emotional disorder and psychiatric care for several months, during which extensive struggle was required, for example, to get him to leave his house, even for a walk.[646]

On the RCP side came the publication of *Revolution and Counter-Revolution*, which among other things reprinted the opposition's formerly internal documents, *verbatim*, including the names of formerly secret RCP leaders, including five members of the Political Committee and six members of the Central Committee.[647] Of course Bergman himself appears to have freely named the unnamed Bill Klingel as the person siding with Avakian on the leading body. All of this was in keeping with the abandonment of any sense of mutual respect and political decorum.

This departure from principle lowered the terms and coarsened the disagreement. Along with the airing of internal dirty laundry, and disregard for heretofore-organizational secrecy, there was a re-writing of the group's history. In language suggestive of Stalin in the Thirties, Bergman and Jarvis were portrayed as party members seeking at every turn to undermine the correct leadership of the Party, specifically the singular leadership of Bob Avakian. RCP documents talked about Bergman and Jarvis' "long-term double-dealing and hatred for Comrade Avakian."[648]

In this was also a radical recasting of the role of Leibel Bergman. The Party now offered only a minimum of credit to Bergman in the group's foundation, allowing that he "had learned some Marxist-Leninist theory in the CPUSA and was able to play a somewhat useful role in the early period of the new communist movement." It then proceeded to politically eviscerate him:

> Instead of studying Marxism-Leninism he boycotted study groups in the Party, preferring instead to coast along with his mishmash of Marxism, revisionism and the "wisdom" of openly bourgeois "authorities." Instead of playing an active role in helping the Party to grapple with new and difficult questions, he simply doled out "advice," and increasingly wrong advice at that.[649]

The broadside concluded with the *ad hominem* attack that, "[h]e saw himself as a 'great mind' floating free while his body wandered about the country in his role as a Condescending Savior or a Confucian Sage." For the Party, Bergman was now a sinister force who "preferred to lurk in the background and engage in Machiavellian maneuvering in hopes of getting his revisionist line across."[650]

Avakian himself would later step back from this assessment, to a degree, describing Bergman as someone who played a "very important role in developing me into a communist and in lending more ideological clarity to our efforts in forming the organization we did in the Bay Area late in 1968."[651] Coming twenty-five odd years after the fact, however, the damage was done. The scorched earth manner of criticism, a literal tearing at its own roots and legacy, meant the RCP would go into its next phase more isolated and sectarian than in its worst periods up to that point.

Bergman's own thoughts in regard to Avakian after the split are a bit more generous, if no less critical. In the notes of a presentation Bergman gave soon after the split, he describes Avakian as "a quick student of Marxism-Leninism," albeit with "a tendency to dogmatism."[652] There is also, in Bergman's comments, a view that serves as a certain counterpoint and accurate predictor of what would come to characterize the view and method of the "new" RCP:[653]

> The other tendency coming to full-flower under [Avakian] was that [the] day-to-day working class is nothing. This was seized on by [Avakian] as combatting rightism. Because it spoke to a real problem the tendency from comrades was to listen [sic]. There were rightist errors but the work was not rightist.[654]

The reality of a Maoist party in the 1970s USA was always a high-wire effort between radicalism and getting drawn into the mainstream. While some did better than others, the labels being heaped on the defectors in this final schism come across as overly simplistic. An entire coterie of comrades—numbering many hundreds—were labeled rightists or "Mensheviks." Most of these cadres too had come through the Sixties, some acquitting themselves quite remarkably in taking courageous and radical positions of the time. Any acknowledgement of this seemed to have disappeared in the immediate aftermath of the split in the efforts to clearly draw the "two lines." Meanwhile, the basis was being laid for what would be left of the RCP to go forward untethered from any basing of itself, not just among the working class, but any section of people within the United States.

The RCP Exits the USCPFA

One of the direct consequences of the split would be the end of the RCP's relationship with the US-China Peoples Friendship Association. By 1977, the USCPFA had a membership of over 11,000 people in 90 chapters.[655] The largest membership was concentrated on the West Coast, where there were 6,930 members, compared to 1,914 on the East Coast, the next largest region. With the split in the RCP, the group's organizational profile would now become highly unsettled.

In the wake of the split, the USCPFA would maintain a sizable membership, but the organization would lose half its footprint on the West Coast, the key stronghold of the RCP.[656] In the Party's view, it was largely responsible for the group's existence and were "instrumental in the formation of the earliest local Friendship Associations in 1971, and had played a significant role in the creation of the national association."[657] Given that, they felt they had a particular responsibility to use their presence as a forum to promote their analysis on events in China, which included denouncing the current leaders as revisionist and noting that the "progressive role played by the Association for several years had necessarily to come to an end with the revisionist coup in China."[658] This was, however, at direct odds with the mandate of the organization, and led to all manner of conflict. In Seattle, for example, where the RCP had a disproportionate representation in the local chapter, and used that to exercise organizational control,[659] the national organization in turn, in June 1978, demoted the chapter to an

Organizing Committee.[660] This all came to a head at the USCPFA national meeting in September 1978. RCP supporters attended the convention, attempting to promote the RCP's position. In this, they promoted upcoming programs set to explain events in China from the RCP's view. They also challenged speakers they disagreed with by chanting from the floor, "Five! Five! Mao Makes Five!"[661] All of this was wildly unsettling and disorienting to much of the Association's rank and file.

Regardless, it was a new day for the group. The time of promoting a Maoist alternative to capitalism was largely at an end. In that respect, the RCP's view that the "Friendship Association will complete its transformation into a funded staff operation on behalf of the Chinese government in cooperation with US imperialism" was more correct than not. The Party's efforts, however, came down to putting forward their political position in an organization they no longer had any use for—a situation emblematic of the crisis they were in the grip of; one with no easy answers or clear resolution.

The Split in the RCYB

The split also effectively destroyed the newly formed Revolutionary Communist Youth Brigade (RCYB) as it had been constituted. A good chunk of the RCYB's membership were students concentrated in areas in the East and Midwest, by cadre who were never fully on board with the whole concept of the RCYB. In the aftermath of the split, the RCP produced a pamphlet documenting the struggle in the group, before its founding conference in 1977, over what would be the name of this young communist league. The forces that would become the Revolutionary Workers Headquarters had submitted a paper arguing to not have "communist" in the name, because of the prevalence of anti-communism, and the limits it would put on their ability to organize. In this, they argued for the name Revolutionary Youth Brigade. For the RCP, they wanted the communist politics front and center under the name Revolutionary Communist Youth. For them, this was a touchstone question between communism and revisionism and a further justification of their positions in the split that had just occurred, widening the rationale to one beyond the position on China.

Characteristically after the fact, the RCP assessed this struggle as mainly a good thing and that the organization was "growing far stronger in the process,"[662]—a starkly counterfactual characterization. In fact, the split largely signaled the end of the Party's organized presence on US campuses, though the RCYB itself would continue as a smaller, more loosely organized entity.

The Split in VVAW

Perhaps of all the intra-organizational splits, the one within Vietnam Veterans Against the War was the most acrimonious. Unlike the USCPFA, the leadership of VVAW was concentrated in one organization, the RCP. When that organization split into two—consistent with the regional fault lines of the overall rift—the bulk of the leadership went with the Revolutionary Workers Headquarters. In this there was a rapid rushing away from the revolutionary attraction the Party had been to these veterans. A sharp expression of this can be seen in later remarks from Dave Cline, a Vietnam combat veteran who had also, not inconsequentially, been on the Central Committee of the RCP:[663]

> After the split in the RCP, people started examining the shit more closely. I mean, I believe in socialism; I believe that the capitalist system is a system that is as corrupt as the communists were—but eventually people have to come to some cooperative system. But you're not a conveyor belt to recruit someone to nirvana in Marxist-Leninist heaven. We spent a lot of time, after the RCP thing, getting the shit off our shoes.[664]

While Cline pointedly does not fully renounce the cause of socialism, he does not acknowledge his leadership role in a self-professed communist vanguard. This is at once suggestive of the bitterness of his experience, but is also a contributing factor to a certain re-writing—even erasing—of the history of VVAW's time under RCP leadership. This was consistent with the fact VVAW took steps to disassociate itself from the RCP. The organization brought a lawsuit against another fraction of the organization, still sympathetic to the Party, Vietnam Veterans Against the War Anti-Imperialist,[665] to ensure its name not be used. In fact, VVAW still has the court judgement available on its website and identifies the RCP-friendly VVAW-AI (anti-imperialist) as "the creation of an obscure, ultra-left sect"—without naming the RCP specifically. Somewhat discordantly, their website also has a complete archive of the newspaper, *The Veteran*, including the years it was most closely associated with the RCP.

The Role of the FBI?

There was, of course, one other element in play during this schism—one that thus far has flown under the radar of disclosure—the activity of the FBI and local police red squads. By 1977, the FBI's penetration of the group had grown in sync with the organization's expansion. The FBI was by then collecting an extensive "album" of RCP members, grouping members both nationally and regionally. An FBI memo in January 1975 instructed certain notations be made in the "NY RU album," and then stipulated coding for Mickey Jarvis, Victoria Garvin, Leibel Bergman and other leading members living in the New York area.[666] The fuller content of this album is still secret. In response to a Freedom of Information query, the FBI claims its file on the New York branch of the RU "[w]as destroyed in 1990."[667]

While the specifics of what the authorities were doing at this time—including operating in the troubled waters of this acrimonious split—remains largely hidden, it is the case that the turn in China away from revolutionary Maoism solved a formidable problem. If the FBI played no role in the airing of the dirty laundry, internal secrets, and the war of words between the RCP and RWH—an unlikely prospect given everything they had been able to do before that point—then it must have taken pleasure in the fact that the two factions were essentially undertaking mutually destructive work, in a better way than they ever could.

Regardless, events in the world had a far more decisive effect than anything they attempted in all the years and effort they had expended on the RU and the RCP. One can reasonably liken it to the climactic battle scene in *Gangs of New York* where the two sides square off—chains, clubs, and fists at the ready for the final showdown, only to look up in baffled amazement as canon-balls fired from US military gunboats in the harbor hurtle toward them. The FBI and the RCP may have been locked in battle, but in the end larger forces decided the war.

The Mao Memorial

To mark the second anniversary of Mao's death on September 9 and 10, 1978, the Revolutionary Communist Party held two major "memorials," one in New York and one in San Francisco, to commemorate Mao Zedong and his revolutionary contributions.[668]

The events attracted 1,100 people in New York and 1,200 in San Francisco and were notable for the heavy security and massive postering effort to publicize the event. The extent of publicity on the part of the Party was such that one news profile reported on how "[p]olice from San Francisco to Albany, NY to Tampa, Fla. have arrested poster pasters or begun investigations into the groups responsible for their placement."[669] The poster campaign, ads, and other promotion were the RCP trying to stake its claim to the future, upholding Mao and arguing that they were the true inheritors of his legacy.

Introducing Avakian, the featured speaker at both events, were Bill Klingel and Joanne Psihountas[670]—identified as leaders of the Central Committee of the Party, signaling the change in leadership in the wake of the exit of Leibel Bergman and Mickey Jarvis. The speech, later published as *The Loss in China and the Revolutionary Legacy of Mao Tse-tung*, elaborated on Avakian's earlier thesis of what had happened in China, based on his reading of official documents coming out of China before and after the coup. While there was a general suggestion that the reversal in China might be a more long-term circumstance, it emphasized that ultimately communism would be successful and the need for "Mao's successors" to carry out his legacy—a call that would set the terms for what the RCP would do going forward.

Rebuilding/Rectification

Under Avakian's leadership, a rectification campaign was launched inside the remaining organization. There had already been weeks of concentrated study and meetings for cadre to get steeped in Avakian's position. This would soon give way to a dramatic transformation of how the group went about its work.

Throughout the Seventies, the organization had taken on many of the trappings of US society, including no small amount of listlessness, malaise, and even decadence. This was compounded by the fact that it had gone into the heart of the American mainstream, the stable US working class. For the previous five to seven years, most cadre were in monogamous relationships, many with young children, living in working-class neighborhoods, drawing union salaries, and attempting to assimilate into the lifestyle of those they were organizing. They took out mortgages, listened to country music, and drank on weekends. Along the way, not a few developed drinking problems, didn't have much time for reading, and were dragged down by the politics of the shop floor. This was to be no more, as a singular focus on "revolution" was reintroduced and emphasized—albeit without the social upheaval of the previous decade. Meantime, the Party organization in key parts of the country had been decimated. In New York, only a handful of members remained loyal to the Party—and they were mainly cadre living in New Jersey. A few Asian-American cadre, who had moved East from the Bay Area a few years earlier, remained loyal, but by-in-large the RCP had lost its footprint in the largest city in the country. The organization's presence in Philadelphia, too, given the stature garnered during the Bicentennial struggle, was entirely gone (though there were still Party cadres in northeast Pennsylvania's Allentown Pottstown and Reading), likewise Milwaukee had been decimated and Chicago—the Party's center—was bifurcated. There were other losses in smaller cities and towns, which aggregated up to a significantly diminished organization. This was a situation the RCP would never completely recover from. The upsurge of the 1960s and 1970s was now in the past, with no similar historic confluence forthcoming. The lost cadre would not be replaced.

The Party, however, tried to adjust. Cadres were re-assigned from the untouched areas of the Bay Area, Los Angeles, and the Pacific Northwest. They undertook construction of a new Revolution Books, in New York City to take the place of the now antagonistic China Books, which had served the Party's purposes, but now followed the current leadership of the CCP. More cadre would follow, as the Party started closing up shop in places such as the coalfields and moved those cadres and others to the East Coast and Midwest. But an organization that likely never had more than 900-1,100 had been cut down by a third, and the years that would follow would see negative attrition reduce that further still.

The Aftermath

It seems the RCP passed through its last schism naïve, in the largest sense, as to what was happening in the world and to the implications for its organization. An article written by the Revolutionary Workers Headquarters calling out what it considered the low politics and methods behind the split, was notably signed "by a veteran comrade who has been through this kind of thing before"—almost surely Leibel Bergman. In a similar vein, Avakian, toward the end of his Central Committee report on China, stated, "It is inevitable that socialism will eventually replace capitalism and communism will ultimately be achieved in every country, throughout the whole world. Nothing that has happened in China changes this."[671] Such facile, even quasi-religious, analysis looked past something important. There had never before been anything like what happened in China, and that historic event held sweeping implications, not the least of which was the presaging of the end of the socialist project of the twentieth century. Far from either shard of the former organization coming out stronger, this event would be devastating to both, albeit with different dynamics and temporal frameworks. It also effectively signaled the end of the vibrancy of the new communist movement in the US. This was, in sum, a world-shifting event—and one that could not be understood with any depth at the moment, or even the immediate years surrounding it. It constituted a paradigm shift that even today has largely not been appropriately understood, or even fully acknowledged by still-existing Maoist forces. In that respect, the change in China and the resulting split in the RCP necessitated and offered an opportunity for first-order questions to be asked. The Party would ask *some* hard questions in its wake, but only within the framework of building on what Mao had brought forward.[672] In this way, it would retain continuity, but at the expense of a fuller and much needed engagement of the universe of questions in front of it.

* * *

By any definition, the schism of 1977-78 was a devastating blow to the organizational reach and influence of the Revolutionary Communist Party. The US-China Peoples Friendship Association as an organization promoting revolutionary socialism and influencing many thousands was for all intents and purposes at an end. Vietnam Veterans Against the War, while not nearly the organization it had been at the beginning of the Seventies, was significantly diminished and was quickly putting distance between itself and any kind of radicalism. The Revolutionary Student Brigade/Revolutionary Communist Youth Brigade as a national organization of discrete chapters was no more. As for the Revolutionary Communist Party, it would continue, but would become something quite different.

Chapter 10

After the Fall

A great and historic step was taken on May Day 1980.
— *Revolutionary Worker,* May 5, 1980.

Cleveland office workers, meanwhile, threw rocks, bottles, and eggs, at about 50 communist demonstrators on a flatbed truck
— News report, May 2, 1980.[673]

The period after the split was a transformative one for the remains of the Party. On one level, the period from 1978 through 1980 was one where it attempted to recover from its most serious schism and maintain its vibrancy. On the other, the steps it took to overcome what it had identified as the shortcomings of the pre-split organization would seal its fate as a marginal group in the larger political universe. Along the way, it would endure a wave of political repression—including the killing of one of its members—along with the exit of a large number of veteran cadre. For his part, Bob Avakian would consolidate a spot as sole head of the Party. Ironically, he would occupy that position from outside the US, living in self-imposed exile.

The Deng Demo

In early 1979, Chinese Vice Premier of the State Council, Deng Xiaoping came to the United States to tour the country, meet with President Jimmy Carter, and solidify his ties with the US. For the RCP, Deng's visit was both an affront and a gauntlet—and they resolved to confront him. Thus, in January 1979, they assembled the "Committee for a Fitting Welcome" for Deng, and sent an advance team to Washington, DC to begin planning the protest.

This would be a different kind of demonstration. The RCP

hadn't undertaken a protest of this nature since the days of the anti-Nixon action in San Jose—if even then. One of the preparatory actions, occurring five days before Deng's arrival, involved five supporters of the RCP hurling red paint at the Chinese liaison office (soon to become the Chinese Embassy). They also broke windows with lead fishing weights and hurled an effigy of Deng onto the steps. A spokesperson for the action—in the manner of issuing a communiqué—called the *Associated Press* and said, "We wanted to insult the revisionist leadership in China. We wanted it to be a warning to Deng that he can expect a lot of opposition from revolutionaries."[674] This action was a reference point for Avakian who in a press conference on January 25, 1979 said, "The kind of thing that happened at the embassy yesterday is an example of a 'fitting welcome.'"[675]

In a more modest and direct protest, on January 29, two Party supporters using *Revolutionary Worker* press credentials were able to briefly disrupt a press conference and wave copies of *Quotations from Mao Tse-tung* at Deng and Carter[676] before being arrested for disorderly conduct, charges that were later dropped.[677]

On the same day, a rally to prepare for the march on the White House was held in DC's All Souls Church; there Avakian gave an impassioned speech:

> What they hate and what they fear, and what they want to crush is the banner of revolution, the banner of the Revolutionary Communist Party and its revolutionary line, the banner of Mao Tse-tung. It's the banner of working every day for revolution, of seeing beyond the superficial and down to the essence of what this hellish society, and its mad-dog prison-house that they call democracy, is all about. And we gotta hold up that banner, we gotta hold it up today and rally the revolutionary-minded people, all people who look and long for a way out of this madness.[678]

The RCP had no illusions about changing the course of events in China in the short term—though it had referred to the change in China as a "temporary setback." However, the "now or never" message implicit in Avakian's speech made clear the Party felt making a sharp statement upholding Mao was an absolute necessity—and this needed to be done in a bold and aggressive way. [679]

At the start, the protest march after the rally wound its way toward the White House in conventional style, with militant chanting and marching. However, as the front of the march entered Lafayette Park, across the street from the White House things changed. Here the Party and the established press offer conflicting versions. According to the *Washington Post*:

> Suddenly, as they approached the park from the east along Pennsylvania Avenue, they broke into a run, shouting "Death, Death to Teng Tsiao-Ping"[sic] and began hurling bottles, poles, lighted road flares, and hundreds of nails, heavy washers and fishing sinkers at both D.C. and U.S. Park Police gathered near the parks. Police, apparently caught off guard, quickly recovered and with reinforcements charged into the crowd swinging their clubs wildly. Many demonstrators swung back with their improvised clubs.[680]

The Party's account makes no mention of demonstrators throwing things at police and rather suggests a determined self-defense against an unprovoked attack:

> As the cops began their attack, the marchers suddenly broke into a run toward the White House. A thundering cry reverberated down Pennsylvania Avenue, "DEATH, DEATH, TO TENG HSIAO-PING!" As the police moved on the crowd clubbing and beating, hundreds stood their ground.[681]

The demonstration was short, violent, and bloody. In the end, at least 38 demonstrators were treated at local hospitals along with 13 police officers.[682] Seventy-eight demonstrators were arrested, with slightly more men than women taken into custody. Initial charges were on the level of disorderly conduct, but over the next couple of days they were upgraded to felony assault on a police officer.[683]

At first the Party exhibited a certain triumphalism. The lead article in the *Revolutionary Worker* announced: "Traitor Deng Given Fitting Welcome: Revolutionaries in Fierce Clash with DC Cops." The coverage, along with pictures of the march, included a picture of two demonstrators with 2 x 2 clubs running away from a police officer lying on the ground next to his motorcycle.[684] The report cast the overall scene in heroic terms:

> While the march was a source of inspiration to revolutionary minded people around the world, it was a nightmare for the bourgeoisie. The intensity of the police attack and the severity of the charges –felony assault thrown at the 78 arrested – only underscored the desperation of the bourgeoisie that they were not able to stop this powerful statement from being made. It was definitely a "fitting welcome" for the ratfaced traitor Teng Hsiao-ping.[685]

As the enormity of the response by the state began to sink in, the Party shifted its focus to highlighting the viciousness of the police attack. Eventually, the RCP would omit self-defense entirely from the narrative. In 2005, Avakian recounted how, "[a]s we began the march, it was already very clear that the authorities really didn't like this demonstration. And as we got to the area of Lafayette Park, the police unleashed a violent attack, beating as many people as they could and finally succeeded in breaking up the march."[686] The change in tack had to do with the severity of the fallout. The Party's chief leader was facing multiple felony charges that, if upheld, would mean decades in prison, a situation that would take several years and undue energy to fight off. Further, the federal government was able to place a formidable legal Damocles sword over a number of dedicated cadre. Along with this, the arrests in the run up and aftermath of the march meant the government had an audit on scores of other Party members and supporters—many who had largely been off the political police's radar since the heyday of the Sixties.

After the Deng Demo

Under Avakian's leadership, the RCP was redefining itself. It began to reject the whole strategy of having cadre working among the industrial proletariat in favor of the more amorphous strategy of "Create Public Opinion/Seize Power," taken from a saying by Mao: "Before you make a revolution, you must first create public opinion."[687] This also flowed from a reading of Lenin's pamphlet *What Is To Be Done*, that the communist "ideal should not be the trade union secretary, but *the tribune of the people* [emphasis original], who is able to react to every manifestation of tyranny and oppression, no matter where it appears, no matter what stratum or class of the people it affects."[688] As a result the RCP began extricating itself from building a base among the more stable unionized working class in favor of what increasingly was being defined as the "real proletariat"—a term Avakian would popularize to describe the "strategic orientation that Lenin stressed, of going down *lower and deeper to the basic sections of the proletariat,* whose interests more conform to and give rise to an inclination or gravitation toward proletarian revolution."[689] Here the work of creating "revolutionary public opinion" through a weekly newspaper distributed in the housing projects as well as among immigrant workers and lower paid industrial workers, along with key demographics like youth and other social groups, was the primary focus. From this point on, the Party no longer would attempt to base cadre—in any meaningful way—among what it identified as strategic sections of the working class. Rather, they would attempt to "build a base" through a network of connections made via their newspaper.

The other component of the changed strategy was bound up with the specific targeting of Avakian. In this, the RCP began to purposefully build a "cult of personality" around Avakian, as a means not only to build support for him legally but also to also popularize the RCP as the most thoroughly revolutionary organization in the US. In building this cult, the RCP was drawing not only upon communist history going back to Stalin's time and Mao's cult but also to the Free Huey! campaign that Avakian and other early RU members had played active roles in.

In this they reached for a theoretical justification in the work of the Russian Social-Democrat, Georgy Plekhanov:

> Carlyle, in his well-known book on heroes and hero-worship, calls great men *beginners*. This is a very apt description. A great man is precisely a beginner because he sees *further* than others, and desires things *more strongly* than others.[690]

This offered an explanation for the "specialness" of Avakian at a time when the political repression aimed at him was quite pronounced and when the RCP no longer had China to look to for inspiration.

As time went on, this would assume more and more exaggerated proportions. For the moment, however, it marked a final divide between what had been a more collective leadership, and one where Avakian served as the guiding counsel, visionary leader, and last word. This at once ensured continuity for the organization but also a rigidity and inflexibility in doctrine—to say nothing of opening it up to all manner of ridicule on the larger left. In this it appears Avakian himself was highly responsible for the promotion of his own cult. As he wrote:

> I remember, for example, being challenged by someone interviewing me—I believe this was on a college radio station in Madison, Wisconsin—who asked insistently: "Is there a 'cult of personality' developing around Bob Avakian?' And I replied: 'I certainly hope so—we've been working very hard to create one."[691]

This was put forward not as a matter of egotism but as a "scientific" assessment, bolstered by organizational approbation, that such a cult could be a helpful instrument for advancing the aims of the group. Such a rationale, however, is largely beside the point. In the end, it could be no more than what it actually was—the promotion of an individual over and above (including largely above criticism) everyone else in the organization. More significantly, it was a sign of the weakened state of the group: only an outsize character could continue to cohere it.[692]

Regardless, as part of the emphasis, there was a campaign focused on promoting and defending Avakian—above the other arrestees—from the charges stemming from the Deng demonstration. Posters were done up with his image under the headline "The Revolutionary Communist Party and its Chairman, Bob Avakian, are target of the most vicious attack by the government since the '60s." As part of the implementation of this, the May Day celebration in 1979, three months after the Deng demonstration, was held in Washington, DC, with the goal of beating back Avakian's prosecution given his prominent position. It was at the conclusion of this May Day march and rally that Avakian gave a speech announcing a year-long campaign for a Revolutionary May 1, 1980, with the stated intention of the RCP and Avakian being much more influential and well known in a year's time.

Before that, however, the Party put out a call for volunteers to come to DC in November 1979 to "Turn DC Upside Down" in an effort to overturn the charges against Avakian and his remaining co-defendants—their number having been reduced after the government dropped charges on all but 17 of the original 78.[693] In the midst of this initiative, an appeals court judge dismissed the charges saying the government had overstepped, engaging in prosecutorial vindictiveness.[694] The Party and volunteers held a celebration on the announcement, but it was premature. Less than a year later, the charges would be reinstated.[695]

Meanwhile, events in the world were spinning at a feverish pace. In Nicaragua, Anastasio Somoza was chased from office by the revolutionary Sandinista forces. In Iran, the pro-US Shah fled, leading to Iranian students occupying the US Embassy. In Greensboro, North Carolina, at a "Death to the Klan" rally, five members of the Communist Workers Party—a smaller entity in the larger new communist movement—were shot dead in broad daylight by Klan members and domestic Nazis. Events seemed to justify the RCP's amplified sense of urgency. The level of confrontation, street fighting, and arrests would soon escalate to levels never before confronted by the RU/RCP. This, in turn, upped the ante. Steve Hamilton, writing now as a former RU member, noted developments with some alarm:

> Now, in 1979, RCP seems to have regressed to a kind of left adventurism that is reminiscent of the Weatherman days, also reminiscent of the later years of PL as well when it found itself an isolated sect and a kind of "go for broke" mentality set in.[696]

From his step back position, Hamilton's assessment seems apt.

May Day 1980

In the early months of 1980, May Day Brigades were formed on the West and East coasts. They were to be mobile squads of a couple dozen cadre and close supporters who would descend on areas announcing and organizing for mass demonstrations on May 1. From the very beginning, the squads were targeted by both local police and other government authorities.

On February 14, 1980, ten members of the May Day Brigade were arrested outside an unemployment office in Youngstown, Ohio, then held in jail for several days with their bail being raised from a modest $625 to $4500 each.[697] On March 4, members of the May Day Brigades "burst into the office of the US Attorney" and read an "indictment" by the working class of the government in this case, they then went outside and joined a demonstration demanding the charges against Avakian be dropped.[698] In West Virginia, 18 people were arrested under an arcane state law that made the display of the red or black flag illegal.[699] In another action in the coalfields, the "May Day brigade was run into hiding by reactionary mobs in Beckley, West Virginia."[700] The incidents and confrontations were relentless.

In this time, the RCP was also becoming known for its provocative and high profile public burnings of American flags. In one case, on March 27, 1980, two RCP supporters burned a flag outside the federal courthouse in Greensboro, North Carolina, to protest the prosecution of Avakian for the Deng demonstration. The response from the government was Draconian. The two, Teresa Kime and Donald Bonwell, were tried under a 1968 federal flag desecration law and were later convicted after a jury trial, on July 17, 1980. They were, in turn, sentenced to eight months in jail. They lost on appeal and went to jail after the US Supreme Court refused to review their case in October 1982.[701]

Incidents like these and other evidence suggest a major offensive aimed at the RCP. The previous fall, Avakian had undertaken a national speaking tour as a way of bolstering his profile and supporting efforts to beat back the legal charges stemming from the Deng demonstration. In the course of the tour, Avakian spoke extensively with the press, and even made an appearance on the late night show *Tomorrow*, hosted by Tom Snyder. While in Los Angeles, Avakian spoke with a reporter from the *Los Angeles Times* who in turn ran a story misconstruing Avakian's political statement as a potential criminal threat. As the Party's press reported:

> The Secret Service used that article as a pretext for an investigation into Avakian. After being threatened with a lawsuit, the *L.A. Times* printed a partial retraction, and the Secret Service investigation into Avakian was challenged in court. Avakian was never charged in connection with this investigation.[702]

In challenging that effort, the Party sought disclosure of what the Secret Service was doing. One result was the release of 534 pages of Secret Service documents after an FOIA request. According to the Party's press, the material presented:

> Clear indication of both informants and actual government agents infiltrating RCP activity; prosecution being actively considered against RCP and its members on charges on advocating the violent overthrow of the government; "Look Out Lists" maintained by the Secret Service as well as by other government police agencies on RCP connected cars in Washington, DC during the campaign to turn DC upside down; "criminal/mental checks" ordered by the Secret Service on arrested RCP members and supporters; open cooperation between reactionary organizations and the Secret Service and local police agencies to sabotage RCP led demonstrations and set revolutionaries up for possible arrests; cooperation between national wire services, well known newspapers and the Secret Service to provide the Secret Service with information on RCP activity[703]

Unfortunately the Party's press did not cite specific references from the FOIA material or share this information with the wider public, or even the broader ranks of the Party—however everything listed is consistent with what had been leveled at the RU/RCP up to that point.

The level of attention was so intense that by the end of March the campaign for May Day 1980 had led to 207 arrests of RCP members and supporters.[704] Confrontation with the police in this period was regular to the point of routine. On the one hand, the pronounced leftism, the willingness to step outside the bounds of certain laws on the part of the Party, was laying it much more open to the repressive moves by authorities. On the other, there was a pronounced shift within the political realm in the US. By the late 1970s, the world had become a different place. The US now had a political alliance with China, was confronting a heightened geopolitical challenge by the Soviet Union, was dealing with the debacle of the fall of the Shah of Iran, along with the shaking of their grip on key countries in Central America. All of this created a certain necessity to shut down whatever remaining radicalism of the Sixties still existed.

It was in this context that the RCP was experiencing the most serious repression it had ever seen. It was here too, only weeks before May Day 1980, that an internal struggle broke out that threatened to destroy the Party.

The May Day "Farrago"

Mike Ely, a former editor of the *Revolutionary Worker*, describes what the Party would later refer to as a "farrago" that ensued in late February and peaked in March 1980:

> A line came to the fore that argued that the main obstacle and problem in the May Day 1980 campaign was the opposition by "rightists" within the party. And a "farrago" erupted (farrago meaning a "mish mash" of things, but in party jargon it meant a big blowup). This farrago was a vicious turning inward – the launching of a "war on

> the right" within the movement for May Day 1980, that involved "pulling out rightists" (including leaders) for public criticism (not only in party meetings but in public meetings that included non-member activists).[705]

The Party never wrote publicly about all that happened during this "farrago," though internal bulletins would later ascribe it as a matter of a line that appeared "left" but was in essence "right." This farrago, lasting only a matter of weeks, peaked in March 1980, one month before the May Day demonstrations were to occur, but did a good deal of damage in its short run. It was particularly feverish within the East Coast May Day brigade. In a *public* mass meeting in New York, comrades were criticized and expelled from the Party. The tone was ugly and dangerous. On a visit to Philadelphia, the leaders of the May Day brigade joked about one comrade being upset to the point of wanting to commit suicide and laughingly remarking it would "be a good thing for her to do just that."[706] Leaders were removed, and new leaders installed, actions the Party had encouraged a few weeks earlier were now denounced as "rightist." Overall, the bearings of the group were running amok. As Ely describes:

> This farrago (this "war on the right") almost pulled the party apart. The campaign for May Day 1980 was suddenly in danger of collapsing into a public and embarrassing free-for-all. And Avakian angrily called the farrago off–saying that it ran counter to the plans for a successful May Day event and that it had not been authorized.[707]

This largely unknown event remains shrouded in a certain mystery. It was certainly true that by this time the Party had become adept at vicious internal infighting, but it is no less true that the FBI and other police agencies had accumulated a long track record of fostering and promoting an atmosphere in furtherance of rending divisions—in that respect it is hard to imagine political police operatives or informers *not* involved in some way. It is, on the whole, a matter yet to be fully explored.

No sooner had this "War on the Right" been brought to heel, than another crisis gripped the Party. On March 20, 1980, RCP cadre, Damián García, and two other members of the May Day Brigade, Abigail Bayer and Hayden Steel Fisher, ascended to the heights of the US Alamo, lowered the Texas state and American flags, and raised a red flag and May Day Banner saying "Take History Into Our Hands." This was an incident, with an iconic photo, that was splashed on newspapers across the country—an anomaly given the press's reticence to acknowledge the Party's existence most of the time. The three were initially charged with flag desecration, charges that were soon dropped.[708] They would, however, later be convicted and fined for disorderly conduct.[709]

The Killing of Damián García

Little more than a month later, when May Day volunteers—including García and Fisher—went into the Pico Aliso Gardens housing project in Los Angeles, on April 22, the outcome was far graver. Initially the Brigade marched through the various units of the project distributing flyers for May Day 1980. Close at hand were police cars monitoring their activity. According to the RCP's press, when they got to the last unit in the project, the police were absent.[710]

In his doctoral dissertation, David Morgan writes a narrative version of these events that includes an interview of someone he calls "Luisia." Though he presents it as a fictionalized account, it is one that appears to correspond to the known facts. He describes how the Brigade was confronted with some gang members who seemed to come out of nowhere:

They looked like gang members but they weren't any of the

> gang members we'd seen before. There were just two of them at first. They were drinking from pint flasks. One of them started yelling shit at us. "Get the red flag outa' here. Get the fuck outa my territory."
>
> Our tactical leader went up to him. She said, "This ain't your territory. The pigs run it. The working class has no borderline."
>
> Then he said, "You guys are against the government, well, I am the government. You guys are the fucking red flag. Mine is the red, white and blue."[711]

What happened next was a confusion of events, with gang members grabbing the Brigade's banner and turning a water hose on them. When Damián García approached one of them with the newspaper, "[t]he first guy tried to knock the papers out of Damián's hand. The guy that seemed to be in charge held onto the guy with the hose until six to eight more guys came around the corner to make a total of twelve to fifteen. Then he said, 'Okay, fuck 'em up.'"[712] When the smoke cleared, Damián García lay dead, fatally stabbed. RCP member, and Vietnam veteran, Hayden Fisher was also stabbed—though he survived the attack. Two days after the stabbing, Rosalio Gomez was quoted in the *Los Angeles Times* saying, "The US imperialist ruling class has lashed out in an act of cowardly desperation. This was a police hit."[713] The party's press struck the same tone, claiming García was "knifed to death by a police agent."[714] For their part, LAPD homicide Lt. Jerry Trent claimed the Party "didn't take into account the territorial imperative of the barrio gang environment"[715]—an argument that would turn out to be both convenient and deceptive.

What Trent did not disclose was that the LAPD had an officer working undercover within the May Day Brigade. The officer's name was Fabian Lizarraga, and he had infiltrated the RCP's work in LA, beginning in January 1979. As the *Los Angeles*

Times would report, Lizarraga "was present when the principal subject of his investigation [García] was murdered."[716] As part of his information gathering, Lizarraga had told his superiors that the Brigade would be in the project the day of García's killing. Lizarraga's zeal in doing his job also lead to his striking up a relationship with a Party member:

> After first consulting his superiors, he regularly engaged in sexual intercourse with a woman party member, because he believed that if they had sex he could get more information out of her.[717]

Lizarraga would go on to be part of the RCP's May Day in LA, marching at the front of the procession on a bullhorn, but disappeared when the police moved in on the demonstrators in a later clash. Lizarraga's identity as an informant became public accidentally—though apparently the result of amateurishness. The LAPD, on the one hand, tried to conceal his identity, but at the same time had assigned him to uniform duty; a Party member subsequently spotted him while he was walking a beat in Westwood.[718]

Two months after García was killed, 23-year-old George Arrellano was stabbed to death in the same project where García was killed. According to the *Los Angeles Times,* "Eduardo Aceves, 22, was arrested and charged with murdering Arellano." The paper, citing the LAPD, noted that "[b]oth Arellano and Aceves are members of the Primero Flats gang," which it said operated near the housing project. It also reported that they had already known Arellano was the man who stabbed García: "[t]he residents had told police earlier that Arellano was the killer, but refused to sign affidavits for fear of retribution." The police claimed that now that he was dead, people felt they could speak openly about this. The identity of the killer before then, however, was a detail they did not share with the Party.[719] Though Arellano was charged with Aceves' killing, those charges were later dropped, due to lack of evidence.[720]

For its part, the RCP's narrative emphasizes certain things while obscuring others. According to Bob Avakian, the García murder was "a planned execution by agents of the political police."[721] The RCP version generally omits the gang component that seems to have been in play in the projects (albeit one ripe for manipulation by police).[722] They also largely omit mention of the actual person who appears to have done the stabbing. When they do, as in Avakian's memoir, it is only to suggest it was part of a greater conspiracy, noting that García's killer was "mysteriously murdered (in what may well have been part of a cover-up)."[723] The Party also came to obscure Lizarraga's role as an RCP-infiltrator,[724] instead referring to him repeatedly as "the pig who stood five feet from Damián when he was stabbed."[725] The net result in this telling is one of a conspiracy by government forces to premeditatedly murder Damián García, full stop. While this version is in the realm of possibility, the absence of evidence to back up the more dramatic claims makes it one that seems less than definitive.

As a result of the limits of the LAPD and the RCP narratives, the full story of events surrounding the killing of García remains shrouded in a certain fog. Whether Lizarraga's intelligence work inadvertently—which is not to say his intentions were ever benign—set a chain of events in motion that led to García's killing, or whether the murder was the plan all along, remains unclear. The outcome, however, was undeniable. García was dead, and a pall had been cast over the upcoming May Day demonstrations.

Red Squads and Private Security

The activity of the LAPD's intelligence arm underscores a certain type of police spying in operation during the May Day 1980 campaign. The exposure came amid a stepped up role of private intelligence in the early to mid 1980s, particularly with the group Western Goals. Western Goals was an entity started by the John Birch Society member and sitting US Congressman, Larry McDonald. Working with McDonald were two people with a long track record of targeting the left and the RU/RCP, John and Sheila Rees, the latter being the former FBI informant who had infiltrated the Washington, DC, Revolutionary Union.[726] Western Goals would cease operations in 1986 after a congressional hearing revealed its role in the Iran-Contra scandal. However, in the early Eighties they appear to have their hand in all manner of malfeasance[727]—filling a gap left by the limits imposed on the FBI, and the increased scrutiny of local police red squads.

All this came amid revelations of LAPD spying. One thing revealed was that Jay Paul, an officer in LA's Public Disorder and Intelligence Division, had in fact stored intelligence files at his home and garage,[728] to evade scrutiny. Paul was also shown to have shared information with Western Goals.

Further up the Coast, in Portland, Oregon, red squad officer Winfield Falk had also stored Portland police intelligence files off-site. His files, dating from 1965 up to the early 1980s, were kept in his garage—the files being discovered in 2002, 15 years after his death. Falk too had shared information with Western Goals.[729]

The Portland files were ultimately moved to the Portland City Archives. What they show is that by the early 1980s the police and Western Goals were sharing information directly related to the RCP. In Portland, the arrest records, complete with mug shots and fingerprints of May Day Brigade members arrested in San Antonio, are included in the files.[730] Also included is a document by the San Antonio Police Department Intelligence Division titled "Texas Revolutionary May Day Brigade Demonstration, March 20, 1980." The document stipulates that it "is intended for law enforcement agencies only" and "not

[to] be disseminated to any person or agency outside of the law enforcement profession." The memo helps explain the level of attention heaped on the May Day Brigade as they traveled around the country; police and local right-wing forces had advance notice of their activity, they were expecting them.[731]

For its part, the RCP continued to the end to push the envelope. Their last "advanced action"—as the Party came to call politically symbolic undertakings often involving stepping over legal limits—occurred on April 30 at the United Nations. Steve Yip and Glenn Gan, two self-identified Party supporters who had gained access to the UN through press passes, threw red paint on Soviet Ambassador Oleg Troyanovsky and US Ambassador William vanden Heuvel. As they did, they shouted, "Our flag is red, not red, white and blue!" and "Down with Soviet-American war moves!"—the inevitability of World War III and the revolutionary possibilities that might emerge as a result being an emerging focus of the group's work.[732] They were immediately taken into custody, held in jail on $100,000 bail, and hit with federal charges of conspiring to assault internationally protected persons.[733] In turn, they were quickly brought to trial and convicted. By March 1981, all appeals, including up to the US Supreme Court, having been exhausted, the two began serving their one-year sentences.[734]

May Day itself was an anticlimax and disappointment. Despite the *Revolutionary Workers'* headline of "A Great Leap on May 1st,"[735] the demonstrations, rather than pulling out the projected 10,000, appear to have never aggregated past the hundreds nationwide. In Los Angeles—with the help of police infiltrators—the demonstrators clashed with police after being denied a permit to march downtown. As the press would later report, "[w]itnesses said the marchers clearly were outnumbered by the police. One observer estimated there were at least 250 uniformed and plainclothes officers at the park and along the parade route."[736] Twenty-eight of the marchers were arrested.

In Chicago, where 100 plus people turned out, 13 were arrested for disorderly conduct and obstruction of justice. The press reported that Avakian spoke in Oakland to a crowd of around 200. The small numbers were of a similar scale elsewhere, with reports of 50 people in Portland, 75 in Washington, and 15 in West Virginia.[737] For its part, the Party's press was sketchy about actual numbers, saying "hundreds of workers" turned out in Los Angeles (likely the largest demonstration.) Regardless, it proclaimed it

> [a] great and historic step was taken on May Day 1980. Powerful political demonstrations exploded onto the scene to mark May Day in the major cities of the United States. Who would have expected a working class so infatuated with what's in front of their nose that the best it was capable of was perhaps to run a little after a piece of cheese in a maze.[738]

Such language could not change the fact that the Party had been politically damaged—their claims going into this and the outcome being so at odds. The disconnect was the final straw for more than a few cadre who left soon after. For those who stayed, by the autumn of 1980, things had gotten unsustainable. People were not working, many had accumulated considerable debt or cashed in what reserves they had, and scores faced criminal charges—some quite serious. Still, the Party attempted to up the ante following May Day with a campaign to raise the level of distribution of its newspaper to the wholly unrealistic level of 100,000 copies a week—an effort that reaped similar results to May Day.

To compound things, the charges against Avakian and the other remaining "Mao Defendants," which had been dropped because a judge ruled the prosecution was "motivated by vindictiveness,"[739] were reinstated. The prospect of going to trial and losing appeared to be weighing heavily on the Party leadership to such a degree that at the end of the year Avakian left the country. In December 1980, he arrived in Paris and applied for political refugee status. The move ended up being premature, given that a year and a half later the government dropped all charges against him in exchange for guilty pleas by his 10 co-defendants (they were sentenced to fines and probation). The reason for dropping charges against Avakian in particular was not just because he was going to be a much more difficult subject to convict (there appears to have been little evidence against him). As the lead attorney in the case Russell F. Canand told the press, "damaging evidence" about wiretapping and harassment of Avakian and the Revolutionary Communist Party would have come out.[740]

Avakian, however, on his own decision, would not return to the US in any public way from that point on, the rationale being the government would continue to try to jail or kill him. This was consistent with the Party's view that the agents of the FBI and other police intelligence divisions continued to target the Party with the same intensity they had done in its peak years. Given the dramatically changed situation in the United States, to say nothing of the diminished size and influence of the Party, this would seem a specious assessment.

Bob Avakian's exit also signaled a retrenchment on the part of the Party and a stepping away from sharper confrontational tactics. This, in turn, led to an easing to a degree of its ability to function. At the same time, cadre continued to exit. It was not just the toll of the repression, or the schisms, or the political infighting, but the gradual realization on the part of a good number of formerly dedicated members that things had changed. Unlike earlier episodes of mass exit, this loss of membership was not focused on a particular political fault line or organizational split, but rather individual decisions. This was accelerated by the disconnect with the assessment coming from the top of the Party, which insisted on the more or less standing possibility of a revolutionary situation arising. As Avakian argued, the group needed to be ready to seize on events "whenever a revolutionary situation does develop—which, as we've seen from experience, can develop suddenly and without much warning."[741]

This gets at something basic in the group's thinking. At one point in his memoir, Avakian refers to Leibel Bergman's inability to accept what had happened in China after Mao's death:

> Leibel might just as well have said, and in effect he did say: "Well, these people won out, so what can we do? That's the way it is, and we might as well 'make a virtue out of necessity.' It's much better if we can still say that China is socialist. So let's not get into all this stuff about analyzing what's going on.[742]

Leaving aside the liberties Avakian takes in reconstructing Bergman's thinking, the matter of how to relate to the dramatic changes in China did lead to a rush for pat answers. In that respect, denying anything had essentially changed was one way of dealing with things. The irony is that Avakian, and the Party he led, undertook another kind of denial. One of the slogans put forward after the final split was, "Mao Tse-tung Did Not Fail, Revolution Will Prevail," which was soon followed by, "If you liked the '60s, you'll love the '80s."[743] Given everything going on—the abandoning of socialism in China, the frailty of the Soviet Union's already highly fraught model (which would soon assert itself), and the United States' ascendance as the bastion of global capitalism—such a confident vision of a revolutionary near-future was striking in its almost magical thinking. This was, however, what the Party embraced—as a diminished entity—as it went forward.

Chapter 11

Conclusion

But as we have often said, while the road ahead is tortuous, the future is bright.
— Mao Tse-tung, *On the Ten Major Relationships*, April 1956.[744]

In a word, oppressor and oppressed, stood in constant opposition to one another, carried on an uninterrupted, now hidden, now open fight, a fight that each time ended, either in a revolutionary reconstitution of society at large, or in the common ruin of the contending classes.
— Karl Marx and Frederick Engels, *Manifesto of the Communist Party*, February 1948.[745]

The story of the Revolutionary Union / Revolutionary Communist Party is a major piece of Sixties history that has largely been overlooked, minimized, or ignored. It is history that operates first as a story on its own. It is one of the advances, missteps, challenges and errors, of a sizable group of domestic US Maoists, taking inspiration from the unprecedented events in China, and in turn attempting to lay a basis—through strategically organizing in the working-class and other sections of society—for an eventual seizure of power and establishment of socialism in the US. It is also, however, the story of one of the biggest undertakings of the FBI in this tumultuous period. A campaign drawing on decades of experience—especially its efforts against the Communist Party USA—relentlessly conducting informant penetration, data collection and launching destabilizing initiatives, all with the aim of undermining and weakening the group in the near term, while laying the basis, when the time came, to fully destroy it.

The absence of the RU/RCP in most published histories of the period has thus created a situation in which the radicalism of the Sixties/Seventies period itself has not been fully accounted for. This stands out clearly in such things as their role in SDS, their work with groups like VVAW and the USCPFA, and their cohering of a large component of Sixties radicals to cross the bridge of radicalism into the Seventies. While it can be argued that the organization was so politically problematic as to not be desirable—that does not deal with the fact of its existence, attraction, and impact. The fact that the RU was *there* is a critical thing.

There is, of course, the matter of the group's politics and what one makes of it. In all candor there was a hope in undertaking this project of finding something better than what we did. Here things broke two ways. There was never a question about the sincerity of intentions of those who made up this group. There were, in our view, good things here; the daring to conceive of a socialist society as a fundamental negation of the rapacity of capitalism, a renouncing of American exceptionalism and willingness to call out the crimes of the US government rather than making accommodation with them, the feeling that the dispossessed need to be brought into the center of the levers that run society. This is a list that could be added to in multiples. This group was not whimsical, but was called forth by great wrongs and towering inequality.

In the end, however, one needs to look at the piece as a whole. The controversies that made up the nodal points and their resolution are definitive here: the struggle against urban guerrilla warfare that led to a heightened organizational authoritarianism, the inherent reactive response in opposition to the complex debate around nationalism, the dogmatic methodology used to analyze the intricate, complex, and shifting events in China. Such things, among not a few others, serve as points of transformation, largely in the wrong direction. While nothing here was ever so simple as "all bad" or "all good," there was a clear trajectory.

The sectarianism, dogmatism, and voluntarism, eventually came to characterize the group, diminishing and overwhelming much of the critical grounding, liberatory vision, and communal spirit that had made it attractive in its beginnings. The reasons for this are many, but the overriding one being its willingness from inception to tie itself so uncritically to the communist legacy dating back to the Russian Revolution. Here is the paradox: had they not taken inspiration from the socialism of China, which in its time was the most formidable model available, they likely would have withered on the vine. But the Maoism of mid-to-late Sixties China, for all its lofty goals and some of the real good it did for its people, was, on the terms it was constituted, unsustainable—to say nothing of the universe of controversies and very bad things that happened in the same period. By the Seventies, however, it was in transition toward something else. Thus the RU/RCP's future was tethered to the rise and fall of a model that was about to hit its limits.

Of course the rise and fall of this group is not wholly a story of China. It is also one of the US war and eventual defeat in Vietnam, the upsurge of struggles for national liberation worldwide, and the revolutionary Black freedom movement within the US. Such things were the raw fuel impelling the creation of this organization, but such things were a moving target. By the mid-Seventies the resurgent conservatism that would accompany the US as it entered onto a neoliberal path was limiting what a revolutionary communist group could do "in the working class" and the wider society. As we have noted, what was possible in Richmond, California in 1968, was not possible in West Virginia in 1977.

It also needs to be noted that the RU/RCP's willingness, indeed its exulting, in entering into divisive two-line struggle and in relatively quickly drawing schismatic lines, was highly problematic, coinciding as it did with the Bureau's preeminent strategy of splitting organizations. It will be the work of future researchers to determine the full scope of how this group was affected, but our investigation shows definitively, and repeatedly, that when they were challenged in this way, they came out the other side the worse for wear.

One last point in this regard. The RU/RCP prided itself on, and had among the wider left, a certain reputation for a solid security culture. Certainly the remarks of people like Larry Goff on its rigorous discipline are telling. The paradox, of course, is that this came from Goff, *the informant*. Indeed for all its extolling of discipline and adhering to democratic centralism, it was too often the case—and this from the very beginning—that the two entities with the fullest understanding of the group were the small number of leaders at the top of the organization and the FBI. While such principles of discipline could be effective, potentially in keeping certain matters secret, the fact of informants at the *top* of the organization meant that such practices were too often nothing more than an exercise. Worse, it created the perilous situation where RU/RCP cadre and supporters knew far less about the group than the Bureau did.

As for the Bureau, no study up to now has explored the enormity of the effort it leveled against the RU/RCP. Indeed no study—outside of those of the FBI and the House Internal Security Committee—has acknowledged in any meaningful way (Max Elbaum's work and a few less-than-mainstream publications aside). Here what has been in play is an operating principle in US society, one that refuses to acknowledge, not just the legitimacy of the communist ideology, but whenever possible its very existence as an organized entity within the US; failing that, such entities are cast as the most marginal (and ridiculous) expression of fringe politics.

In order to get a truer picture, one has to go to the US secret police. In that regard the following exchange in the 1980 Felt-Miller trial, between US Attorney John Nields and the FBI's David Ryan is highly instructive:

Q. You were in charge of the Leibel Bergman investigation?
A. Yes, Sir.
Q. And just to give the jury an idea, would you indicate, if you took the Leibel Bergman files and piled them one on top of the other, all the pieces of paper in the files, how high would it stack.
A. I have no idea. I think that you probably could tell me better.
Q. About, four, five, six feet high. Something like that.[746]

Ryan did not answer the question, instead saying the "FBI never judges the validity of its investigation by the size of its files."[747] Such dissembling aside, as is clear from his testimony, and the investigation done for this book, this effort was massive. Yet Bergman—one of the most significant radicals of the Sixties/Seventies era—for all intents and purposes is absent from the history books.

And here it is our view that the FBI needs to be understood differently than it has been up to now. In this two popular tendencies stand out. One dismisses the Bureau as paranoid, over-reactive, and largely ineffective. The other too often mystifies the Bureau's power, ascribing too much agency to "COINTELPRO" and other covert undertakings—suggesting its hand in all outrages and unexplained events. In what we have written it ought to be clear the actual situation is not so cut and dried—all real FBI absurdities and nefarious (and outlandish) undertakings aside. The Bureau we met in relation to the RU/RCP was a largely sophisticated entity, albeit one arguably most effective when employing tried-and-true methods. They had the foresight to see the RU as an emerging "threat" even before it became a publicly known organization. Not only did they penetrate the group's executive committee by early 1968, they appear to have gotten an informant to the level of the National Central Committee by 1971. That is beyond the not inconsequential lesser informants and casual snitches who came and went throughout this period. While they were largely unable to staunch the emergence of the group, and its expansion into a national organization—such successes were no small matter. Yes, the FBI often came across as "unhip" and absurd, as befit J. Edgar Hoover's organizational culture, but that did not mean they could not recruit people who were unrecognizable as FBI operatives, and keep them in place for significant blocks of time. All that taken into account that was not, in the end what led to the RU/RCP's ultimate decline; bigger forces, as we have shown, were responsible for that. We do, however, give more credit to the initiative exhibited by the Bureau in shaping this group and affecting how it interacted with the larger world. To put it more directly, it is not possible to understand this grouping—and this is likely a point applicable to quite a number of organizations in that time—without understanding the role of the Bureau in relationship to it.

It can be argued that all this was justified given the group's stated aims, which were certainly extreme, as the FBI was quick to outline in justifying their efforts, invoking such laws against "Rebellion or Insurrection," "Seditious Conspiracy" and "Advocating the Overthrow of the Government."[748] Yet for all such incendiary charges, there were no corresponding indictments, arrests, or court cases. The RU/RCP was direct about its aims, and how they saw achieving them, but they also largely stayed "between the lines" of legally protected activity. One could argue that such is the absurd nature of the US legal system—but it is the system in place, one the Bureau willingly disregarded when it became inconvenient.

* * *

In our introduction, we noted that a number of people questioned what relevance there was to looking at a US Maoist group that existed decades ago—in a time and world long gone.

It is our hope that we have shown in the depth and breadth of that experience how integral it was to a proper understanding of that period. There is, however, another point. In a fundamental way the world that gave rise to this grouping still exists. For those who question not only the desirability of it continuing as is, to say nothing of its bedrock ability to sustain human civilization, the need to advance beyond it remains. Whether or not it will be possible to achieve something better—as the two quotes above counterpose—is a question that can be answered with no certainty. But if it is to be so—and here is where history imposes itself—it will be so in no small measure because of the experience of those who already tried to advance beyond it. In that respect it is our hope that what we have set down here will be of some use.

Postscript

Bob Avakian remains as Chairman of the RCP, USA. In 2005, he published *From Ike to Mao and Beyond: My Journey From Mainstream America to Revolutionary Communist,* a personal memoir and political history of the RU/RCP. An invitation to interview representatives of the RCP for this project was declined.

Leibel Bergman died in 1988 after a long illness; he was 73. His former comrades, mostly those who had left the RCP after 1978, along with his family, came together to raise funds to pay for his medical bills. As part of the fundraising efforts, a collection of Bergman's poetry, *Will We Remember?*, was published by "Friends of Leibel Bergman."

Bruce Franklin is currently a professor of English and American Studies at Rutgers University. He has written numerous books and articles spanning topics from Melville, Vietnam, to science fiction. He declined to be interviewed for this project.

After leaving the RU, Steve Hamilton continued his political activism in other organizations. In his later years, he also became a therapist in the interest of "better[ing] the mental health system in which his father had suffered."[749] He died of a heart attack in 2009 at the age of 64.

APPENDIX

Interview With Danielle Zora

Below is an interview with Danielle Zora, née Zuraitis, one of eight Revolutionary Union members to visit China in the fall of 1971, several months before Richard Nixon's historic visit in February 1972.[1]

RU Delegation and Others, China 1971

1st Row, 3rd from left, Mary Lou Greenberg, Leibel Bergman, Geng Biao, Bob Avakian, Pablo Guzman

2nd Row, 2nd from left, Doug Monica, Unidentified, Danielle Zora, Joanne Psihounstas, Donald H. Wright

Aaron Leonard: How did you get picked to be part of the trip?

Danielle Zora:. The Chinese invited people to visit to see socialism in action and to hear China's view as to their need to break out of isolation.

At the time, I was one of the co-chairs of a Bronx collective of the Revolutionary Union. The other chair—Mickey Jarvis—had no interest in going. I had been part of the organization from its beginning. Five of us from New York City had driven to California to be part of the first national meeting of the Revolutionary Union. The other four had quit within months of our return, this for both political reasons and out of fear of the visible surveillance we were under. So, I was an obvious choice in some ways.

On the other hand, I had a number of chronic health issues that were not diagnosed until years later, so it was not an obvious choice for me. I felt my healthy husband, a better speaker and debater, was a better choice. Leibel Bergman convinced me that China would be an educational experience that would inspire and motivate me for years—which it did—and that it would give the organization strength. He believed that I could go to China and return to union organizing work. He assured me that my future plans and goals would be largely unaffected. As things turned out, I was never a successful organizer. In fact, I spent many years on unemployment. At the time, I believed it was a result of my own weaknesses until I got my FBI and CIA files in the early 1980s. It turns out they were opened because of my travel to China. The FBI was unaware of my activity before that.

AL: How did you travel there?

DZ: Passport laws had just been changed to allow travel to China. I took a bus to Montreal and flew from there to Paris. In Paris, Leibel took us to the graveyard of the Communards. The next day we all flew to Beijing—though there were several stops on the way, including Cairo. It was uneventful. I do not remember arriving in China. We were settled into a nice hotel in Beijing. After I went out on the street looking for a candy bar—and the Chinese learned of this—I was given a plate of candy daily.

The return flight, however, was a nightmare. While the inbound flight was a normal mix of passengers, the return consisted of a majority of communist sympathizers, including a PLO contingent, the Albanian gymnast team, etc. There was a very bad storm as we entered European airspace, with the plane being tossed about like a feather. Everyone started singing Chinese (Peoples Liberation Army-PLA) army songs about being brave and fearing no adversity. We feared that few governments would care about our safety, and with the bad weather, it made it impossible to stop at any of our continental stops, including Tirana, Albania. We were supposed to return to Paris, but that was also impossible. We were allowed to land in London since we were running out of gas. Everyone was fearful. Albanians particularly feared losing their athletes to defection. Ironically, we all made it safely through the lightning storm and English customs. Given events in the following decade or so, it is my sense that many of these China visitors, including many among the Palestinian contingent, are no longer with us.

AL: How long did you spend in China?

DZ: I believe we were there for six weeks.

AL: Where did you travel and what did you see?

DZ: Looking back, I see what a well-planned and well-rounded trip had been organized for us. We went to historic sites like Yan'an where the Communist Party rebuilt their strength after the Long March, and the famous Red Boat, where a handful of people founded the Chinese Communist Party in 1921. We went to rural areas where there were successful socialist projects such as the Red Flag Canal and Dazhai Commune. There we talked to the peasant leader, Chen Yonggui, at length. He was a former illiterate peasant who had become a member of the Politburo and a Vice Premier of the People's Republic of China. We also visited rural areas that were struggling to make transformations. We visited factories, schools, universities, and urban neighborhood organizations. We also visited tourist sites, for example, the terracotta soldiers. These were terracotta sculptures depicting the armies of Qin Shi Huang, the first emperor of China, which had just been unearthed. The delegation also walked the Great Wall — though I personally missed that due to illness.

We spoke to people who survived Japanese occupation, people who fought and behaved nobly. We also spoke with people—we were told—who had behaved poorly during the early Cultural Revolution. Beyond that, we visited a surgical theater to see acupuncture at work in several surgeries. And we also went to the theater to see the new Beijing operas.

AL: Who were the prominent Chinese leaders you met?

DZ: Our early meeting with Geng Biao, a former major general in the PLA, and veteran of the Long March, who was also in party leadership, set a tone of mutual respect and serious conversation. However, we were refocused back to the Chinese people. As I remember, Chen Yonggui and Zhou Enlai were the only other "prominent leaders" we met. Many people we interacted with had impressive histories. For example, our lead translator had been a "little devil," a street kid that had followed the Red Army to Yan'an.

AL: What other Chinese people did you meet?

DZ: We met people from all walks of life, peasants, workers, soldiers, party members, students, children, and teachers. To me, there was a sense of a very robust democracy. People were engaged and opinionated. Many knew American left and labor history. I recall that in one remote rural village, we were serenaded by a Chinese man who sang us Paul Robeson's "hits." In general, everyday people were engaged in politics and had opinions on world events.

For example, in 1971, I still considered myself an "ethnic" American, Lithuanian-American. As a result, I was asked about Lithuania's abandonment of China in more than one city and meeting.

Many people we met in rural areas had not met non-Chinese people previous to our visit. Everyone was very hospitable and gracious and thanked us for visiting. The children hugged us and called us uncle and auntie. They tried to accommodate our food preferences and surprised us with an American "barbecue." Everyone was warned that I had not mastered the use of chopsticks, so there was always a fork and spoon ready for me.

AL: Who else was part of this visit – individuals and organizations?

DZ: The RU was an invited delegation, as were the Black Panthers, and the pacifist American Friends Service Committee. Beyond that, there were people such as Leibel Bergman, William Hinton, Richard Frank and Susan Warren, who had lived in China or visited before. I know that Bill Epton—who had recently been expelled from Progressive Labor Party—was at the Zhou-Enlai meeting. The Black Panthers sent Huey Newton, Elaine Brown, and Robert Bay (Newton's bodyguard)—we briefly crossed paths with them.[2] The Chinese also introduced a few Americans that had been in China since the war. Aside from one meeting though—where we were greeted by Zhou—we did not all gather together.

AL: What did you think of Maoism at the time?

DZ: I was a believer. Maoist slogans still shape my world. Some that come immediately to mind: "Serve the people," "Unite all who can be united to defeat the common enemy," "A single spark can start a prairie fire," and "Do not treat contradictions among the people like contradictions between the people and the enemy." There are many more. It is striking to me that these basic ideas seem controversial today.

AL: What was your sense of women's role as you toured the different areas?

DZ: The slogan women hold up half the sky was ubiquitous and women were visibly in leadership everywhere, including previously all male work spaces like the Shanghai docks. I would never have guessed that 50 years later Chinese politics would be male dominated in the way it is today.

When we were in China, women of all ages were in leadership. The wives of top Chinese leaders like Zhou Enlai and Liu Shaoqi were longtime activists and fighters and were also in leadership. The Chinese spoke respectfully of female Prime Ministers, such as Sirimavo Bandaranaike of Sri Lanka.

Beyond that, there was childcare and communal kitchens to free women from housework and to maximize their work opportunities. Women were encouraged in most careers.

While foot binding had been outlawed by the Nationalists, it had continued. It was class-based, among those who hoped or expected to marry into wealth. The 1949 revolution criticized the practice as oppressing women, limiting their movement. Other laws were passed that opposed the physical abuse of women and promoted their body autonomy.

On the other hand, it was a conservative culture, premarital sex was discouraged. Childbirth in marriage in the mid-twenties was promoted. We heard snark against middle-aged actresses at the theater as their waistlines had expanded with age. The fact that I was married, at the age of twenty, was questioned—it was thought to be too young—and my wearing my hair long and braided was criticized. Married women cut their hair.

AL: Did you get a sense of the social welfare of people—for example, how were the Chinese dealing with crime, drug addiction, and healthcare?

DZ: These were the issues that drew me to investigate Chinese socialism. Street crime, which addiction and inequality breed, was absent from our view. We were aware of the terrible history of the British East India Company flooding China with opium for their own financial gain. Opium addiction was a major problem until 1949, but Mao took a strong stand against drugs. There was little, if any, opium smoking during Mao's time. The CCP focused on basic rights for all—housing, food, and jobs while also exerting a pervasive culture of community control. By some accounts, today, with billionaires flourishing, inequality growing, and opportunities receding, drug addiction has returned, and it has brought back some of the crimes and social disorder.

As for healthcare, there were two big, internationally

recognized successes that I looked forward to investigating. The first was the development of "barefoot" doctors in the 1960s and 1970s as a public health prevention force. There were millions of peasants and only 40,000 trained doctors in China, mostly in the cities. The barefoot doctors were peasants trained in basic Western and traditional Chinese medicine. One million were trained. They could identify and treat some diseases, outreach and educate, and make referrals to doctors when appropriate. Medical experts worldwide respected China's success against infectious diseases like polio and schistosomiasis with the barefoot doctors. It was remarkable, especially when compared to other countries with comparable wealth and resources. They were an impressive and effective force—I have been a supporter of peer healthcare and service delivery programs my whole life. The Chinese, however, abandoned the program in the 1980s, in favor of a fee system as more doctors were available and people began moving from the rural areas.

The other big success was their early elimination of pests and the diseases they carried by mobilizing the public—paying them a bounty—to capture vermin. The "Four Pests" campaign of 1958 was directed at mosquitoes as a transmitter of malaria, rats and rodents that spread the plague, flies which can transmit sixty-five illnesses, including typhoid fever, dysentery, cholera, leprosy and tuberculosis, and sparrows that ate the grain and fruit.

A pest free community was remarkable in a poor country. Health was improved. The success was still being felt and heralded in 1971. However, what was not admitted then, which we now understand, is that the attack on sparrows caused an ecological catastrophe. Sparrows were a natural predator of locust, and without sparrows, locusts overran the fields, all of which exacerbated the famine of the late 1950s. At least 15 million people died of starvation during that period. The year 1958 was the beginning of the Great Leap Forward, or the "Big Fall on Our Face" as most people referred to it on our trip.

By 1960, the sparrows were removed from the campaign and replaced by the less ambiguous scourge, bedbugs. This was the sanitized Four Pests campaign that was promoted on our trip. The famine could not be hidden, but the two events were treated as distinct—the success against pests and the problem of famine.

AL: This trip happened while Lin Biao died in a plane crash, on September 13, 1971. How did this impact your visit? Were there conversations about it among your various hosts?

DZ: We could speak or question about many topics, but questions about Lin Biao always got the same answer—no matter where you were in the country or who you were with—"We don't know much about that."

AL: In your tour of the country, what impressed you the most?

DZ: Every proof that the people united can achieve miracles, move mountains, impressed me. Excited factory workers showing us how they were capturing the heat from the machines to warm their homes. Driving through mountains of rocks, dirt, and dust to arrive at a blooming, beautifully tiered Dazhai Agricultural Commune. Seeing the power stations from waterwheels in irrigation canals built with hand chisels, that opened a waterway through a mountain, inspired by the Red Flag Canal. That socialism was really supporting normal people to improve their common situation with the tools and resources they already had impressed me.

AL: What is your assessment, or impression, of the Cultural Revolution, particularly at the time you were there?

DZ: There was a great deal of class conflict evident on the microaggression level. When we went into the countryside, we interacted with the "popular" classes, people who were enthusiastic about the things they had built and the changes they had made. When we returned to Beijing, the people we interacted with were bureaucrats, most of whom had been trained academically and had traveled internationally. Most of those people were imperious to our translators and snobby and disdainful of the level of progress that had been made in the country materially. That there was a difference in opinion between the "popular" classes and the bureaucrats was obvious—that the bureaucrats believed that they were the rightful leaders was obvious—that some kind of action was necessary to strengthen working class leadership and viewpoints was also obvious.

We went to Tsinghua University. The students wanted to do exactly that—to strengthen working class leadership in the academy. The Cultural Revolution took off here with the students becoming Red Guards. In 1966, they promoted the campaign against the "Four Olds," Old thinking, Old customs, Old habits, Old culture, and supported the "Four News." [New customs, New culture, New habits, and New ideas]

By 1967, the movement had split into two factions. Both believed they were the correct proletarian leadership. Their differences were over important questions: What is the Cultural Revolution? How do we assess it to date? How should cadre be treated?

Yet the factions were one-sided, arrogant, and unable to apply Mao Zedong Thought in dealing with contradictions among the people. By 1968, matters had devolved into 100 days of armed clashes on campus. They were an engineering school, and they used their skills and resources to make grenades, toxic arrows, cannons, and they made armored vehicles into tanks. They actually caused the death of eighteen people and the permanent disability of another thirty. A propaganda and reeducation team was sent into the university to stop the violence and one faction killed five of their members.

Now the whole city of Beijing was shocked and Mao himself stepped in to end the fighting. A working class propaganda team was put in charge of the university. Manual labor and reeducation was added to university life, although the physical work of the students was never very competent or effective. Students were sent out to do farming. There were suicides. The excesses were on all sides. The lesson of common action can devolve into traumatic action, was out there.

We talked to students and propaganda team members. In some ways, in the fall of 1971, they were still all in shock. The Cultural Revolution had not found its footing and did not find its footing. Meanwhile, nationalist middle class bureaucrats fought for power.

AL: How would you contrast visiting China in 1971 to what it was like in the United States at the same time?

DZ: We had things, a thriving manufacturing economy in the US with many good-paying jobs, homes, cars and other material possessions. The Chinese were just developing their manufacturing economy and developing jobs. Many homes were very humble, with few material possessions. There were far more bikes than cars. I thought this would be an environmental boon, a role model for the world, but car culture came to China.

US finance capital was developing white-collar jobs at all skill levels. I worked as a clerk in an insurance company and my job, and insurance, was incomprehensible to most Chinese with whom I spoke. The rural economy in China was strong and still developing. The majority of the people were peasants. Farmers were a minority in the US, farms in the country had been lost in the US in record numbers between 1950 and 1970.

Local government, especially in the countryside, was not that different from that in the US. In China, a party chapter was the local bureaucracy. My hometown in New England had had an open town meeting style of governance from 1780 to 1961, when it changed to a town manager bureaucracy, as had many others.

There was a strong anti-war sentiment in China. World War II was remembered much more viscerally as the country had suffered a brutal Japanese occupation. There was an anti-war movement in the US, but it was not really connected to WWII.

The US was proud to be both diverse and a melting pot. The Chinese had many minority nationalities, and they supported a certain level of self-determination. They had the ability to retain customs, traditions, clothing, and transportation choices. On the other hand, the country seemed homogeneous—Mao jackets and hats made everyone look very similar on the street.

I recently watched a documentary about Shanghai in the 1930s and realized how different and conservative the culture of China was in 1971. Shanghai had been a very cosmopolitan city—middle class clothes and hairstyles were indistinguishable from Western Europe or America. There was a club culture and homosexuals were visible. On the other hand, working people looked poor and overworked. The new culture of equality meant workers and farmers were celebrated on posters, movies, and set the fashion style. Everyone looked well fed and clothed, but everyone looked the same.

On the matter of disabilities, in the US in the early 1970s, the movement had some success in getting disabled people integrated into schools and workplaces – blind newsstand operators, wheelchair users in offices. This was not the case in China. On the other hand, we did not see disabled people abused or demonized, as was the case in other areas of the world.

AL: In hindsight, how do you view this trip?

DZ: I was 20 years old at the time, I am now 70—this is the biggest thing that ever happened in my life. Despite 50 years of defeats throughout the world, I know another world is possible. My fire for change may have dimmed, but the pilot light is still on.

Zora, today, is a health advocate—personally acquainted with several rare diseases. She describes herself as "supportive of anti-imperialist struggle and international working class solidarity for a future that frees and feeds us all." She occasionally blogs at violetsinthegrass and podcasts at cvcradio-ROOT, Running out of Time

Glossary of Organizational Acronyms

AB – Attica Brigade [acronym not used in book], founded in 1971, later became the RSB and official youth group of the RU/RCP before changing its name to the RCYB

AHC – the Ad Hoc Committee for a Scientific Socialist Line, later the Ad Hoc Committee for a Marxist-Leninist Party

BARU – Bay Area Revolutionary Union, founded in 1968; changed its name to the Revolution Union in 1970—referred to as RU in the text [acronym not used in book]

BPP — the Black Panther Party for Self Defense, later the Black Panther Party

BWC – International Black Workers Congress

CCP – Chinese Communist Party

CHICOM – FBI's abbreviation for Chinese Communist

COINTELPRO – abbreviation for the FBI's Counter Intelligence Program

CPUSA – the Communist Party USA

CPML – Communist Party (Marxist-Leninist)

HUAC – the House Committee on Un-American Activities, later the House of Internal Security Committee

NLC – the National Liaison Committee

NUWO – the National United Workers Organization

OL – the October League, later the CPML

PFP – the Peace and Freedom Movement, later the Peace and Freedom Party

PLP – the Progressive Labor Movement, later the Progressive Labor Party

PRRWO – the Puerto Rican Revolutionary Workers Organization, previously the YLP

RCP – the Revolutionary Communist Party, previously the RU

RCYB – the Revolutionary Communist Youth Brigade

RSB – the Revolutionary Student Brigade

RU – the Revolutionary Union, later the RCP

RYM – the Revolutionary Youth Movement, split into RYM I and RYM II

SDS – Students for a Democratic Society

USCPFA – the US-China Peoples Friendship Association

UWOC – Unemployed Workers Organizing Committee

VDC – the Vietnam Day Committee

VO – Venceremos Organization, a group formed in 1970 from the merger of the Franklin section of BARU and Chicano grouping around the free university, Venceremos College [acronym not used in book]

VVAW – Vietnam Veterans Against the War, later the Vietnam Veterans Against the War-Winter Soldier Organization

WMS – Wei Min She. Radical Asian activist organization in the Bay Area.

YLP/YLO – Young Lords Organization later the Young Lords Party and then the PRRWO [acronym not used in book]

Also note, the RU/RCP referred to its ideology as Marxism-Leninism, Mao-Tse-tung Thought. For simplicity we refer to this simply as Maoism.

Bibliography

Books

Asian Community Center Archive Group. *Stand Up: An Archive Collection of the Bay Area Asian American Movement 1968-1974.* to Berkeley: Eastwind Books of Berkeley, 2009.

Avakian, Bob. *From Ike To Mao and Beyond: My Journey from Mainstream America to Revolutionary Communist: a Memoir.* Chicago: Insight Press, 2005.

Adelson, Alan. *SDS: A Profile.* New York: Charles Scribner's Sons, 1972.

Allan, Joe. *Vietnam: The (Last) War the U.S. Lost.* Chicago: Haymarket, 2008.

Barber, David. *A Hard Rain Fell: SDS and Why it Failed.* Jackson: University Press of Mississippi, 2010.

Barrett, Wayne. *Rudy: An Investigative Biography of Rudy Giuliani.* New York: Basic Books, 2000.

Bergman, Leibel. *I Cannot See Their Faces and Keep Silent.* Saint Paul: Prometheus Press, 1946.

Bergman, Leibel. *Will We Remember?* Friends of Leibel Bergman, 1984.

Bloom, Joshua and Waldo E. Martin, Jr.. *Black Against Empire: The History and Politics of the Black Panther Party.* Berkeley: University of California Press, 2013.

Cleaver, Eldridge, Kathleen Cleaver, ed. *Target Zero: A Life in Writing.* Basingstoke: Palgrave Macmillan, 2007.

Didion, Joan. *Slouching Towards Bethlehem: Essays.* New York: Farrar, Straus and Giroux, 1990.

Donner, Frank. *Protectors of the Privilege: Red Squads and Police Repression in Urban America.* Berkeley: University of California Press, 1990.

Dunbar-Ortiz, Roxanne. *Outlaw Woman: A Memoir of the War Years, 1960-1975.* San Francisco: City Lights Publishers, 2002.

Elbaum, Max. *Revolution in the Air: Sixties Radicals Turn to Lenin, Mao and Che.* London, New York: Verso Books, 2002.

Elwood, Ralph Carter. *Roman Malinovsky, A Life Without a Cause.* Newton, MA: Oriental Research Partners, 1977.

Esherick, Joseph W., Paul G. Pickowicz, and Andrew G. Walder, eds. *The Chinese Cultural Revolution as History (Studies of the Walter H. Shorenstein Asia-Pacific Research Center).* Palo Alto: Stanford University Press, 2006.

Foley, Michael S. *Confronting the War Machine.* Durham, NC: University of North Carolina Press, 2003.

Franklin, H. Bruce. *Back Where You Came From: One Life in the Death of the Empire.* New York: Harper's Magazine Press, 1975.

Franklin, H. Bruce (ed.). *From the Movement Toward the Revolution.* New York: Van Nostrand Reinhold, 1971.

Franklin, H. Bruce. *Vietnam and Other American Fantasies.* Amherst: University of Massachusetts Press, 2001.

Getty, J. Arch and Oleg V. Naumov. *The Road to Terror: Stalin and the Self-Destruction of the Bolsheviks, 1932-39.* New Haven: Yale University Press, 2002.

Georgakas, Dan and Marvin Surkin. *Detroit: I Do Mind Dying.* Chicago: Haymarket Books, 2012.

Gitlin, Todd. *The Sixties: Years of Hope, Days of Rage.* New York: Bantam, 1993.

Hilliard, David & Donald Weise (eds.). *The Huey P. Newton Reader.* New York: Seven Stories Press, 2002.

Hinton, William. *Fanshen: A Documentary of a Revolution in a Chinese Village.* New York: Monthly Review Press, 1966.

Hinton, William. *Turning Point in China: An Essay on the Cultural Revolution.* New York: Monthly Review Press, 1972

Ho, Fred (ed.). *Legacy to Liberation: Politics and Culture of Revolutionary Asian Pacific America.* Chicago: Haymarket Books, 2006.

Horn, Joshua, *Away With All Pests: An English Surgeon in People's China, 1954-1969.* New York: Monthly Review Press,1971.

Hunt, Andrew E. *The Turning: A History of Vietnam Veterans Against the War.* New York: NYU Press, 1999.

Jones, Charles (ed.). *The Black Panther Party Reconsidered.* Baltimore: Black Classic Press, 1998.

Kerry, John and Vietnam Veterans Against the War. *The New Soldier.* New York: Collier Books, October 1971.

Kraus, Richard Curt. *The Cultural Revolution: A Very Short Introduction.* New York: Oxford University Press, 2012.

Leese, Daniel. *Mao Cult: Rhetoric And Ritual In China's Cultural Revolution.* Cambridge: Cambridge University Press, 2013.

Lüthi, Lorenz M. *The Sino-Soviet Split: Cold War in the Communist World.* Princeton: University of Princeton Press, 2008.

Mailer, Norman. *Miami and the Siege of Chicago.* New York: NYRB Books, 2008.

Mao Tse-tung. *Quotations From Chairman Mao Tse-Tung*. Peking: Foreign Language Press, 1966.

Mao Tse-tung. *Selected Works of Mao Tse Tung. Volume I-IV.* Peking: Foreign Language Press, 1965.

Mao Tse-tung. *Selected Works of Mao Tse Tung. Volume V.* Peking: Foreign Language Press, 1977.

Meisner, Maurice. *The Deng Xiaoping Era: An Inquiry into the Fate of Chinese Socialism, 1978-1994.* New York: Hill and Wang, 1996.

Meisner, Maurice. *Mao Zedong: A Political and Intellectual Portrait.* Cambridge: Polity, 2006.

Nicosia, Gerald. *Home to War: A History of the Vietnam Veterans Movement*. New York: Crown, 2001.

Noyes, Henry. *China Born: Adventures of a Maverick Bookman.* San Francisco: China Books & Periodicals, 1989.

Richardson, Peter. *A Bomb in Every Issue: How the Short, Unruly Life of Ramparts Magazine Changed America.* New York: New Press, 2010.

Rudd, Mark. *Underground: My Life with SDS and the Weathermen.* New York: HarperCollins, 2009.

Sale, Kirkpatrick. *SDS: The Rise and Development of Students for a*

Democratic Society. New York: Vintage, 1974.

Schram, Stuart (ed.). *Chairman Mao Talks To The People: Talks and Letters: 1956-1971*. New York: Pantheon Books, 1975.

Schram, Stuart, ed. *The Thought of Mao Tse-tung*. Cambridge: Cambridge University Press, 1989.

Seale, Bobby. *Seize the Time: The Story of the Black Panther Party and Huey P. Newton*. New York: Random House, 1970.

Stacewicz, Richard. *Winter Soldiers: An Oral History of the Vietnam Veterans Against the War*. Chicago: Haymarket Books, 2008.

Starr, Kevin. *Golden Dreams: California in an Age of Abundance, 1950-1963*. New York: Oxford University Press, 2009.

Theoharis, Athan G. *The FBI: A Comprehensive Reference Guide*. Phoenix, AZ: Oryx Press, 1999.

Teiwes, Fredrick C. and Warren Sun. *The End of the Maoist Era: Chinese Politics During the Twilight of the Cultural Revolution, 1972-1976*. New York: M.E. Sharpe, 2008.

Pamphlets and Major Periodical Sources

Avakian, Bob. "Summing up the Black Panther Party." Chicago: RCP Publications, 1979.

Editorial Departments of Renmin Ribao (People's Daily) and Hongqui (Red Flag). *On Khrushchov's Phoney Communism and Its Historical Lessons for the World: Comment on the Open Letter of the Central Committee of the CPSU (IX)*. Peking: Foreign Languages Press, 1964.

Editorial Departments of Renmin Ribao (People's Daily) and Hongqi (Red Flag). *Is Yugoslavia a Socialist Country? Comment on the Open Letter of the Central Committee of the CPSU (III)* September 26, 1963. New York: Liberation Books, 1979.

Klingel, Bill and Joanne Psihountas. *Important Struggles in Building the Revolutionary Communist Party, USA*. Chicago: RCP Publications, 1978.

Progressive Labor Party. *Revolution Today*. New York: Exposition Press, 1970.

Bay Area Revolutionary Union. *The Red Papers,* 1969.

Bay Area Revolutionary Union. *Red Papers 2,* 1969.

Revolutionary Union. *Red Papers 3: Women Fight for Liberation,* 1970.

Revolutionary Union. *Red Papers 4: Proletarian Revolution vs. Revolutionary Adventurism,* 1972.

Revolutionary Union. *Red Papers 5: National Liberation and Proletarian Revolution in the US,* 1972.

Revolutionary Union. *Red Papers 6: Build the Leadership of the Proletariat and its Party,* 1974.

Revolutionary Union, *Red Papers 7: How Capitalism Has Been Restored in the Soviet Union and What This Means for the World Struggle,* 1974.

Revolutionary Workers Headquarters. *Red Papers 8: China Advances on the Socialist Road,* 1978.

Revolution (monthly newspaper, magazine from 1979 on).

Revolutionary Union (1973-1975).

Revolutionary Communist Party (1975-1978).

Revolutionary Worker (weekly newspaper), Revolutionary Communist Party (1979 on).

Government Sources

Federal Bureau of Investigation. FBI Records: The Vault vault.fbi.gov

COINTELPRO: New Left (Various), 1968-1970.

U.S. House of Representatives, Committee on Internal Security. *America's Maoists: The Revolutionary Union, the Venceremos Organization. Report by the* Committee on Internal Security, House of Representatives, Ninety-Second Congress, Second Session. U.S.A. Congress. Washington: US Government Printing Office, 1972.

U.S. House of Representatives, Committee on Internal Security. *Progressive Labor Party.* Hearings Before the Committee On Internal Security House of Representatives, Ninety-Second

Congress. First Session, April 13,14 and November 18, 1971. Washington: US Government Printing Office, 1972.

U.S. House of Representatives, Committee on Internal Security. *Investigation of Attempts to Subvert the United States Armed Services, Part 1.* Hearings Before the House of Representatives, Ninety-Second Congress, First Session. Hearings, October 20, 21, 22, 27, and 28, 1971. Washington: US Government Printing Office, 1972.

U.S. House of Representatives, Committee on Un-American Activities. *Hearings H.R. 12047, H.R. 14925, H.R. 16175, H.R. 171401714,0. AND H.R. 171794 to Make Punishable Assistance to Enemies of U.S. in Times of Undeclared War*. August 19, 1966. United States Subcommittee on Un-American Activities. Washington: Government Printing Office, 1966.

U.S. House of Representatives, Committee on Un-American Activities. *The Northern California District of the Communist Party of California: Structure—Objectives—Leadership.* Eighty-Sixth Congress, Second Session, Part 2, May 13, 1960. Washington: US Government Printing Office, 1960.

U.S. Senate Committee of the Judiciary. *Threats to the Peaceful Observance of the Bicentennial.* Hearing Before the Subcommittee to Investigate the Administration of the Internal Security Act and Other Internal Security Laws of the Committee on the Judiciary, United States Ninety-Fourth Congress. Second Session, June 18, 1976. Washington: US Government Printing Office, 1976.

U.S. Senate. *Final Report on the Select Committee to Study Governmental Operation with Respect to Intelligence Activities.* 94th Congress. Senate Report. 2d Session, No. 94-755. "Supplementary Detailed Staff Reports on Intelligence Activities and the Rights of Americans." Book III. United States Senate, April 23, 1976. Washington: US Government Printing Office, 1976.

Court Papers

Deposition, ACLU v. City of Chicago et. al. 1980, David Ryan, Washington, DC April 10, 1980. Sullivan TAM.528 Box 8, Folder 46.

U.S. District Court for the Northern District of Illinois Eastern District. American Civil Liberties Union et al., Plaintiff v. City of Chicago et. al. Defendants. Joseph A. Burton Affidavit. July 22, 1980.

United States Court of Appeals, Third Circuit. 479 F.2d 569 William P. Biggin, Petitioner, v. Immigration and Naturalization Service. Respondent. No. 72-1120. United States Court of Appeals, Third Circuit. Argued February 13, 1973. Decided May 23, 1973.

Film & Video Footage

Conference for a United Front Against Fascism. San Francisco Bay Area Television Archive. KPIX Eyewitness news report from the Oakland Auditorium on July 19th, 1969.

Huey! American Documentary Films, in Cooperation with the Black Panther Party, 1968.

Endnotes

New Introduction

1. For examples of where Maoism garners brief mention—as opposed to full omission—see: Mark Hamilton Lytle, *America's Uncivil Wars: The Sixties Era from Elvis to the Fall of Richard Nixon*, New York: Oxford University Press, 2006, 194, Mike Davis and Jon Wiener, *Set the Night on Fire: LA in The Sixties* New York: Verso, 2020, 413 & 719, and Maurice Isserman and Michael Kazin, *America Divided: The Civil War of the 1960s*, New York: Oxford University Press, 2020, 180.
2. See, for example, Julia Lovell, "Maoism Marches on: The Revolutionary idea that still shapes the world," *The Guardian*, March 16, 2019.
3. To minimize confusion, we have updated the RU/RCP's size estimates in the text and corresponding footnote. See page 7, 221, and footnote 10 in this volume.
4. The other major informant discussed in this volume, though he is not named, was Darrell Grover. We were only able to reveal his identity in our second book. See this volume, 38-42 and Aaron J. Leonard and Conor A. Gallagher, *A Threat of the First Magnitude: FBI Counterintelligence & Infiltration From the Communist Party to the Revolutionary Union 1962-1974*, London: Repeater, 106-118.
5. Jefferson Morley, "CIA Reveals Name of Former Spy in JFK Files—And He's Still Alive", *Newsweek*, May 15, 2018, accessed February 4, 2022. https://www.newsweek.com/richard-gibson-cia-spies-james-baldwin-amiri-baraka-richard-wright-cuba-926428
6. FBI Memo, Richard Gibson: Information Concerning, June 13, 1969. https://www.maryferrell.org/showDoc.htm

l?docId=167124#relPageId=65&search=sugar_davida%20fineman%20gibson

7. Director FBI, to SAC Chicago, Ad Hoc Committee for a Marxist-Leninist Party, IS-C 11/22/66 https://www.maryferrell.org/showDoc.html?docId=167124#relPageId=68&search=sugar_davida%20fineman%20gibson
8. CIA Report, Subject: Donald Wright, Black Panther Party Member, Travel to Algiers, February 6, 1970. https://www.maryferrell.org/showDoc.html?docId=167124#relPageId=55&search=wright
9. Director, FBI to SAC Chicago, 2/20/70 DN 447-S (Research Section). https://www.maryferrell.org/showDoc.html?docId=167124#relPageId=54&search=wright
10. Wright's codename for the Chicago field office CG-7262-S, Leonard and Gallagher, *Threat of the First Magnitude*, 132.
11. CIA Memo, Subject: Leibel Berman, Herb Block, Reference: Our memorandum of 6 February 1970, Subjects Davida Fineman and Leibel Bergman. https://www.maryferrell.org/showDoc.html?docId=167124#relPageId=53&search=%22Herb_Block%22%20AHC%20%22Leibel%22%20PLP%20David%20Fineman
12. Richard J. Ott to SAC Chicago, Subject AD-HOC COMMITTEE FOR A MARXIST-LENINIST PARTY, IS-C. Report received from [informant] CG 7015-S 4/17/1968. From the David Sullivan US Maoism Collection, NYU-Tamiment Library. TAM.527, Box 23 Folders: 5-6.
13. Hearings Before the Subcommittee to Investigate the Administration of the Internal Security Act and Other Internal Security Laws of the Committee on the Judiciary. United States Senate. Ninety-First Congress, Second Session Part 3, March 11, 1970. Testimony of Gerald Kirk, 234-235.
14. Director, FBI to SAC New York, Counterintelligence & Special Operation (Research Section) 4/17/70.

15. Ibid.
16. The term New Communist Movement entered circulation in the mid-Seventies, at a point when China was moving away from the radical Maoism of the previous decade. The word "New" in the term has to do with its rejection of the staunchly pro-Soviet (old) Communist Party, USA.
17. The FBI in the mid-1970s also gave considerable attention to The National Caucus of Labor Committees, led by perennial presidential candidate Lyndon LaRouche. NCLC was an organization steeped in conspiracy theories and provocative behavior. Like the Weathermen, the FBI's attention to them stemmed from what they saw as the group's criminal activities. "The group is engaged in a harassment program called "Operation Counter-Punch" directed against big business and law enforcement. Its members have also been involved in beatings, kidnappings, and other forms of intimidation of members of other domestic revolutionary organizations." Clarence M. Kelley, "Federal Bureau of Investigation," Attorney General. Annual Report. U.S. Department of Justice 1976 (1976): 147-166.
18. J. Edgar Hoover, "Federal Bureau of Investigation," Attorney General. Annual Report, U.S. Department of Justice 1971 (1971): 114-122.
19. Clarence M. Kelley, "Federal Bureau of Investigation," Attorney General. Annual Report. U.S. Department of Justice 1976 (1976): 147-166.
20. See current edition, footnote 10, page 262-263.
21. Report of Richard J. Hanf, Los Angeles Office, 3/12/74, Title: October League (Marxist-Leninist), Internal Security-China, FBI Atlanta office October League file.
22. FBI Report, Communist League, Jan. 26, 1973, Joe Burton FBI file, Sec. 2, 33-34.

23. According to PRRWO member, Richie Perez. Leonard and Gallagher, *Threat of the First Magnitude*, 183.
24. Report of Charles R. Poplinger, 12/5/73, FBI IBWC file (file courtesy of David Goldberg).
25. Max Elbaum estimates the new communist movement "held the allegiance of roughly 10,000 core activists." This seems a significant overestimation. As noted above, after the RU/RCP, groups descended in size considerably. Based on what we have learned, a more reasonable estimate for the totality of the new communist movement—including the RU/RCP—would be in the range of 2000-2500. Elbaum, *Revolution in the Air*, 4.
26. See, for example, Van Gosse, *Rethinking the New Left: An Interpretative History*. New York: Palgrave Macmillan, 2005, 195.
27. When introducing the term, Elbaum acknowledges its tenuousness, writing it was "sometimes explicitly termed Third World Marxism, sometimes not." He does not, however, offer evidence of its explicit use. Elbaum, *Revolution in the Air*, 2.
28. Elbaum, *Revolution in the Air*, 140.
29. Leonard and Gallagher, *Heavy Radicals*, 109.
30. Leonard and Gallagher, *A Threat of the First Magnitude*, 109.
31. "Delegation Meets with Chairman Hua," *The Call*, Vol. 6, No. 30, August 1, 1977. Reprinted on Marxists.org, accessed March 18, 2022. https://www.marxists.org/history/erol/ncm-3/cpml-hua.htm
32. John Fraser, "Peking posters: new boldness in talk of rights: 'Propaganda teams' take message to main cities," *The Christian Science Monitor*, December 28, 1978.
33. Linda Matthews, "A New Leap: Modernizing China: Teng's Daring Drive," *Los Angeles Times*, February 8, 1979.

Notes: *Heavy Radicals*

1. Michele Meeks, Information and Privacy Coordinator Central Intelligence Agency, to Connor Gallagher, February 14, 2014.
2. Leibel Bergman, *Will We Remember,* Friends of Leibel Bergman, 1984, 39.
3. FBI, Chicago Illinois, "Revolutionary Communist Party," September 6, 1976. David Sullivan U.S. Maoism Collection, TAM.527, Box 23 Folders 5-6.
4. Author interview with a participant in the demonstration, San Francisco, May 2012.
5. Steve Roberts, "Coast Chief Tells of Fear for Nixon," *New York Times,* November 1, 1970.
6. Tom Devries, "Nixon Wasn't Stoned," *Village Voice,* November 5, 1970.
7. Mary McGrory, "Mr. Nixon gets his showdown," *Boston Globe,* October 31, 1970.
8. Author interview, San Francisco, May 2012.
9. "Pro-Maoists Behind Anti-Nixon Violence in San Jose, Pair Say: Couple Tell House Committee They Joined Group Called the Revolutionary Union as Under Cover Informants for the FBI." *Los Angeles Times,* October 22, 1971.
10. The RCP never issued membership numbers. J. Edgar Hoover, in 1972, also did not give a specific number for membership of the RU, writing that it was "not large, perhaps several hundred." "Mao's Red Shadow," reprinted in *Boston Globe,* August 18, 1971. In 1976, the Bureau stated: "The current membership of the RCP is now approximately 650; RSB, 500, VVAW, 100. The exact number of RCP members in the USCPFA is unknown." FBI, Chicago Illinois, "Revolutionary Communist Party," September 6, 1976. David Sullivan U.S. Maoism Collection, TAM.527, Box 23 Folders 5-6. The Party's high point, a

demonstration in Philadelphia in July 1976, produced 3,500-4,000 demonstrators. *Philadelphia Tribune,* "RCP draws 3500 to rally." July 10, 1976. *The Guardian,* "RCP draws 3500 to rally," July 14, 1976. "In the first national show of strength of the RCP, 3500 to 4000 people marched in an action of the 'Rich Off Our Backs–July 4 Coalition.'" A significant percentage of the Rich Off Our Backs demonstrators were cadre (perhaps 25% or higher)—and this would have included most all cadre from the eastern half of the US. The west, where the group was historically larger, sent only token representatives, leaving perhaps several hundred cadre who did not attend. Given that, it seems reasonable to project that the actual peak cadre level corresponds roughly with the FBI's aggregated RCP/RSB/VVAW numbers (even though all RSB and VVAW members were not in the Party), i.e., a number in the high hundreds to low-thousands. Total members passing through the group between the 1968-1977 period would likely have approached or crossed the 2,000 cadre threshold.

11. Ellen Hume, "The 'heavy' radicals: The intellectual cadres plant ideas—not bombs; terrorists considered less important to the cause," *Boston Globe,* September 27, 1975. Also singled out in the article was the October League, which, next to the RU, was the second largest new communist organization.
12. FBI Report on RCP, Chicago, September 6, 1976.
13. "The Northern California District of the Communist Party of California: Structure—Objectives—Leadership," Hearings Before the Committee on Un-American Activities, House of Representatives, Eighty-Sixth Congress, Second Session, Part 2, May 13, 1960, US Government Printing Office, Washington, 1960. https://ia600202.us.archive.org/1/items/northerncaliforn02unit/

northerncaliforn02unit.pdf

14. U.S. Congress, Committee on Un-American Activities. "Hearing on H.R. 12047, H.R. 14925, H.R. 16175, H.R. 17140, AND H.R. 17194—Bills to Make Punishable Assistance to Enemies of the U.S in Times of Undeclared War," August 16-19, 1966, 1184. https://ia600301.us.archive.org/21/items/hearingsonhr120401unit/hearingsonhr120401unit.pdf, 1181.
15. Joan Didion, *Slouching Towards Bethlehem: Essays.* New York: Farrar, Straus and Giroux, 1968, 61.
16. Leibel Bergman, *I Cannot See Their Faces and Keep Silent,* Saint Paul: Prometheus Press, 1946. See back cover for biographical information.
17. Stipulation entered into the record at the Felt-Miller trial, 1980. Record Group 21, Records of the District Courts of the United States, District of Columbia, Criminal Case File 78-00179, *United States v. W Mark Felt and Edward S. Miller.* Location in NARA Stacks: 16W3/15/05/05-06. Box 30, 3938.
18. Bergman, *I Cannot See Their Faces.*
19. Notes from Lincoln Bergman.
20. Nikita Khrushchev, Speech to 20th Congress of the C.P.S.U., marxists.org. http://www.marxists.org/archive/khrushchev/1956/02/24.htm
21. For a fuller examination, see, for example, Lorenz M. Lüthi, *The Sino-Soviet Split: Cold War in the Communist World,* Princeton: University of Princeton Press, 2008.
22. "An American Proposal," *Fortune,* May 1942.
23. Mao Zedong, *Selected Works of Mao Tse Tung. Volume 5,* "U.S. Imperialism is a Paper Tiger," July 14, 1956, marxists.org. http://www.marxists.org/reference/archive/mao/selected-works/volume-5/mswv5_52.htm
24. Bergman, *Will We Remember,* 6.
25. The Northern California District of the Communist Party, 2009.

26. "San Francisco Rioting Blamed on Agitators: Police Chief Says Older Individuals Stirred Demonstrators into a Mob Frenzy," *Los Angeles Times,* May 15, 1960.
27. Jim Dann and Hari Dillon, "The Five Retreats: A History of the Failure of the Progressive Labor Party", 1977. marxists.org. http://www.marxists.org/history/erol/1960-1970/5retreats/chapter1.htm
28. Bergman, *Will We Remember.*
29. Deposition, ACLU v. City of Chicago et. al 1980, David Ryan, Washington, DC, April 10, 1980. Sullivan TAM.528 Box 8, Folder 46.
30. Victoria Holmes Garvin, Bureau file, 100-HQ-379895.
31. Bergman, *Will We Remember*, 7-8 and Garvin Bureau file, 656.
32. FBI, Chicago, September 6, 1976, 2.
33. Ibid.
34. Seth Rosenfeld, "Anti-war activist Steve Hamilton dies," *San Francisco Chronicle,* March 30, 2009. http://www.sfgate.com/bayarea/article/Anti-war-activist-Steve-Hamilton-dies-3246417.php
35. "In Memory of Steven Charles Hamilton." Remarks by Shirley (Hamilton) Metcalf, Southgate High School website, http://www.southgatheigh.org/MemSHamilton62.htm
36. Mario Savio, Speech before Free Speech Movement Sit-In, December 3, 1964. http://www.fsm-a.org/stacks/mario/mario_speech.html
37. To Director, FBI. From San Francisco, Subject Steven Charles Hamilton, 5/26/1966, FBI Steve Hamilton file 100-54915, 18.
38. Athan G. Theoharis, *The FBI: A Comprehensive Reference Guide*, Phoenix, AZ: Oryx Press, 1999, 20.
39. SAC San Francisco, to Director, FBI, 12/27/1971, Steve Hamilton file 100-54915, 136. "Subject's activities warrants such tabbing because (state reasons) of Subject's

membership in the RU Regional Central Committee, which represents secondary leadership capacity."

40. To Director, FBI. From San Francisco, Subject Steven Charles Hamilton 5/26/1966, FBI Steve Hamilton file 100-54915, 21.
41. Rosenfeld, "Anti-war activist Steve Hamilton dies."
42. Hearings on H.R. 12047, H.R. 14925, H.R. 16175, H.R. 17140 and H.R. 17194, 1232 and Stephen D. Lerner, "8 Protesters Called Before HUAC Board: Local Radicals Fear 'They Will Be Next,'" *Harvard Crimson,* August 9, 1966.
43. Willard Clopton, "Hailing 'Victory,' Demonstrators 'Dream of Joe Pool' in New Song," *Washington Post,* August 21, 1966, A19.
44. Saul Bellow, Julian Bond, Irving However, Robert Lowell and Daniel Bell, et al. "HUAC" *New York Review of Books,* September 1966. http://www.nybooks.com/articles/archives/1966/sep/08/huac/?pagination=false
45. "Hearing on H.R. 12047, H.R. 14925, H.R. 16175, H.R. 17140, AND H.R. 17194, 1184. https://ia600301.us.archive.org/21/items/hearingsonhr120401unit/hearingsonhr120401unit.pdf
46. San Francisco Office, FBI. Title "Steven Charles Hamilton," 5/1/196, FBI Steve Hamilton file 100-54915, 48.
47. Michael S. Foley, *Confronting the War Machine,* Chapel Hill: University of North Carolina Press, 2003, 88.
48. Ibid., 77.
49. Rosenfeld, "Anti-war activist Steve Hamilton dies."
50. "As a political science grad student at Berkeley fighting for the Free Speech Movement and against the Vietnam War, he was one of the Oakland Seven against the draft in 1967. He learned from Maoist students supporting the Black Panthers and soon went on to organize the

Bay Area Revolutionary Union (BARU). Still in Berkeley in 1969..." John Womack, Jr., "Trampling Out the Sanctimony," *Monthly Review On-Line*, September 1, 2012. http://monthlyreview.org/2012/09/01/trampling-out-the-sanctimony

51. Rosenfeld, "Anti-war activist Steve Hamilton dies."
52. Emma Rothschild, "Notes from a Political Trial," *New York Review of Books*, July 10, 1969. http://www.nybooks.com/articles/archives/1969/jul/10/notes-from-a-political-trial/?pagination=false
53. Foley, *Confronting the War Machine*, 88.
54. Steve Hamilton, "On the History of the Revolutionary Union, Part I." First Published: *Theoretical Review* No. 13, November-December 1979. Reprinted marxists.org. http://www.marxists.org/history/erol/ncm-1/hamilton1.htm
55. Rick Del Vecchio, "'Sparky' Avakian: Racism Fighting Judge," *San Francisco Chronicle*, February 2, 2002. http://www.sfgate.com/news/article/Sparky-Avakian-racism-fighting-judge-2877881.php
56. Bob Avakian, *From Ike To Mao and Beyond: My Journey from Mainstream America to Revolutionary Communist: A Memoir*, Chicago: Insight Press, 2005, 1-6.
57. Bob Avakian, "FSM Reflections: On Becoming a Revolutionary," *Revolutionary Worker*, November 17, 1996, Reprinted Free Speech Archives. http://www.fsm-a.org/stacks/avakian.html
58. Daryl E. Lembke, "Viet Group Splits on Berkeley Clash: Crowd of 2,000 Hears Criticism of Militants at UC Campus Rally," *Los Angeles Times*, April 14, 1966.
59. Avakian, *Ike to Mao*, 144.
60. Aaron Leonard, "How the Short, Unruly Life of 'Ramparts' Magazine Changed America: An Interview with Peter Richardson," *History News Network*, hnn.us, September,

2009. http://hnn.us/node/118028

61. Avakian, *Ike to Mao,* 144.
62. Bob Avakian, "Summing up the Black Panther Party," Chicago: RCP Publications, 1979, 3.
63. "What's That Lad Doing," Committee of New Politics Communique broadsheet, March 30, 1967.
64. Avakian, *Ike to Mao,* 155.
65. Black Panther Party for Self Defense, "Ten Point Program." From marxists.org. http://www.marxists.org/history/usa/workers/black-panthers/1966/10/15.htm
66. Joshua Bloom and Waldo E. Martin, Jr. *Black Against Empire: The History and Politics of the Black Panther Party.* Berkeley: University of California Press, 2013, 311.
67. Garrett Epps, "Huey Newton Speaks at Boston College, Presents Theory of 'Intercommunalism.'" *The Harvard Crimson,* November 19, 1970. http://www.thecrimson.com/article/1970/11/19/huey-newton-speaks-at-boston-college/

    Also, David Hilliard and Donald Wiese. "If colonies cannot 'decolonize' and return to their original existence as nations, then nations no longer exist. Nor, we believe, will they ever exist again. And since there must be nations for revolutionary nationalism or internationalism to make sense, we decided that we would have to call ourselves something new." *The Huey P Newton Reader,* Intercommunalism, February 1971, New York: Seven Stories Press, 2002,187.
68. Elsa Knight program on KPFA Radio, Panel, Bobby Seale (Black Panther Party), Bob Avakian and Mike Parker (Peace and Freedom Party) February 15, 1968, UC Berkeley Library Social Activism Sound Recording Project:
    The Black Panther Party.
    http://www.lib.berkeley.edu/MRC/pacificapanthers.html# 1968

69. Eldridge Cleaver, *On the Ideology of the Black Panther Party, Part I,* Black Panther Party pamphlet. San Francisco, 1970, 7.
70. Joel Wilson, *In Search of the Black Panther Party: New Perspectives on a Revolutionary Movement.* Durham, NC: Duke University Press, 2006, 220-221.
71. Flyer, "Endorsers: Peace and Freedom," November 7, 1967, author collection.
72. Bloom and Martin, *Black Against Empire,* 108.
73. Wilson, *In Search of the Black Panther Party*, 204.
74. "Letters: Cleaver for President. Eldridge Cleaver for President Fund," *New York Review of Books,* November 7. 1968. http://www.nybooks.com/articles/archives/1968/nov/07/cleaver-for-president/
75. Bloom and Martin, *Black Against Empire,* 101.
76. W.J. Rorabaugh, *Berkeley at War: The 1960s,* New York: Oxford University Press, 1989, 83.
77. *Huey!* American Documentary Films, in Cooperation with the Black Panther Party, 1968. San Francisco Bay Area Television Archives. https://diva.sfsu.edu/collections/sfbatv/bundles/191359
78. Ibid., transcription, Aaron Leonard.
79. "Avakian Given 30 Days in Desecration of Flag," *Oakland Tribune,* October 21, 1968.
80. Bloom and Martin, *Black Against Empire*, 81.
81. Avakian, *Ike to Mao*, 188.
82. H. Bruce Franklin, *Back Where You Came From: One Life in the Death of the Empire,* New York: Harper's Magazine Press, 1975, 38-39.
83. Ibid., 56.
84. Ibid., 110-111.
85. Ibid., 226.
86. H. Bruce Franklin, *Vietnam and Other American Fantasies,* Boston: University of Massachusetts Press, 2001, 74-75.

87. Franklin, *Back Where You Come From,* 153.
88. Kenneth Lamott, "In the Matter of H. Bruce Franklin," *New York Times,* January 23, 1972.
89. *America's Maoists - The Revolutionary Union, The Venceremos Organization.* Report by the Committee on Internal Security, House of Representatives, Ninety-Second Congress, Second Session. U.S.A. Congress. US Government Printing Office, Washington, 1972. pp. 11-12.
90. Bob Avakian, "Talking About Huey P. Newton and the Black Panther Party—the Early Years," *Revolutionary Worker* #1213, September 21, 2003. "I thought it was much better to develop things to the point where you could merge and openly have a party that had everybody in it who was serious about revolution and wanted to implement a program of proletarian revolution." From revcom.us. http://revcom.us/a/1213/bahuey.htm
   Also Hamilton, *History of the RU, Part I.* "The RU had avoided recruiting Black members but instead encouraged them to join the Panthers."
91. Report of Brent T. Palmer, San Francisco, FBI. Re: "Steven Charles Hamilton—Security Matter Revolutionary Union," 4/10/70—Appendix Page 26—Description of SDS. BU file, Steve Hamilton, 100-45639. Document release, 163.
92. Jack Weinberg and Jack Gerson, "The SPLIT IN SDS," *I.S.,* September 1969, Reprinted in US Congress, *America's Maoists,* 173-175.
93. Kirkpatrick Sale, *SDS: The Rise and Development of Students for a Democratic Society.* New York: Vintage, 1974, 16-17.
94. League for Industrial Democracy website. http://industrialdemocracy.org/
95. Port Huron Statement of the Students for a Democratic Society, 1962, New Insurgency: The Port Huron Statement in Its Time and Ours website. http://www.lsa.umich.edu/

phs/resources/porthuronstatementfulltext

96. Mark Rudd, "The Death of SDS." Mark Rudd website markrudd.com, 2007. www.markrudd.com/?sds-and-weather/the-death-of-sds.html
97. Jack Newfield, *Village Voice,* September 5 1968. Taken from Norman Mailer, *Miami and the Siege of Chicago,* New York: NYRB Books, 2008, 170-171.
98. Joe Allen, *Vietnam The (Last) War the U.S. Lost.* Chicago: Haymarket Books, 2008, 189.
99. Progressive Labor Party, *Revolution Today.* New York: Exposition Press, 1970, 263.
100. Ibid., 265.
101. See for example: David Landau, *The Harvard Crimson,* "Is PL Killing SDS," March 8, 1971. http://www.thecrimson.com/article/1971/3/8/is-pl-killing-sds-plate-last/#
102. Avakian, *Ike to Mao,*187.
103. Hamilton, *RU History,* Part I.
104. Steve Hamilton, "Summation of Experience in Revolutionary Union and Bay Area Communist Union," Forum Speech, Bay Area, April 7, 1976. Reprinted marxists.org. http://www.marxists.org/history/erol/ncm-1/hamilton-speech.htm
105. Director, FBI, to SAC San Francisco Re: Revolutionary Union, aka Red Union IS— CH 8/15/68: Bureau File, Steve Hamilton 100-445639, 312.
106. Ibid.
107. Director, FBI, to SAC San Francisco, August 29, 1968, Subject: CHANGED: Revolutionary Union, aka Red Union, Internal Security RU Bureau File, Steve Hamilton 100-445639. Document release, 299.
108. Ibid., 300.
109. Ibid.
110. Director, FBI to SAC San Francisco "Revolutionary Union (RU) IS-CH Nationalities Intelligence," Bureau File, Steve

Hamilton 100-445639, Document release, 267.

111. Contact with REDACTED, 7/24/68. Report dated July 25, 1968, Bureau File, Steve Hamilton 100-445639. Document release, 319.
112. Ibid, 322.
113. Ibid.
114. Contact with REDACTED. 9/10/68. Submitted September 11, 1968. Bureau File, Steve Hamilton 100-445639. Document release, 289-290.
115. Ibid.
116. Contact with REDACTED, 7/24/68. Report dated July 25, 1968. Bureau File, Steve Hamilton 100-445639. Document release, 319.
117. Area Meeting of the Revolutionary Union (RU) 1/19/69. Bureau File, Steve Hamilton 100-445639. Document release, 222.
118. Executive Committee Meeting. June 20, 1969. Bureau File, Steve Hamilton 100-445639. Document release, 46.
119. Ibid.
120. Director, FBI to SAC San Francisco 9/11/68. "Revolutionary Union, aka Red Union Internal Security - Revolutionary Union. Bureau File, Steve Hamilton 100-445639. Document release, 284.
121. "On March 2, 1969, an Executive Committee meeting of the RU was held at 620 Waller Street, San Francisco, California, in which STEVE HAMILTON was present. SF T-1, 3/10/69." and "On March 9, 1969, an Executive Committee meeting of the RU was held at 6A Downey, San Francisco, California, in which the East Bay Local of the RU was represented by STEVE HAMILTON and two other individuals." T-3, 3/10/69. Report of Brent T Palmer, FBI, 4/10/70. Bureau File, Steve Hamilton, 100-54915. NARA Document release, 15.
122. RU Executive Committee Meeting, San Francisco,

California, 4/6/69, submitted, April 14, 1969. Bureau File, Steve Hamilton 100-445639. Document release, 118.

123. Ibid.
124. Jon Hillson, Denver Branch, SWP, "American Maoism: Re-emergence and Regroupment." *SWP Discussion Bulletin*, Vol. 31, No. 6, May 1973. From marxists.org. http://www.marxists.org/history/erol/ncm-1/hillson.htm
125. Weinberg and Gerson, "The Split in SDS."
126. Mike Ely, email exchange with Aaron Leonard, February 21, 2012.
127. *The Red Papers.* The Revolutionary Union 1969. From marxists.org. http://www.marxists.org/history/erol/ncm-1/red-papers-1/against.htm
128. Mao Zedong, "Statement Supporting the American Negroes In Their Just Struggle Against Racial Discrimination by U.S. Imperialism," *Peking Review,* August 8, 1963.
129. Revolutionary Union, *The Red Papers.*
130. Ibid.
131. For a good historical accounting see J. Arch Getty and Oleg V. Naumov. *The Road to Terror: Stalin and the Self-Destruction of the Bolsheviks, 1932-39*. New Haven: Yale University Press, 2002, 590-91.
132. Sale, *SDS,* 522.
133. Stuart Schram, *The Thoughts of Mao Tse-tung.* Cambridge: Cambridge University Press, 1989, 151.
134. See, Lorenz, *The Sino-Soviet Split.*
135. RU, *The Red Papers.*
136. Ibid.
137. RU Executive Committee Meeting, San Francisco, California, 2/23/69, Report dated March 3, 1969. Bureau File, Steve Hamilton 100-445639. Document release, 172.
138. SA Bertram Worthington TO SAC, San Francisco, 3/5/69. Bureau File, Steve Hamilton 100-445639. Document release, 177.

139. RU Executive Committee Meeting, San Francisco, California, 4/6/1969, Report dated April 14, 1969. Bureau File, Steve Hamilton 100-445639. Document release, 119.
140. SAC, San Francisco (100-61281) to Director, FBI (105-184369), "Revolutionary Union." April 30, 1969.
141. Ron Koziol, "Red Unit Seeks SDS Rule," *Chicago Tribune,* June 17, 1969.
142. Ibid.
143. Chicago, To Director, FBI, 6/30/69 Subject: COINTELPRO New Left. Freedom of Information and Privacy Acts Subject (COINTELPRO) New Left, Chicago Division. 100-449698-9, document pp. 28-30.
144. SAC, Chicago to Director FBI, Subject COINTELPRO - New Left, 6/24/1969. Freedom of Information and Privacy Acts Subject (COINTELPRO) New Left, Chicago Division. 1,00-449698-9, document pp. 31-32.
145. SAC Chicago, to Director FBI "Counterintelligence and Special Operations (Nationalities Intelligence)." 5/14/1969. David Sullivan U.S. Maoism Collection, TAM.527, Box 8, Folder 45.
146. The RU, in the Bureau's parlance, was labeled "Internal-Security," or IS - RU for short. Director, FBI, to SAC San Francisco. August 29, 1968. Subject: <u>CHANGED</u>: Revolutionary Union, aka Red Union, Internal Security - RU Bureau File, Steve Hamilton 100-445639. Document release, 299.
147. C.D. Brennan, to W. C. Sullivan, "Subject: Counterintelligence Program Internal Security Disruption of the New Left." May 9, 1968. Ward Churchill. *The COINTELPRO Papers*. Boston: South End Press, 1990, 177.
148. Ibid.
149. "You Don't Need A Weatherman To Know Which Way The Wind Blows." Submitted by Karin Ashley, Bill Ayers, Bernardine Dohrn, John Jacobs, Jeff Jones, Gerry Long,

Howard Machtinger, Jim Mellen, Terry Robbins, Mark Rudd and Steve Tappis. *New Left Notes,* June 18, 1969.

150. Ibid.
151. Ibid.
152. RU Executive Committee Meeting, San Francisco, California, 7/6/1969, Report dated July 11, 1969. Bureau File, Steve Hamilton 100-445639. Document release, p 33.
153. Mao Tse-tung, "Problems of Strategy in Guerrilla War Against Japan," *Selected Works of Mao Tse-tung.* May 1938. From marxists.org. http://www.marxists.org/reference/archive/mao/selected-works/volume-2/mswv2_08.htm
154. David Barber, *A Hard Rain Fell: SDS and Why it Failed.* Jackson, MS: University Press of Mississippi, 2008, 219-220.
155. Jack Smith, "SDS Ousts PLP," *The Guardian,* June 28, 1969. From marxists.org. http://www.marxists.org/history/erol/ncm-1/sds-ousts-plp.htm
156. "Revolution in the Revolution: Interview with Chris Milton," *The Movement,* February 1969.
157. FBI, "Mao Tse-tung Influence on SDS Factions at the June 1969 National Convention." vault.fbi.gov, Weather Underground (Weathermen) Part 2 of 6, 24. http://vault.fbi.gov/Weather%20Underground%20%28Weathermen%29/Weather%20Underground%20%28Weathermen%29%20Part%202%20of%206/view
158. Sale, *SDS,* 531.
159. Charles Jones, *The Black Panther Party Reconsidered.* Baltimore: Black Classic Press, 1998. 33.
160. Smith, "SDS Ousts PLP."
161. Mary-Alice Waters, "The split at the SDS national convention," *The Militant,* Vol. 33, No. 27, July 4, 1969. Reprinted marxists.org,. http://www.marxists.org/history/erol/ncm-1/militant-sds.htm

162. SAC Cleveland, To Director, FBI, " 8/1/1969. New Left, Cleveland Division. Bureau file, 100-449698-11.
163. Ibid.
164. markrudd.com. and Rudd, *My Life Underground*, 172-174.
165. John Kifner, "S.D.S. Protestors Tried in Chicago," *New York Times*, November 2, 1969.
166. For more see Alan Adelson, *SDS: A Profile.* New York: Charles Scribner & Sons. 1972.
167. SAC San Francisco to Director, FBI, 8/11/70. Dept. of Special Collections and University Archives Stanford University Libraries. SC664. Robert Beyers Papers. Bruce Franklin FBI documents. Box 6. Folders 8-9.
168. Ibid.
169. Ross K. Baker. "Weathermen: Bringing the War Back Home," *Winnipeg Free Press*, citing a Liberation News Service report, December 1970.
170. Steve Hamilton, "Serve the People, Learn From the People, Become One With the People," *The Movement*, January 1969, reprinted in *The Red Papers.*
171. Avakian, *Ike to Mao*, 199.
172. Record Group 21, Records of the District Courts of the United States, District of Columbia, Criminal Case File 78-00179, *United States v. W Mark Felt and Edward S. Miller.* Location in NARA Stacks: 16W3/15/05/05-06. Box 30, p 4049.
173. Informant Report received by SA Gary L. Penrith. Subject: RYM II Convention in Atlanta Georgia, November 27-30-1969. Report dated 12/18/1969. Bureau File, Steve Hamilton, 100-445639. Document release 96-97.
174. Hoover Institution Archives Stanford University. *New Left Collection:* Peace and Freedom Party, Box 40, 59. Copy on file with authors.
175. Contact with REDACTED. 9/10/68. Submitted September 11, 1968. Bureau File, Steve Hamilton 100-445639.

Document release, 289-290.

176. Revolutionary Union (RU), Executive Committee Meeting 7/6/69. Submitted July 11, 1969. Bureau File, Steve Hamilton 100-445639. Document release, 32.
177. Ibid.
178. "Conference for a United Front Against Fascism," KPIX Eyewitness news report from the Oakland Auditorium on July 19th, 1969. Francisco Bay Area Television Archive. https://diva.sfsu.edu/collections/sfbatv/bundles/207569
179. "New Leftists, Reds, Call for Alliance," *Oxnard Press Courier,* July 7, 1969.
180. Hamilton. "RU History, Part I."
181. Ibid.
182. Hamilton, "Learn From the People."
183. Stipulation entered into the record at the Felt-Miller trial, 1980. Record Group 21, Records of the District Courts of the United States, District of Columbia, Criminal Case File 78-00179, *United States v. W Mark Felt and Edward S. Miller*. Location in NARA Stacks: 16W3/15/05/05-06. Box 30, p. 3993.
184. Hamilton, "RU History, Part I."
185. US Congress, *America's Maoists*, 14.
186. Ibid.
187. H. Bruce Franklin, *From the Movement Toward the Revolution,* "Young Partisans Speaks, Articles from Free You, The Redwood City Young Partisans," New York: Van Nostrand Reinhold, 1971, 129 & 133-37.
188. Robert Avakian, "The People v. Standard Oil," *The Movement,* March 1969, Vol 5. No. 2 p 3, 22
189. Ibid.
190. Ibid.
191. US Congress, *America's Maoists,* reprint of Ed Montgomery column, the June 2, 1969, *San Francisco Examiner*. pp. 14-15.

192. Richard W. Lyman, "Stanford in Turmoil," *Sandstone & Tile,* Winter 2011, Stanford Historical Society Vol. 35, Number 1, 5-15. https://purl.stanford.edu/xd213kr2527
193. "Richard W. Lyman, Stanford's seventh president, dead at 88," *Stanford News* (Newsletter), Stanford Report, May 27, 2012. http://news.stanford.edu/news/2012/may/richard-lyman-obit-052712.html
194. Lyman, "Stanford in Turmoil."
195. Paul Rupert, "You Guys Were Fantastic," *Peninsula Observer,* through March 31 1969.
194. Lyman, "Stanford in Turmoil."
197. Dave Pugh, "Stanford Anti-War and Justice Movements (1966-1969),"*Stanford Reorientation Guide 09-10,* 35-36.
198. Ibid.
194. Lyman, "Stanford in Turmoil."
200. Ibid.
201. Steve Weissman, "Occupy This: Crazy Tom the FBI Provocateur," *Reader Supported News,* November 27, 2011. http://readersupportednews.org/opinion2/275-42/8619-occupy-this-crazy-tom-the-fbi-provocateur
202. Ibid.
203. Testimony of Thomas Edward Mosher, "Subcommittee to Investigate the Administration of Internal Security Act and Other Internal Security Laws," Committee on the Judiciary, U.S. Senate. Part I March 19, 1971. US Government Printing Office, Washington, D.C. 1971.
204. Director, FBI (105-173280). to SAC, San Francisco (105-22316). Subject redacted. 5/8/1969.
205. US Congress, *America's Maoists,* 26.
206. Ibid., ix.
207. Ibid,. 26.
208. Ibid., 27.
209. Ibid., 27.

210. Ibid., 53.
211. Ibid., 28.
212. US House of Representatives, Committee on Internal Security, *Investigation of Attempts to Subvert the United States Armed Services, Part 1,* Hearings Before the House of Representatives, Ninety-Second Congress, First Session. Hearings, October 20, 21, 22, 27, and 28, 1971, US Government Printing Office 1972, 6463.
213. SJRUWC, Workers Collective Meeting, 7/12/70 (Notes). Report Submitted. 7/16/1970, by REDACTED. FBI file, SF-67080 Mid-Peninsula Workers Committee.
214. US Congress, *Investigation of Attempts to Subvert the United States Armed Services*, 6439.
215. Ibid., 6444.
216. Ibid.
217. Ibid., 6426.
218. Ibid., 6440.
219. Ibid., 6432.
220. SJRUWC, Workers Collective Meeting, 7/12/70.
221. See, for example, Mao Zedong, "Talks With Responsible Comrades At Various Places During Provincial Tour," from the middle of August to 12 September 1971. "This Party of ours already has fifty years' history, during which time we have had ten big struggles on the question of our line. During these ten struggles there were people who wanted to split our Party, but none of them were able to do so." *Selected Works of Mao Tse-tung Vol. I*, at marxists.org. http://www.marxists.org/reference/archive/mao/selected-works/volume-9/mswv9_88.htm
222. Bill Klingel and Joanne Psihountas, *Important Struggles in Building the Revolutionary Communist Party, USA*. Chicago: RCP Publications, 1978. Reprinted marxists.org. http://www.marxists.org/history/erol/ncm-3/rcp-history.htm
223. SAC, San Francisco. SA Bertram Worthington,

Revolutionary Union IS - RU 11/22/68, Bureau File, Steve Hamilton 100-445639. Document release, 262-263.

224. Ibid
225. Ibid.
226. The following year, Avakian would be added to a list of speakers Congress felt were 'inflaming' campuses—along with people such as Bobby Seale, Benjamin Spock, and Nat Hentoff. "House Unit Says 57 Inflamed Campuses," *Chicago Tribune,* October 15, 1970.
227. Montgomery, June 2 1969.
228. Hamilton. *RU History Part I.*
229. Ibid.
230. Klingel and Psihountas, *Important Struggles.*
231. See, for example, Treiger polemics in Spartacist pamphlet, *Marxist Bulletin Number 10. From Maoism to Trotskyism.* https://www.marxists.org/history//etol/document/icl-spartacists/marxist-bulletins/MB-10.pdf
   Also *Workers Vanguard* No. 1023, "An Appreciation of Tweet Carter" for his departure from the Spartacist League.
   http://www.icl-fi.org/english/wv/1023/tweet.html
232. David Sullivan Maoism Collection, TAM-527, Box 1, Folder 52.
233. Email exchange, Ted Franklin with Aaron Leonard July 23, 2013.
234. SAC, San Francisco, Director, FBI 4/3/1970. David Sullivan Maoism Collection. TAM.527. Box 8, Folder 46.
235. SAC San Francisco to Director FBI. 4/28/1970. David Sullivan Maoism Collection. TAM.527. Box 8, Folder 46.
236. Avakian, *Ike to Mao,* 218.
237. US Congress, *America's Maoists,* 16. Avakian, *Ike to Mao,* 219.
238. Area Meeting of the Revolutionary Union (RU) 7/6/69. Submitted July 11, 1969. Bureau File, Steve Hamilton 100-

445639. Document release, 34.

239. See SAC Chicago, to Director, FBI. "Subject: Revolutionary Union,"12/23/1970, David Sullivan U.S. Maoism Collection. TAM.527 Box 23, Folder 6.
240. Ronald Koziol, "Investigators Bare Reds' Recruitment of Chicago Radicals," *Chicago Tribune*, October 13, 1970.
241. Aaron Leonard email exchange with former RU comrade. June 2013.
242. US Senate, "Final Report on the Select Committee to Study Governmental Operation with Respect to Intelligence Actives," 94th Congress, Senate Report, 2d Session, No. 94-755. "Supplementary Detailed Staff Reports on Intelligence Activities and the Rights of Americans," Book III, United States Senate, April 23, 1976. http://repositories.lib.utexas.edu/bitstream/handle/2152/13804/ChurchCommittee_BookIII.pdf.txt;jsessionid=6ED0B9D3A4F435641ECA430E867248A4?sequence=3
243. Guide to the Marc Lendler Revolutionary Union/Revolutionary Communist Party Collection, TAM.631. http://dlib.nyu.edu/findingaids/html/tamwag/tam_631/bioghist.html
244. SAC Cincinnati, FBI Director, "Subject: Revolutionary Union - RU COINTELPRO - New Left," 10/28/70. SAC, Cincinnati Bureau File 100-449698-10.
245. Ibid.
246. US Congress, *America's Maoists*, 15.
247. SAC, San Francisco, To Director, FBI. 8/12/70. Special Collection Research Center, Temple University Library, Paley Library, Liberation News Services Library Records, Record Group MSS SP 003. Box 4. Folders 1-5.
248. Ibid.
249. There was a story passed around the RCP the author heard repeatedly, of the Tsarist police agent, and Bolshevik Central Committee member, Roman Malinovsky, with

the accompanying folktale that Lenin and the Bolsheviks ultimately were able to use his position in the Tsarist DUMA to further their aims—a rather serious misreading of the actual damage Malinovsky did. For a concise and helpful account, see Ralph Carter Elwood, *Roman Malinovsky: Life Without A Cause*. Newtonville, Mass.: Oriental Research Partners, 1977.

250. Roxanne Dunbar, *Outlaw Woman*. San Francisco: City Lights Publishers, 2002, 297.
251. *San Jose Mercury*, October 22, 1971, reprinted in US Congress, *America's Maoists*, 32.
252. Felt-Miller transcript, 3947.
253. US Congress, *America's Maoists*, 16-17.
254. Revolutionary Union, "The Military Strategy for the United States: Protracted Urban War (A Draft), The Franklin Group," as printed in *Red Papers 4*, 1970. http://www.marxists.org/history/erol/ncm-1/red-papers-4/article1.htm
255. San Francisco (105-22479), Special Collection Research Center, Temple University Library, Paley Library. Liberation News Services Library Records. Record Group MSS SP 003. Box 4. Folders 1-5.
256. Area Meeting of the Revolutionary Union (RU) 7/6/69. Submitted July 11, 1969. Bureau File, Steve Hamilton 100-445639, 290.
257. Area Meeting of the Revolutionary Union (RU) 7/6/69. Submitted July 11, 1969. Bureau File, Steve Hamilton 100-445639, 70.
258. Contact with REDACTED. 9/10/68. Submitted September 11, 1968. Bureau File, Steve Hamilton 100-445639, 289-290.
259. Revolutionary Union, "Revolutionary Adventurism or Proletarian Revolution," *Red Papers 4*, The R.U. Leadership. http://www.marxists.org/history/erol/ncm-1/red-papers-4/article2.htm

260. Ibid.
261. Revolutionary Union, *Red Papers 4.*
262. See Newton, Huey P. "War Against The Panthers: A Study Of Repression In America" Section - Fostering a Newton-Cleaver Split. Doctoral Dissertation, UC Santa Cruz, June 1, 1980.
263. American Documentary Films, *Huey!*
264. "On the Revolutionary Union's Current Struggle Against Left Adventurism," RU Internal document, David Sullivan U.S. Maoism Collection. TAM.527 Box 1, Folder 23.
265. Hamilton, *RU History, Part I.* See also, Eldridge Cleaver, "On Lumpen Ideology," *Black Scholar* 3, November-December 1972: 9, 37.
266. Ibid.
267. Ibid.
268. Revolutionary Union, *Red Papers 4,* "The Franklin Group It is Right to Rebel. Local Cadre Leave the Revolutionary Union." Originally published December 16, 1970, *THE FREE YOU,* Palo Alto, California.
269. US Congress, *America's Maoists,* 27
270. SAC San Francisco (105-22479), To Director, FBI 11/24/1970. Special Collection Research Center, Temple University Library, Paley Library. Liberation News Services Library Records. Record Group MSS SP 003. Box 4. Folders 1-5.
271. Robert M. Horner to Donald G. Sanders, Chief Counsel, Re: Revolutionary Union, August 17, 1973, University Archives, University of Missouri, Columbia, C.22/9/1 Box 7 FF21.
272. San Francisco to Director, 11/24/1970.
273. SAC Chicago, to Director, FBI. "Subject: Revolutionary Union,"12/23/1970, David Sullivan U.S. Maoism Collection. TAM.527 Box 23, Folder 6.
274. Avakian, *Ike to Mao,* 223.
275. SAC Chicago to Director, FBI, 12/23/1970.

276. Ibid.
277. SAC, San Francisco, Director FBI, "Howard Bruce Franklin IS - RU (Nationalities Intelligence)" 5/14/1969. Dept. of Special Collections and University Archives Stanford University Libraries. SC664. Robert Beyers Papers. Bruce Franklin FBI documents. Box 6. Folders 8-9.
278. FBI Memo, SAC, San Francisco, to Director, FBI, Date (illegible). Subject Counterintelligence and Special Operations (Nationalities Intelligence), Cover, SFO to Director FBI, 9/10/69.
279. SAC, San Francisco (105 22479), to Director, FBI. (105-174254) "Counterintelligence and Special Operations (Research Section)," 9/28/1970.
280. SAC, San Francisco, to Director, FBI, 9/5/1969, Airtel, Dept. of Special Collections and University Archives Stanford University Libraries. SC664. Robert Beyers Papers. Bruce Franklin FBI documents. Box 6. Folders 8-9.
281. SAC San Francisco to Director, FBI, 10/14/69. Dept. of Special Collections and University Archives Stanford University Libraries, SC664. Robert Beyers Papers, Bruce Franklin FBI documents. Box 6. Folders 8-9.
282. Acting Director, FBI to SAC Chicago, Newark, San Francisco, "Revolutionary Union" 1/18/1973, David Sullivan U.S. Maoism Collection, TAM.527. Box 23, Folder 5-6.
283. Author interview with former RU comrade, May 2012.
284. "Party Routs Revisionist Clique: The High Road vs. The Well-Worn Rut," *Revolution*, Vol. 3, No. 7-8, April-May 1978.
285. RU, *Red Papers 4*.
286. "On the Revolutionary Union's Current Struggle Against Left Adventurism," RU Internal document, David Sullivan U.S. Maoism Collection, TAM.527 Box 1, Folder 23.
287. US Congress, *America's Maoists,* 91 and 94. Klingel and

Pshihountas, *Important Struggles in Building the RCP.*

288. Franklin, *From the Movement Toward the Revolution,* 129.
289. US Congress, *America's Maoists*, 94-95.
290. Ibid.
291. US Congress, *America's Maoists,* 88.
292. Ibid., 89.
293. Ibid., 28.
294. Ibid., 29.
295. Ibid., 89
296. *Stanford Daily,* September 27, 1971, cited in US Congress, *America's Maoists*, 115.
297. US Congress, *America's Maoists,* 115.
298. Alan M. Dershowitz, *The Best Defense,* New York: Vintage, 1983, 217-221.
299. "Stanford Teacher Fired in 1972 Loses Appeal for Reinstatement," *Associated Press*, September 21, 1985.
300. Kenneth Lamott, "In the Matter Of H. Bruce Franklin: Franklin and academic tenure," *New York Times,* Jan 23, 1972.
301. US Congress, *America's Maoists*, 143.
302. paloaltohistory.com "Venceremos: Arming for Fight." http://www.paloaltohistory.com/venceremos.php
303. Ibid.
304. Donna DiNovelli, "Professor Named Fellow," *Hartford Courant,* 4/3/1975.
305. "Conviction of Two Radicals for Aiding in Escape Upheld," *Los Angeles Times*, Jun 28, 1975.
306. Report of Robert C. Wannamaker, FBI, San Francisco, 10/26/1973. Title: Aaron Manganiello. Bureau file 100-HQ-451992. Document release,154.
307. Franklin, *Back Where We Came From,* xiii.
308. "Review: *Back Where We Came From,*" *Village Voice* May 5, 1975.
309. Director FBI, to SAC, San Francisco. 11/3/1972, Transcript

of interview by SA Kent O. Brisby and SA Robert C. Wanamaker 10/18/1972, Manganiello. Bureau file 100-HQ-451992. Document release, 113.

310. FBI, San Francisco, Report on Aaron Joseph Manganiello, 8/23/1974. Interview with SA Michael. SA G. Kealey, Robert C. Wanamaker, and SA Kent O Brisby. Interview date 8/13/1974. Manganiello FBI file, "He knew no one in the Symbionese Liberation Army with the exception of JOSEPH REMIRO. He met REMIRO several years ago in Oakland, California, on two occasions. He was unaware that REMIRO had joined the Venceremos Organization until after he was arrested and charged with the murder of MARCUS FOSTER. Manganiello Bureau file 100-HQ-451992. Document release, 165.
311. Ibid.,167.
312. From San Francisco, to Director. Teletype August 8, 1975, Manganiello. Bureau file 100-HQ-451992, File release, 183.
313. R.L. Shackelford to W. R. Wannall, Subject CONF. INF. SF 82170POS (SPECTAR) SM – WEATHERMAN. Stamped, August 26, 1975. Manganiello. Bureau file 100-HQ-451992, 191.
314. SAC San Francisco, to Director FBI 11/6/1975. Transcript of interview by SA Kent O. Brisby and SA Robert C. Wanamaker 10/18/1972. Manganiello file, 190. Group acronyms are as follows: Weather Underground (WU), New World Liberation Front (NWLF), the Red Guerrilla Family (RGF), Americans for Justice (AFJ), Chicano Liberation Front (CLF). Manganiello FBI file.
315. SAC San Francisco, To Director FBI, 11/6/75, Manganiello Bureau file 100-HQ-451992. Document release, 194.
316. Max Weber, "Politics as a Vocation." "Today, however, we have to say that a state is a human community that (successfully) claims the monopoly of the legitimate use

of physical force within a given territory." http://www.sscnet.ucla.edu/polisci/ethos/Weber-vocation.pdf

317. Revolutionary Union, *Red Papers 4,* The RU Leadership, "Marxism vs. Opportunism, The Class Struggle Within our Organization." http://www.marxists.org/history/erol/ncm-1/red-papers-4/article5.htm
318. Mao Zedong, "On Practice," July 1937, Selected Works, Vol. I, Foreign Language Press, Peking, 299-300.
319. Mao Zedong, "Talks With Responsible Comrades."
320. "Correct Line Achieved Through Study, Struggle, Criticism," *Revolution*, January 1974.
321. Mao Tse-tung, "Get Organized!" November 29, 1943, Selected Works, Vol. III, p.158. Taken from marxists.org. http://www.marxists.org/reference/archive/mao/works/red-book/ch11.htm
322. "Mass Line Is Key To Lead Masses In Making Revolution," *Revolution,* December 15, 1975. Reprinted in RCP pamphlet *The Mass Line.* 1976. Taken from massline.info. http://www.massline.info/rcp/ml_art1.htm
323. Josef Stalin, *Foundation of Leninism,* marxists.org. http://www.marxists.org/reference/archive/stalin/works/1924/foundations-leninism/ch08.htm
324. Hamilton, *RU History, Part II.*
325. Klingel & Pshihountas, *Important Struggles in Building the RCP.* http://www.marxists.org/history/erol/ncm-5/rcp-history.htm
326. Hamilton. *RU History, Part II.*
327. US Congress, *America's Maoists,* ix.
328. *Quotations from Mao Tse Tung.* "Patriotism and Internationalism," marxists.org. http://www.marxists.org/reference/archive/mao/works/red-book/ch18.htm
329. SAC New York to Director, FBI. "Subject: Victoria Holmes

Garvin, aka SM-C," 8/24/71. Bureau File, Victoria Garvin 100-HQ-379895, 400.

330. W.A. Branigan to A.H. Belmont. "Subject Joan Chase Hinton Atomic Energy Act." July 23, 1953. FBI Bureau File, William Hinton, 100-HQ-351197.
331. FBI: Albany, To Director, FBI. 11/2/1953. FBI Bureau File, William Hinton, 100-HQ-351197.
332. Bob Wittman, Jr., "Notes Told Daring Tale Of China Life," *Sunday Call-Chronicle*, Allentown, PA. April 08, 1984.
333. "Hearings Before the Subcommittee to Investigate the Administration of the Internal Security Act and Other Internal Security Laws," The Committee on the Judiciary, United States Senate Eighty-Fourth Congress, Second Session, "Scope of Soviet Activities in the United States," March 7 and 8, 1956, United States Government Printing Office, Washington, 1956. https://ia600304.us.archive.org/11/items/scopeofsovietact07unit/scopeofsovietact07unit.pdf
334. Ibid., 241.
335. Whitman, "Notes Told Daring Tale."
336. Background notes to *Fanshen*, Monthly Review Press website, monthlyreview.org. monthlyreview.org/2003/10/01/background-notes-to-fanshen
337. William Hinton, *Fanshen: A Documentary of Revolution in a Chinese Village,* New York: Monthly Review Press, 1966, vii.
338. Ibid., 42-43.
339. Ibid., 602.
340. Ibid., 604.
341. Ibid., 608
342. See, for example, Jack Belden, *China Shakes the World,* New York: Monthly Review Press 1970, Alan and Adele Rickett, *Prisoners of Liberation: Four years in a Chinese*

Communist prison, New York: Anchor Press, 1973, and William Hinton, *Hundred Days War,* New York: Monthly Review Press, 1972.

343. Joshua Horn, *Away With All Pests: An English Surgeon In People's China 1954-1969,* New York: Monthly Review Press, 1971. 18-19.
344. Frank Rich, "Stage: Hare's 'Fanshen' The Chinese Revolution," *New York Times,* February 3, 1983.
345. *Sunday Call Chronicle,* "Notes Told Daring Tale."
346. After a seven year legal battle the FBI was forced to produce its file on Hinton in 1988. It consisted of 10,462 pages (excluding duplicates). William H. HINTON v. The DEPARTMENT OF JUSTICE and the Federal Bureau of Investigation, Appellants. No. 87-1390. United States Court of Appeals, Third Circuit. Argued December 15, 1987. Decided April 14, 1988. However, shortly afterwards, the FBI destroyed records in Hinton's files, February 1, 1993 and June 11, 1993, "pursuant to the agency's record retention and disposition schedules," Sean R. O'Neill, Administrative Appeals Staff, USDOJ, Office of Information Policy to Conor Gallagher, June 7 2013. Of the 598 pages released to this book's authors, 77 pages consisted of the transcript of Hinton's public testimony before the Senate Internal Security Committee on July 27, 1954 and the 294 page manuscript of Hinton's book *Iron Oxen.*
347. There are also brief references to Hinton in the FBI file of Susan Warren, a former CPUSA member, and onetime chair of the New York Chapter of US-China Peoples Friendship Association.
348. Christopher Wallace, "From Putney to Peking: Carmelita Hinton at 82," Excerpted by permission from the *Boston Globe Sunday Magazine,* November 26, 1972.
349. Report of Hal H. Bremer, Office: Philadelphia, PA, April

5, 1968. Field Office File 161-1199. "Special Inquiry Robert Sargent Shriver," Unclassified.

350. Ibid.
351. US House of Representatives, Committee on Internal Security. *Investigation of Attempts to Subvert the United States Armed Services, Part 1.* Hearings Before the House of Representatives, Ninety-Second Congress, First Session. Hearings, October 20, 21, 22, 27, and 28, 1971. US Government Printing Office 1972. p. 6467.
352. Raymond Lotta, "Remembering William Hinton," *Revolutionary Worker* #1253, October 3, 2004.
353. Mar Rudd, *Underground: My Life with SDS and the Weathermen.* New York: William Morrow, 2010, 161.
354. K.M. Wilford, to Colin Wilson, Esq., Far Eastern Department, Foreign and Commonwealth, London, October 30, 1968. File No. FEC13/1, Part A, Intelligence and Information Miscellaneous Sources.
355. Venessa Hua, "Henry Halsey Noyes - distributor of Chinese Books," Obituary. *San Francisco Chronicle.* July 8, 2005. http://www.sfgate.com/cgi-bin/article.cgi?f=/c/a/2005/07/08/BAGHJDKP001.DTL&feed=rss.bayarea
356. Henry Noyes, *China Born: Adventures of a Maverick Bookman.* San Francisco: China Books & Periodicals, 1989, 74-75.
357. "Radicals Aided By Church Plea: Communists Win Lease of Auditorium for Lenin Program," *Milwaukee Journal,* January 16, 1936.
358. Director, FBI, to SAC Chicago Re: Henry Halsey Noyes, May 18, 1954. Bureau File, Henry Halsey Noyes 100-PH-31003, 10.
359. J. Edgar Hoover to Honorable Clement J. Zablocki January 21, 1965. FBI file "Victor Riesel."
360. Copy of stamp, personal collection.
361. Contact with REDACTED, 9/1068. Submitted September

11, 1968. Bureau File, Steve Hamilton 100-445639, 288.

362. Author interview, former RU comrade, May 2012.
363. *Revolution*, February 1973, 15.
364. Huston, Tom Charles Special Report for the President, "Foreign Communist Support of the Revolutionary Protest Movement in the United States," NLN 06-0811 NARA, 20.
365. Ibid.
366. Ibid.
367. SAC Newark to Acting Director FBI 10/20/27, Bureau File, Victoria Garvin 100-HQ-379895.
368. Tim Weiner, "W. Mark Felt, Watergate Deep Throat, Dies at 95," *New York Times,* December 19, 2008. *nytimes* online. http://www.nytimes.com/2008/12/19/washington/19felt.html?pagewanted=all&_r=0
369. Ronald Reagan, "Statement on Granting Pardons to W. Mark Felt and Edward S. Miller," April 15, 1981 http://www.reagan.utexas.edu/archives/speeches/1981/41581d.htm
370. Record Group 21, Records of the District Courts of the United States, District of Columbia, Criminal Case File 78-00179, *United States v. W Mark Felt and Edward S. Miller.* Location in NARA Stacks: 16W3/15/05/05-06. Box 30, 3952.
371. Ibid., 3949.
372. Ibid., 3951.
373. Ibid., 3954-3955.
374. Ibid., 3962.
375. Ibid., 3963.
376. Ibid., 4000.
377. US Congress, *America's Maoists,* 17-19.
378. CIA record, C/CI/SO. "Summary on: Meeting Between Chou en-Lai and the Americans," 26 November 1971. NARA JFK Box # JPK14.
379. *PL Magazine,* "Road to Revolution: The Continuing

Struggle Against Revisionism," Progressive Labor Party, 1970.

380. CIA, CI/SO Summary.
381. Daniel Leese, *Mao Cult: Rhetoric And Ritual In China's Cultural Revolution. Cambridge:* Cambridge University Press, 2013, 109.
382. Avakian, *Ike to Mao,* 251.
383. Ibid.
384. Ibid., 252-253.
385. Informant report of public meeting at Long March in Los Angeles, received by S.A. W. Don Roger 5/5/1972. Bureau File, Steven Hamilton 100-HQ-445639, 83.
386. Ibid.
387. Kissinger, Clark, C. "A working man's China: Adultery is rare and frowned upon. So is premarital sex," *Chicago Tribune,* July 29, 1973.
388. Ibid.
389. Ibid.
390. Ibid.
391. Ibid.
392. U.S. District Court for the Northern District of Illinois Eastern District. American Civil Liberties Union et al., Plaintiff v. City of Chicago et. al. Defendants. Joseph A. Burton Affidavit. July 22, 1980. p. 2. David Sullivan Maoism Collection TAM.527, Box 23, folders 5-6.
393. *Avakian, Ike to Mao,* 261.
394. SAC New York, To Acting Director FBI. Re: Victoria Holmes Garvin. March 22, 1973. Bureau File, Victoria Holmes Garvin, 100-NK-37220, 510.
395. US Congress, *America's Maoists,* 24.
396. Revolutionary Union. *Red Papers 6.* "Build the Leadership of the Proletariat and its Party."
   Reprinted marxists.org.
   http://www.marxists.org/history/erol/ncm-2/rp-6/

section11.htm

397. Email exchange with a former RU cadre February 2014.
398. San Francisco Bay Area Farah Support Committee, "Union Drive in the Southwest: Chicanos Strike at Farah," United Front Press, January 1974.
399. Theoharis, *The FBI: A Comprehensive Reference Guide*, 886.
400. Ibid., 886.
401 Ibid., 887.
402. The NLG sued the FBI in 1977. In 2007, after years of wrangling, the courts ruled such surveillance documents should be turned over to the Guild, with a copy to be housed in New York University's Tamiment Library. Colin Moynihan, "Trove of F.B.I. Files on Lawyers Guild Shows Scope of Secret Surveillance," *New York Times*, June 25, 2007. http://www.nytimes.com/2007/06/25/nyregion/25archives.html?_r=0
403. Memo to Director, FBI, From SAC WFO (134 NEW), 8/24/73. Tamiment Collection, New York University. From the National Lawyers Guild records, TAM.191, Box 205. Folders 11-14.
404. Letter to WFO et al., Re: Revolutionary Union, 2/3/1974. National Lawyers Guild Records, NYU-TAM.191, Box 205, folders 11-14.
405. Sheila Louise O'Connor, handwritten statement, August 30, 1974.4. National Lawyers Guild Records, NYU-TAM.191, Box 205, folders 11-14.
406. Informant Report - undated. 4. National Lawyers Guild Records, NYU- TAM.191, Box 205, folders 11-14.
407. To Director, FBI From SAC WFO, 11/7/1973. 4. National Lawyers Guild Records, NYU- TAM.191, Box 205, folders 11-14.
408. FBI Informant Report 5/23/74. 4. National Lawyers Guild Records, NYU-TAM.191, Box 205, folders 11-14.
409. FBI Informant Report 3/28/1974. 4. National Lawyers

Guild Records, NYU-TAM.191, Box 205, folders 11-14.

410. Report 5/29/1974. 4. National Lawyers Guild Records, NYU-TAM.191, Box 205, folders 11-14.

411. Informant Report 7/16/74. 4. National Lawyers Guild Records, NYU-TAM.191, Box 205, folders 11-14.

412. Informant Report 8/6/1974. National Lawyers Guild Records, NYU-TAM.191, Box 205, folders 11-14.

413. SAC, WFO to Director FBI, 4/16/1975. 4. National Lawyers Guild Records, NYU-TAM.191, Box 205, folders 11-14.

414. SAC, WFO, to Director FBI 3/1/1976. 4. National Lawyers Guild Records, NYU-TAM.191, Box 205, folders 11-14.

415. "1,200 at forum on new party," . *The Guardian,* April 4, 1973.
From marxists.org.
http://www.marxists.org/history/erol/ncm-2/g-forum-1.htm

416. Assastashakur.org "Chronology of Political Events. http//www.assatashakur.org/forum/breaking-down-understanding-our-enemies/1058-chronology-political-events.html

417. "The New Communist Movement: Initial Party-Building Campaigns, 1973-1974."
Reprinted marxists.org.
http://www.marxists.org/history/erol/ncm-2/index.htm#grdforum

418. Informant Report, 8/7/1974. NYU-TAM.191, Box 205, folders 11-14.

419. Black Workers Congress. Manifesto of the Black Workers Congress. 1970. Reprinted marxists.org. http://www.marxists.org/history/erol/ncm-1/bwc-manifesto.htm

420. Dan Georgakas and Marvin Surkin. *Detroit: I Do Mind Dying*. Chicago: Haymarket Books, 2012, 143.

421. Email exchange with former New York RU cadre February 2014 and *Palante! A Brief History of the Young Lords.*

http://libcom.org/library/palante-brief-history-young-lords

422. *The Puerto Rican Revolutionary Workers Organization.* Committee of the Judiciary United States Senate, Subcommittee to Investigate the Administration of Internal Security Act and other Internal Security Laws. James O. Eastland, Chair. March 1976. Washington: US Government Printing Office, 1976. Also *The Guardian,* "YLP Congress transforms party into workers group," July 12, 1972. Reprinted marxists.org. http://www.marxists.org/history/erol/ncm-1/ylp-cong.htm
423. Elbaum, *Revolution in the Air,* 77.
424. Klingel & Psihountas, *Important Struggles.*
425. Hamilton, *RU History, Part II.*
426. Revolutionary Union. *On Building the Party of the U.S. Working Class and the Struggle Against Dogmatism and Reformism.* Speeches by Bob Avakian Member of the Central Committee of the Revolutionary Union. p. 30.
427. Hamilton, *RU History Part II.*
428. Revolutionary Union, *Red Papers 5: National Liberation and Proletarian Revolution in the U.S.*, 1972.
429. D.B., "Marxism, Nationalism and the Task of Party Building History and Lessons of the National Liaison Committee," *The Communist,* Theoretical Journal of the Central Committee of the Revolutionary Communist Party, USA, Vol. 2, No. 1, Fall/Winter 1977. DB being the pen name of Danny Brown, a former SNCC member who later joined the RCP. Brown was part of one of the many post-NLC splits of the BWC, the Revolutionary Workers Congress. Reprinted marxists.org. https://www.marxists.org/history/erol/ncm-2/ru-nlc.htm
430. Revolutionary Union, *Red Papers 6,* "National Bulletin 13," Reprinted marxists.org. http://www.marxists.org/history/

erol/ncm-2/rp-6/section3.htm

431. Avakian, *Ike to Mao*, 227.
432. Chicago SAC to Director, FBI, "Recommendation for Incentive Increase" 1/22/1964, 2-3. Ernie Lazar FOIA Collection: FBI Employee Requests. FBI Employees: Freyman, Carl N.-4. https://ia601805.us.archive.org/20/items/foia_Freyman_Carl_N.-4/Freyman_Carl_N.-4_text.pdf
433. SAC, Chicago to Acting Director, FBI 8/30/1972. SPECTAR Bureau File 100 472365. (Courtesy of Art Eckstein). Herbert K. Stallings, "Summary of Radical Political Thought": "In early December, 1969, Jeff Jones and Bill Ayers met with a Chicago informant a man of 55 who was a leader in a pro-Chinese communist group in Chicago." Given the ambiguous description, this is likely not PLP or RU, and the age of the informant suggests someone acting as a veteran communist. It is also the case that a memo from SAC in San Francisco to Hoover, on November 6, 1970, in Steve Hamilton's Cleveland files, references "AHC informants in Chicago"—further suggesting its continued development. Bureau File 105-184369.
434. Martha Wagner Murphy, Chief, Special Access and FOIA National Archives at College Park, MD, to Conor Gallagher, May 14, 2014.
435. SAC Chicago, to Director, FBI. "Subject: Revolutionary Union," 12/23/1970. David Sullivan U.S. Maoism Collection. TAM.527 Box 23, Folder 6.
436. SAC Chicago, to Director, FBI. 12/3/1970. Freedom of Information and Privacy Acts Subject (COINTELPRO) New Left Chicago Division 1 00-449698-9. Federal Bureau of Investigation. FBI Records: The Vault, vault.fbi.gov.
437. Memorandum to SAC. Signed, Joseph V. Baker, Inspector. Charles W. Bates. Inspection Date 2/26/71. David Sullivan U.S. Maoism Collection. TAM.527 Box 23, Folder 6.

438. Notes on discussion with Leibel Bergman by David Sullivan. David Sullivan U.S. Maoism Collection, TAM.527, Box 8 Folder 45. The notes also indicate that AHC organized the trip to the Middle East by Bergman and Davida Fineman that was subject of the phony Liberation News Service article referred to in Chapter 3. "L. went w/DH + a woman, thru good ILLEGIBLE at AHC... AHC set up his trip."
439. In reviewing the notes with Bergman's son, Lincoln, he felt these notes read to him as genuine, i.e., a communication between the two men—albeit with the limitations of notes vs. a transcript. Email exchange with Lincoln Bergman May 6, 2014.
440. Avakian, *Ike to Mao,* 228.
441. See, for example, *Revolution,* November 1973, Masthead: "For the National Central Committee of the Revolutionary Union: Bob Avakian, Barry Greenberg, Mary Lou Greenberg, DH Wright."
442. Avakian, *Ike to Mao*, 275.
443. "On the Expulsion of D.H. Wright"—RU Internal Bulletin. David Sullivan U.S. Maoism Collection. TAM 527 Box: 23 Folder 4.
444. Sullivan, Bergman notes.
445. Interview with former RU comrade 7/2013. Also Sullivan's Bergman notes make a reference to Wright, "monkeying around with Gloria Fontanez."
446. Notes of Bergman interview and author interviews with two former RU comrades, August and September 2012.
447. Revolutionary Union, "On the Expulsion of D.H. Wright."
448. SAC, Chicago, Director FBI 11/27/1973. Bureau file, Victoria Holmes Garvin file, 100-NK-37220. Document release, 664.
449. SAC, Chicago to Acting Director 1/30/73. David Sullivan U.S. Maoism Collection, TAM.527 Box: 23 Folder 4.

450. SAC, Chicago to Acting Director, FBI 8/30/1972.
451. File Review and Summary Clerk Regina T. Jankowski. Subject Steve Charles Hamilton, December 26, 1972. Bureau File, LA 100-68370. Document release, 52.
452. Ibid.
453. FBI historian, John F. Fox, email exchange with Conor Gallagher, June 3, 2014.
454. Director, FBI to SAC, San Francisco, "Revolutionary Union, aka Red Union, Internal Security - RU". August 29, 1968. Bureau File, Steve Hamilton 100-445639. Document release, 300.
455. Ibid.
456. Revolutionary Union, "On the Expulsion of D.H. Wright."
457. Interview with former RU comrade, May 2012.
458. Sullivan, Bergman notes.
459. Ibid.
460. Ibid.
461. D.B., "Marxism, Nationalism and the Task of Party Building."
462. Van Buskerk, I.C. "Former Provocateur sues FBI," *Guardian,* February 4, 1976. From marxists.org. http://www.marxists.org/history/erol/ncm-2/cousml-6.htm
463. U.S. District Court for the Northern District of Illinois Eastern District. American Civil Liberties Union et al., Plaintiffs v. City of Chicago et. al. Defendants. Joseph A. Burton Affidavit. July 22, 1980. p. 1. David Sullivan Maoism Collection TAM.527, Box 23, folders 5-6.
464. *The People's Tribune.* "Call for A Conference of North American Marxist-Leninists" Vol. 4, No. 11, December-January 1972-73. From marxists.org. http://www.marxists.org/history/erol/ncm-2/call.htm
465. Glick, Brian. *WAR AT HOME: Covert Action Against U.S. Activists and What We Can Do About It.* Boston: South End

Press. 1999, 28.

466. SAC New Orleans, to Director FBI, 12/21/73. "Revolutionary Union IS-RU" cc: Chicago. Schafer Bureau File 100-HQ-471704. Document release, 2.
467. SAC New Orleans, to Director, FBI 12/21/73. "Red Collective (RC) IS" Schafer Bureau File 100-HQ-471704. Document release, 1.
468. Director, FBI to SAC New Orleans, 11/15/73. "Revolutionary Union IS-RU" cc: Chicago. Schafer Bureau File 100-HQ-471704. Document release, 3.
469. Jack Davis, "Orleans couple: 'extremists' for the FBI...," *States-Item,* New Orleans, March 6, 1975.
470. Burton Affidavit, 2-3.
471. John M. Crewdson, "Ex-Operative Says He Worked for F.B.I. to Disrupt Political Activities Up to '74," *The New York Times,* February 24, 1975.
472. Van Buskerk, "Former Provocateur sues FBI."
473. Burton Affidavit, 3.
474. Hamilton, *RU History, Part II.*
475. Burton Affidavit, 3.
476. See, "The Reactionary Line of the Communist League," *Revolution* Vol. 2. No. 6, CL 1, July 1974. "CL Covers for the Social Imperialist, Portray U.S. Imperialism on the Rise," *Revolution*. Vol. 2. No. 6. July 1974. "Growing Tired of OL's Childish Antics," *Revolution* Vol. 2. No. 6. July 1974, p.4. "The October League (M-L): A Cover for Revisionism," *Revolution* August 1974, Vol. 2. No. 7 p.11. "The Desperate OL Concocts Lurid Tales. *Revolution,*" *Revolution* Vol. 2 No. 11, December 1974. "The Guardian: Rushing Headlong Into the Swamp," *Revolution* Vol. 3. No. 2. March 1975. "Carl Davidson: Creature from The 'White Skin Privilege' Lagoon," *Revolution* Vol. 3. No. 2. March 1975. "Narrow Nationalism: Main Deviation in the Movement On the National Question," *Revolution* Vol. 2.

No. 10. November 1974.

477. *HGSE News.* "Busing in Boston: Looking Back at the History and Legacy," Harvard Graduate School of Education. September 1, 2000. http://www.gse.harvard.edu/news/features/busing09012000_page3.html
478. "People Must Unite to Smash the Boston Busing Plan," *Revolution,* October 1974.
479. Revolutionary Union, "Class Stand Key in Boston Busing Struggle," *Forward to the Party! Struggle for the Party!,* No. 1. From marxists.org. http://www.marxists.org/history/erol/ncm-3/ru-boston.htm
480. "Boston Busing Struggle Sharpens," *Revolution.* Vol. 2, No. 10, November 1974.
481. Robert J. Anglin, "Boston schools desegregated. First day generally peaceful. Some incidents, widest boycott in South Boston," *Boston Globe,* September 13, 1974.
482. Avakian, *Ike to Mao,* 384.
483. Mike Ely, *Ambush at Keystone: Inside the Coalminers' Gas Protest,* Kasmaproject.org. July 26, 2009. PDF Pamphlet, 21. http://kasamaproject.org/history/1515-47ambush-at-keystone-inside-the-coalminers-gas-protest
484. Victor Riesel, "Revolutionary Union Building Activist Marxists Cadres," *Rome News Tribune,* May 14, 1976.
485. Ely, *Ambush at Keyston*e, 4.
486. Ibid.
487. Patricia Sullivan, "War Resister Oliver Hirsch; Was Among 'Nine for Peace.'" *Washington Post,* January 20, 2007.
488. SAC Seattle To Director FBI. "Re: Oliver Vincent Hirsch," 10/10/1974. Case File 100-HQ-480681. Document release, 5.
489. Jim Green, "Holding the Line: Miners' Militancy and the Strike of 1978," *Radical America,* Vol. 12. No. 3.
490. Ely, "Ambush at *Keystone,*" 12.
491. Ibid., 10.

492. David Winder, "Far-right upsurge seen in pressure on schools: Educational groups says..." *The Christian Science Monitor,* April 9, 1975.
493. Mike Ely, "Memories of the 1974 West Virginia Textbook Protest," April 30, 2010, Humanities and Social Sciences Online. http://h-net.msu.edu/cgi-bin/logbrowse.pl?trx=vx&list=H-1960s&month=1004&week=e&msg=O%2BkPGrkC39FUY1Yfw2yamA
494. Curtis Seltzer, "Two Miners, Two Reporters Jailed in W.Va. Coal Strike," *Washington Post,* September 9, 1975.
495. "Judge Jails Strike Leaders: Most Miners Go Back on the Job," UPI, *The Berkshire Eagle,* September 9, 1975.
496. Ben A. Franklin, "Activities of Maoists Revive 'Red-Baiting' In Coalfields: 50 to 10 Organizers from Splinter Group Are Blamed for Turmoil in Mines," *New York Times,* November 25, 1977.
497. Curtis Setzer, *Fire in the Hole: Miners and Managers in the American Coal Industry,* Kentucky: University Press of Kentucky, 1985. 154.
498. Former RU cadre, email correspondence March 2014.
499. Ely, *Keystone,* 11.
500. Baker, *Winnipeg Free Press.* December 1970.
501. Victor Riesel, "Outlaw Strikes," *Indiana Evening Gazette.* September 11, 1975.
502. US Senate. *US Intelligence and the Rights of Americans. Book II.* "Final Report on the Select Committee to Study Governmental Operation with Respect to Intelligence Activities. Together With Supplemental and Separate Views," April 26 (Legislative day, April 14) 1976, US Government Printing Office, Washington 1976. p. 243. http://www.intelligence.senate.gov/pdfs94th/94755_II.pdf
503. Van Gelder, "Victor Riesel, 81, Columnist Blinded by Acid Attack, Dies," *New York Times,* January 05, 1995.

504. See, for example, Victor Navasky, *Naming Names: With a New Afterword by the Author*. Hill and Wang, 2003, 52 and Barranger, Milly S. *Unfriendly Witnesses: Gender, Theater and Film in the McCarthy Era.* Carbondale: Southern Illinois University Press; 2008, 30.
505. See Hugh Sidey, "This is the White House Calling," *Life*, April 2, 1970, 28 and Kiron Skinner, Annelise Anderson, and Martin Anderson, eds., *Reagan, In His Own Hand: The Writings of Ronald Reagan that Reveal His Revolutionary Vision for America,* New York: Free Press, 2011, 246.
506. Cartha D. DeLoach to Victor Riesel, January 4, 1965, Victor Riesel Papers, Tamiment Library and Robert F. Wagner Archives. NYU-TAM.170. Box 11, Folder 5.
507. J. Edgar Hoover to V. Riesel, March 19, 1965, Victor Riesel Papers, NYU-TAM.170. Box 11, Folder 5.
508. J. Edgar Hoover to Riesel, May 27, 1968, Victor Riesel Papers, NYU-TAM.170. Box 11, Folder 5.
509. Clarence Kelly to Victor Riesel, January 15, 1974, Victor Riesel Papers, NYU- TAM.170 Box 11, Folder 5.
510. William Webster to Victor Riesel, June 19, 1978, Victor Riesel Papers, NYU-TAM.170. Box 11, Folder 6.
511. Gerald Fraser, "FBI's Files Reveal Moves Against Black Panthers," *New York Times,* October 19, 1980.
512. Thomas E. Bishop to Victor Riesel, January 25, 1972, David Sullivan U.S. Maoism Collection. NYU-TAM.170, Box 11, Folder 5.
513. Ibid.
514. Thomas E. Bishop to Victor Riesel, June 9, 1969, David Sullivan U.S. Maoism Collection, NYU-TAM.170, Box 11, Folder 5.
515. Ibid.
516. R.D. Cotter to W.C. Sullivan, May 28, 1969, Victor Riesel-FBI file.
517. Victor Riesel, "Some still confuse treason with dissent

and are silent," *Alton Evening News,* October 22, 1971.

518. Victor Riesel, "Revolutionary Union Building Activist Marxists," *Rome News Tribune,* May 14, 1976.
519. Ibid.
520. Victor Riesel, "Castro's Faithful," *Indiana Evening Gazette,* March 3, 1978.
521. Seth Rosenfeld, *Subversives: The FBI's War on Student Radicals, and Reagan's Rise to Power.* New York: Farrar, Straus and Giroux, 85.
522. Testimony of Edward S. Montgomery of *San Francisco Examiner* on June 27, 1968. House Committee on Un-American Activities investigation of *Subversive Influences in Riots, Looting and* Looting, and Burning, pt. 6. Cited in *America's Maoists*, 8.
523. Ed Montgomery, "Leftists Lift Lid on Revolutionary Plans," *San Francisco Examiner,* March 9, 1969.
524. Herb Borock, "Who Really Fired Bruce Franklin," April Third Movement website. http://a3m2009.org/archive/1971-1972/71-72_franklin_fbi/1971-1972_fbi.html
525. SAC, San Francisco, to Director, FBI, "Revolutionary Union (RU) IS-RU" 4/21/1969, David Sullivan U.S. Maoism Collection, Tamiment, TAM.527. Box 23, Folder 5-6.
526. Director, FBI to SAC San Francisco Subject: Revolutionary Union (RU) IS-RU (Nationalities Intelligence) ResFairtel 4/21/69. Letter Date 5/2/69. Bureau File, Steve Hamilton 100-445639. Document release, 88.
527. Rosenfeld, *Subversives*, 214.
528. Matthew Hurd, Attorney Advisor, Administrative Appeals Staff, USDOJ, Office of Information Policy, to Conner Gallagher, September 26, 2013.
529. Director FBI, to SAC San Francisco, "Revolutionary Union," 5/2/1969. Bureau File, Steve Hamilton 100-445639. Document release, 88.

530. Revolutionary Union, *Build the Anti-imperialist Student Movement,* pamphlet. 1972.
531. Revolutionary Student Brigade, "A Short History of the Brigade: 3 Years of Struggle on the Road to a National Student Organization," From marxists.org. http://www.marxists.org/history/erol/ncm-1/rsb/doc2.htm
532. *Columbia Summer Spectator,* "200 Attend Regional Meeting Of Attica Brigade on Campus," June 14, 1973.
533. *Revolution,* "Students Get it on at Nat'l Convention," July 1974.
534. Ibid.
535. Ibid.
536. Vietnam Veterans Against the War, Inc. National Office, VVAW History, vvaw.org.
537. Camile, Scott. Winter Soldier Investigation Testimony given in Detroit, Michigan, on January 31, 1971, February 1 and 2, 1971. http://www2.iath.virginia.edu/sixties/HTML_docs/Resources/Primary/Winter_Soldier/WS_03_1Marine.html
538. John Kerry and Vietnam Veterans Against the War, *The New Soldier.* New York: Collier Books. October 1971.
539. VVAW History.
540. Internal RU report on VVAW, Leibel Bergman's papers.
541. FBI Report: January 7, 1975 Bureau VVAW File, HQ 100-448092, Section 70, 383. Accessed from wintersoldier.com, Complete VVAW FBI files. http://www.wintersoldier.com/index.php?topic=VVAWFBI
542. Ibid., 384-85.
543. Ibid.
544. ADEX, or Administrative Index, was the renamed iteration of the former Security Index. "CUSTODIAL DETENTION SECURITY INDEX," FBI File: 100-358086. See FBI Records: The Vault, Custodial Detention Security

Index. http://vault.fbi.gov/custodial-detention-security-index/section-1/view

545. FBI Report: Chicago Field Office, October 29, 1975, Bureau VVAW File. HQ 100-448092. Section 70, p. 383. Accessed from wintersoldier.com, Complete VVAW FBI files. Section 75, p. 49. http://www.wintersoldier.com/index.php?topic=VVAWFBI
546. Andrew E. Hunt, *The Turning: A History of Vietnam Veterans Against the War.* New York: NYU Press, 1999, 183.
547. Gerald Nicosia, *Home to War: A History of the Vietnam Veterans Movement*. New York: Crown, 2001, 227.
548. Ibid.
549. *Progressive Labor Party.* "Hearings Before the Committee On Internal Security House of Representatives Ninety-Second Congress," First Session, April 13,14 and November 18, 1971. Washington: US Government Printing Office, 1972, 4052.
550. Ibid., 4054.
551. J. Edgar Hoover, "'Mao's Red Shadow': The article that Hoover refused to reprint," *Boston Globe.* August 18, 1971, 17.
552. Ibid.
553. Challenge Editorial: "Workers Will Smash Nixon-Mao/Chou Axis," First Published: *Challenge.* Reprinted: *Progressive Labor,* Vol. 8, No 3, November 1971.
From marxists.org. http://www.marxists.org/history/erol/1960-1970/pl-nixon-mao.htm
554. House Internal Security Committee, *Progressive Labor Party*, 4127.
555. "Maoist Drive in the U.S. Reported by the FBI," *New York Times,* December 12, 1972.
556. Hoover, "Mao's Red Shadow."
557. *Programme of the Revolutionary Communist Party USA.* Reprinted marxists.org Encyclopedia of Anti Revisionism

On-Line. http://www.marxists.org/history/erol/ncm-3/rcp-program/chapter2.htm

558. *RCP Programme,* "The United Front: United All Who Can Be United to Defeat the Real Enemy."
559. *RCP Programme,* "The Emancipation of Women and Proletarian Revolution Cannot Be Separated."
560. *RCP Programme,* "Life Under Socialism."
561. Ibid.
562. "Position Paper of the Revolutionary Union on Homosexuality and Gay Liberation," David Sullivan U.S. Maoism Collection NYU-TAM.527 Box 1 folder 26.
563. Ibid.
564. Seth Rosenfeld, "Anti-war activist Steve Hamilton dies," *San Francisco Chronicle.* March 20, 2009.
565. SAC, Chicago, Director FBI 11/27/1973.
566. Hamilton, *RU History, Part II.*
567. Asian American 1968. Reprint of the handout "What is Wei Min Shei," December 14, 2007. aamblogspot.com. http://aam1968.blogspot.com/search/label/Wei%20Min%20She
568. Wei Min She. Reprinted, description from marxists.org Encyclopedia of Anti Revisionism On-Line. http://www.marxists.org/history/erol/ncm-1a/index.htm#wms
569. *Stand Up: An Archive Collection of the Bay Area Asian American Movement 1968-1974,* Asian Community Center Archive Group. Berkeley: Eastwind Books, 2009, 97.
570. Fred Ho, ed., *Legacy to Liberation: Politics and Culture of Revolutionary Asian Pacific America*. Steve Yip. "Serve the People—Yesterday and Today: The Legacy of Wei Min She." Chicago: Haymarket Books, 2006, 24.
571. Ibid., 16.
572. Wei Min She Appendix—Proposal to WMS By The RCP (reprint from RCP document) David Sullivan US Maoism Collection, TAM.527.
573. Ibid.

574. *Stand Up*, 102.
575. Cicero Estrella, "The I-Hotel rises again / Nearly 26 years later, rebuilt digs offer seniors rooms with a view," *San Francisco Chronicle.* July 22, 2005.
576. US China Peoples Friendship Association, uscpfa.org. http://www.uscpfa.org/whatis.html
577. *US China Review*, Fall 2012. "Remarks by USCPFA Diana Greer," Vol. XXXVI, No. 4. also see C. Clark Kissinger's web page. http://www.dissident.info/.
578. "Aims of the U.S. China Peoples Friendship Association," August-September 1971. The New York Public Library, Humanities and Social Sciences Library Manuscripts and Archives Division US China Peoples Friendship Association Records 1974-2000. MssCol 6176.
579. SAC Newark, To Director, FBI, "Subject: Leibel Bergman, External Security" October 20, 1972. Bureau file, Victoria Holmes Garvin file, 100-NK-37220, 445.
580. New York FBI, Agent [Name redacted]. Report on Victoria Holmes Garvin. September 8, 1975, Appendix Page 7 "US China Peoples Friendship Association," Bureau file, Victoria Holmes Garvin file, 100-NK-37220. Document release, 682.
581. Felt-Miller transcript, 4003.
582. *Peking Review,* Vol. 17, #6, February 8, 1974, 12-16.
583. Revolutionary Union, *How Capitalism Has Been Restored in the Soviet Union, and What This Means for the World Struggle,* Revolutionary Union, 1974, 103.
584. Ibid., 22.
585. Ibid., 2.
586. Though as late as 1972, the RU had uncritically promoted and defended China's foreign policy. See Revolutionary Union, *China's Foreign Policy: A Leninist Policy.* February 1972. From marxists..org Encyclopedia of Anti Revisionism On-Line. http://www.marxists.org/history/erol/ncm-1/

china-foreign.htm

587. Elbaum. *Revolution in the Air*, 220.

588. See, for example, "The Two Hegemonist Powers, the Soviet Union and the United States, Are the Common Enemies of the People of the World; the Soviet Union is the Most Dangerous Source of World War," and "Chairman Mao's Theory of the Differentiation of the Three Worlds is a Major Contribution to Marxism-Leninism."
http://www.marxists.org/history/erol/ncm-5/theory-3-worlds/section2.htm.
Also "On the Question of the Differentiation of the Three Worlds," Mao Zedong in Conversation with President Kenneth Kaunda of Zambia. china.or.cn.
http://www.china.org.cn/china/military/2007-07/30/content_1219042.htm

589. See for example William Joseph, "China's Relations with Chile under Allende: A Case Study of Chinese Foreign Policy in transition," *Studies in Comparative Communism* Vol. XVIII, No. 2/3, Summer/Autumn, 1985, 125-150.

590. See, for example, "China woos Mrs. Marcos," *Sydney Morning Herald.* September 23, 1974.

591. "RCP, Guardian, Hinton 'Debate': 3-Ring Circus Protects Superpowers," *The Call,* Vol. 5, No. 24, October 18, 1976.
http://www.marxists.org/history/erol/ncm-3/call-rcp-conf-3.htm
And "RCP's International Conference: Chorus Against China and Support for the Superpowers," *The Call,* Vol. 5, No. 31, December 6, 1976. From, marxists.org Encyclopedia of Anti Revisionism On-Line.
http://www.marxists.org/history/erol/ncm-3/call-rcp-conf-2.htm

592. Wayne Barrett, *Rudy: An Investigative Biography of Rudy Giuliani.* New York: Basic Books. 2000, 93.

593. "Threats to the Peaceful Observance of the Bicentennial,"

Hearing Before the Subcommittee to Investigate the Administration of the Internal Security Act and Other Internal Security Laws of the Committee on the Judiciary, United States Ninety-Fourth Congress. Second Session, June 18, 1976. Washington: US Government Printing Office, 1976, 24.

594. Ibid., 40
595. Dennis Hevesi, "Frank Rizzo of Philadelphia Dies at 70; A 'Hero' and 'Villain,'" *New York Times,* July 17, 1991.
596. Frank Donner, *Protectors of the Privilege: Red Squads and Police Repression in Urban America.* Berkeley: University of California Press, 1990, 221.
597. US Congress, *America's Maoists,* 171-172.
598. "Young Canadian to Be Deported," *Gettysburg Times,* April 7, 1971.
599. 479 F.2d 569 William P. Biggin, Petitioner, v. Immigration and Naturalization Service. Respondent. No. 72-1120. United States Court of Appeals, Third Circuit. Argued February 13, 1973. Decided May 23, 1973.
600. Len Lear, "July 4 Group Challenges Rizzo To Debate; Calls Mayor 'Liar,'" *Philadelphia Tribune,* June 22, 1976.
601. "Police Enter Permit Issue," *Observer Report.* Washington, PA. June 30, 1976.
602. Len Lear, "Poor Urged to Unite To Perfect Needed Changes," *Philadelphia Tribune.* July 10, 1976, and, "RCP draws 3500 to rally," *The Guardian,* July 14, 1976.
603. *The Worker for Hawaii,* "Unemployed Organize in Hawaii: 'We Won't Scab and We Won't Starve!'", Vol. 1, No. 3, December 1975. From marxists.org Encyclopedia of Anti Revisionism On-Line. http://www.marxists.org/history/erol/ncm-3/rcp-unemployed.htm
604. "Gert Alexander: A Great Loss, A Great Example," *The Milwaukee Worker,* May 1976.
605. Mat Callahan, "Prairie Fire: Rock Maoists," *Bad Subjects,*

Issue #56, Summer 2001. http://bad.eserver.org/issues/2001/56/callahan.html

606. Bob Avakian, "Revolutionary Communist Party Speech July 4th," *The Worker,* for Hawaii, Vol. 1, No. 10, July-August 1976. From marxists.org. Encyclopedia of Anti Revisionism On-Line. http://www.marxists.org/history/erol/ncm-3/rcp-july-4th-avakian.htm
607. FBI, Chicago Illinois, "Revolutionary Communist Party," September 6, 1976. David Sullivan U.S. Maoism Collection, NYU-TAM.527, Box 23 Folders 5-6.
608. Ibid.
609. Conor Gallagher notes on FOIA submissions, returns and pending applications.
610. SAC Cleveland to Director, FBI. 8/1/1969. New Left, Cleveland Division. Bureau file, 100-449698-11.
611. National Workers Organization, *The Worker for Milwaukee Area and Wisconsin.* August 1977 Vol. 2. No. 11.
612. "Founding Convention A Success: National Workers Organization Formed," *The Veteran,* Vietnam Veterans Against the War. November 1977, Vol. 7, Number 5. http://www.vvaw.org/veteran/article/?id=2255
613. Revolutionary Workers' Headquarters. *Red Papers 8: China Advances on the Socialist Road: The Gang of Four, Revolution in the US, and the Split in the Revolutionary Communist Party*. "Campaign To Build A National United Workers Organization." http://www.marxists.org/history/erol/ncm-5/rp-8/campaign.htm
614. *The Veteran*, "Founding Convention a Success."
615. HUAC Investigation. The Northern California District of the Communist Party, 2012.
616. "RCP Speech to NUWO Convention," *Revolution*, Vol. 3, No 1, October 1977.
617. "Proclamation: From the National United Workers

Organization to the Workers of America," *Revolution* October 1977.

618. "Revolutionary Communist Youth Brigade Founded," *Revolution*. Vol.3, No. 3 November 1977, 1.
619. Ibid.
620. SAC Chicago, to Director FBI 11/27/1973. FBI Victoria Holmes Garvin, File,100-HQ-379895. Document release, 662.
621. "Revisionists Are Revisionists And Must Not Be Supported, Revolutionaries Are Revolutionaries and Must Be Supported," Report on China by Bob Avakian, Chairman of the Central Committee of the Revolutionary Communist Party, USA, Adopted by the 3rd Plenary of the 1st Central Committee of the RCP, USA (1977), Affirmed and Adopted by the 2nd Congress of the RCP, USA (1978). Reprinted in Revolutionary Communist Party. *Communism and Revolution Vs. Revisionism and Reformism in the Struggle to Build the Revolutionary Communist Youth Brigade.* 1978. From marxists.org Encyclopedia of Anti Revisionism On-Line. http://www.marxists.org/history/erol/ncm-5/rcp-youth/index.htm
622. James Strebra, "Successor of Mao Replaced in Peking as Party Chairman," *New York Times,* June 30, 1981.
623. Constitution of the Revolutionary Communist Party, 1975. Taken from marxists.org Encyclopedia of Anti Revisionism On-Line. http://www.marxists.org/history/erol/ncm-3/rcp-program/constitution.htm
624. *Red Papers 8: China Advances on the Socialist Road: The Gang of Four, Revolution in the US, and the Split in the Revolutionary Communist Party. "Rush to Judgement,"* Revolutionary Workers Headquarters. Taken from marxists.org Encyclopedia of Anti Revisionism On-Line. http://www.marxists.org/history/erol/ncm-5/rp-8/rush.htm

625. Avakian, *Ike to Mao*, 342.
626. Notes from a presentation by Leibel Bergman—Leibel Bergman's papers.
627. Avakian, *Ike to Mao,* 351.
628. Bob Avakian, *Revolution and Counter Revolution in China.* Chicago: RCP Publications, 1978, 3.
629. RWH, *Red Papers 8: China Advances on the Socialist Road.*
630. SAC Chicago, to Director FBI 11/27/1973. Victoria Holmes Garvin FBI file 100-HQ-379895. Document release, 663.
631. Bergman notes.
632. RCP, *Revolution and Counter Revolution,* 95.
633. For an extensive examination of this period, see Fredrick Teiwes and Warren Sun, *The End of the Maoist Era: Chinese Politics During the Twilight of the Cultural Revolution, 1972-1976*. New York: M.E. Sharpe, Jan 1, 2007. "The Purge of the Gang of Four," 536-594.
634. RWH, *Red Papers 8: China Advances on the Socialist Road,* "Rush to Judgement."
635. Avakian, *Ike to Mao,* 351.
636. It's Right to Rebel—N.Y. - N.J. District Committee. David Sullivan US Maoism Collection, Tamiment Archives. TAM.527 Box 2, Folder 42.
637. Ibid.
638. Avakian, *Ike to Mao,* 357.
639. From the Central Committee and the Regional and District Leadership Under Its Authority—David Sullivan U.S. Maoism Collection, Tamiment Archives. TAM.527 Box 2 Folder 11.
640. RCP, *Revolution and Counter-Revolution*, 139-140.
641. Interviews with two former RU/RCP comrades—on opposite ends of the schism—spring and summer 2013.
642. Author interview with former Central Committee member, July 2012.
643. Avakian, *Ike to Mao*, 328.

644. *Revolution,* "Party Speech at RCYB Convention." Quote is of Bill Klingel. Vol. 3, No. 9, July 1978. From marxists.org. https://www.marxists.org/history/erol/ncm-5/rcyb-speech.htm
645. RCP, *Revolution and Counter Revolution,* "Rectification is Fine; The Mensheviks' Answer is Terrible,"
RCP Reply to Mensheviks on Rectification Adopted by the 2nd Congress of the RCP, 1978. Taken from marxists.org Encyclopedia of Anti Revisionism On-Line.
http://www.marxists.org/history/erol/ncm-5/rcp-split/rectification-is-fine.htm
646. RWH, *Red Papers 8: China Advanceson the Socialist Road.* http://www.marxists.org/history/erol/ncm-5/rp-8/introduction.htm
647. RCP, *Revolution and Counter-Revolution*, 140-141.
648. "Brief Political History of Leibel Bergman," RCP internal document. David Sullivan US Maoism Collection. NYU-TAM.527, Box 2 Folder 5.
649. *Revolution,* "Party Routs Revisionist Clique: The High Road vs. The Well-Worn Rut," Vol. 3, No. 7-8, April-May 1978. http://www.marxists.org/history/erol/ncm-5/rcp-ro ut.htm
650. Ibid.
651. Avakian, *Ike to Mao,* 188.
652. Bergman Papers.
653. Ibid.
654. Ibid.
655. "Membership Report for National Conference, September 1978," US China Peoples Friendship Association Records 1974-2000. Mss Col 6176. The New York Public Library, Humanities and Social Sciences Library Manuscripts and Archives Division.
656. "Minutes of the National Steering Committee Meeting, USCPFA, Miami Florida, June 10, 11, 1978," US China

Peoples Friendship Association Records 1974-2000. MssCol 6176. The New York Public Library, Humanities and Social Sciences Library Manuscripts and Archives Division.

657. "Convention in San Francisco: Struggle Over "Gang of 5" Hits USCPFA." *Revolution,* Vol. 3, No. 13, October 1978.
658. Ibid.
659. Author witness.
660. Fred Pincus, "RCP Disrupts China friendship meet," *The Guardian.* September 20, 1978.
661. Ibid.
662. Revolutionary Communist Party, *Communism and Revolution Vs. Revisionism and Reformism in the Struggle to Build the Revolutionary Communist Youth Brigade,* 1978. Reprinted marxists.org. http://www.marxists.org/history/erol/ncm-5/rcp-youth/index.htm
663. RCP, *Revolution and Counter Revolution,* 140.
664. Andrew E. Hunt, *The Turning: A History of Vietnam Veterans Against the War.* New York: NYU Press, 2001, 386-87.
665. VVAW Website, "Beware of VVAW AI." www.vvaw.org/about/vvawai.php%5D
666. SAC New York, (105-100707), To Director, FBI, 1/30/1975.
667. FBI correspondence to Conor Gallagher, 9/20/2013.
668. *Revolution,* "CPML Caught in Dilemma: How to Attack Mao While Pretending to Uphold Him," Vol. 3, No. 13, October 1978. Reprinted marxists.org. http://www.marxists.org/history/erol/ncm-5/cpml-caught.htm
669. David Johnston, "Mao's Virtues Extolled: The Great Poster War Rages in Chinatown," *Los Angeles Times,,* September 9, 1978.
670. Bob Avakian, *The Loss in China and The Revolutionary Legacy Of Mao Tsetung: Speech by Bob Avakian, Chairman of the Central Committee of the Revolutionary Communist*

Party, USA Delivered at the Mao Tsetung Memorial Meetings. Chicago: RCP Publications, September 1978. Introduction.

671. RCP, *Revolution and Counter Revolution,* 129.
672. See, Avakian, Bob, *Mao's Immortal Contributions,* RCP Publication, 1979, and Bob Avakian, "Conquer the World, The Proletariat Must and Will," *Revolution* #50, Fall, 1981.
673. "Scores Arrested, Injured in May Day Violence," UPI. *The Pharos Tribune,* Logansport Indiana. May 2, 1980.
674. "Attack China's Office in U.S. to Protest Teng Visit," *Los Angeles Times,* January 25, 1979.
675. Christopher Dickey, "Park, D.C. Police Gird For Teng Visit Violence," *Washington Post,* January 26, 1979.
676. "Spectre of Mao on White House Lawn: 'I Waved the Red Book Teng Hsiao-Ping's Face.'" *Revolutionary Worker,* "Special National Edition," February 1979. Reprinted on marxists.org. https://www.marxists.org/history/erol/ncm-5/waved.htm
677. "Shouting at Carter, Teng Ruled No Crime," *Orange County Register,* May 3, 1979.
678. Bob Avakian, "Storms Are Gathering. Carry the Red Flag Forward," *Revolutionary Worker: Special National Edition,* February 1979. Reprinted on marxists.org. http://www.marxists.org/history/erol/ncm-5/avakian-speech.htm
679. Avakian, *Loss in China,* 124.
680. "D.C. Court Orders $10,000 Bonds on Maoist Rioters; D.C. Judge Cracks Down on 70 Arrested Maoists," *Washington Post,* January 31, 1979.
681. "Traitor Teng Given Fitting Welcome," *Revolutionary Worker,* Special National Edition, February 1979. Reprinted on marxists.org. http://marxists.org/history/erol/ncm-5/teng.htm
682. Paul W. Valentine, and Christopher Dickey, "Violence Flares Briefly in Day of Varied Protests," *Washington Post,* January 30, 1979.

683. Joseph, D. Whitaker, "Most of 70 Protestors Freed But Avakian Remains in Jail," *Washington Post,* February 1, 1979.
684. *Revolutionary Worker,* February 1979, Special Edition.
685. Ibid.
686. Avakian, *Ike to Mao*, 364.
687. Mao Tse-tung, "Talk At A Meeting Of The Central Cultural Revolution Group," *Selected Works of Mao Tse-tung*, January 9, 1967. Reprinted marxists.org. http://www.marxists.org/reference/archive/mao/selected-works/volume-9/mswv9_71.htm
688. V.I. Lenin, *What Is To Be Done? Burning Questions of our Movement.* Reprinted marxists.org. http://www.marxists.org/archive/lenin/works/1901/witbd/iii.htm
689. Bob Avakian, "The Basis, The Goals, and The Methods of The Communist Revolution," *Revolution*, revcom.us. http://revcom.us/avakian/basis-goals-methods/
690. G.V. Plekhanov, "On the Role of the Individual in History," First published: Nauchnoye Obrozhniye, Nos. 3 & 4, 1898. Source: Selected Works of G.V. Plekhanov, Volume II. Reprinted marxists.org. http://www.marxists.org/archive/plekhanov/1898/xx/individual.html
691. Avakian, *Ike to Mao*, 393.
692. Of note in this respect, reflecting on the relatively quick demise of the Revolutionary Workers Headquarters, two former comrades, who parted with the RCP after the split, affirmed Avakian's leadership role (while also opposing) was key to the RCP's continuation, while the RWHq did not have an equivalent force. Author interview with former comrades, summer 2012.
693. Athan G. Theoharis, "Symposium: National Security and Civil Liberties: FBI Surveillance, Past and Present," *Cornell Law Review*, April, 1984. 69, 883. LexisNexis *Academic.*

Accessed: Monday, September 09, 2013.

694. Joseph D. Whitaker and Paul W. Valentine, "17 Maoists Freed By D.C. Judge; Judges Releases Maoists; U.S. 'Vendetta' Charged; Charges of Assault And Rioting During Deng Visit Dismissed," *Washington Post,* November 17, 1979.

695. Joe Pichirallo, "Court Reinstates Charges Against Maoist Protestors," *Washington Post,* October 22, 1980.

696. Hamilton, *RU History, Part II.*

697. "May Day Brigade Held Hostage in Youngstown," *Revolutionary Worker,* February 15, 1980.

698. *Revolutionary Work*er, March 7, 1979.

699. West Virginia Code - §61-1-6.—Display of red or black flag unlawful. "It shall be unlawful for any person to have in his possession or to display any red or black flag, or to display any other flag, emblem, device or sign of any nature whatever, indicating sympathy with or support of ideals, institutions or forms of government, hostile, inimical or antagonistic to the form or spirit of the constitution, laws, ideals and institutions of this state or of the United States." http://law.justia.com/codes/west-virginia/2005/61/wvc61-1-6.html
The law was repealed in 2010, by the 81st West Virginia Legislature. State Legislature of West Virginia Website. http://www.legis.state.wv.us/wvcode/ChapterEntire.cfm?chap=61

700. Mike Ely, "RCP: On Farragos, May Day 1980 and the Echoes Today," *Kasama Project,* April 4, 2008. Reprinted on marxists.org. http://www.marxists.org/history/erol/ncm-5/ely.htm

701. Justin Robert Goldstein, "The Revolutionary Communist Party and Flag Burning During Its Forgotten Years, 1979–1989," *Raven: A Journal of Vexillology,* Number: 6 (1999), 38.

702. *Revolutionary Worker* online, "More About Bob Avakian"

revcom.us.
http://revcom.us/avakian/ba-more-about-bob-avakian-en.html

703. "Tip of Secret Service Iceberg," *Revolutionary Worker,* March 21, 1980.
704. "They're Not Playing—and Neither Are We!" *Revolutionary Worker,* March 28, 1980.
705. Ely, "On Farragos."
706. Author/witness.
707. Ely, "On Farragos."
708. "Prosecutors drop charges of flag desecration against 3 activists," *New York Times,* March 30, 1980.
709 "4 More Communists Convicted for 'Occupation' of the Alamo," *New York Times,* June 22, 1980
710. "The Bloody Hand of the Pig," *Revolutionary Worker,* April 25, 1980.
711. David Morgan, *Shooting the Arrow / Stroking the Arrow,* Ph.D. Thesis—University of Newcastle upon Tyne, School of English Literature, Language and Linguistics, 2010, 27. http://hdl.handle.net/10443/934
712. Ibid.
713. Roger Smith and Henry Mendoza, "Was Garcia a Gang Victim or Martyr to the Revolution," *Los Angeles Times,* April 24, 1980.
714. *Revolutionary Worker,* "The Bloody Hand of the Pig."
715. Smith, "Was Garcia a Gang Victim or Martyr to the Revolution."
716. David Johnston, "Use of Special Prosecutor in Spy Case Urged: Revolutionaries Want Probe of LAPD Undercover," *Los Angeles Times*, December 12, 1982.
717. Ibid.
718. Ibid.
719. Roger Smith, "Killer of Communist Also Believed Slain; Fatally Stabbed 3 Weeks Ago, Police Told," *Los Angeles*

Times, June 25, 1980.

720. Johnston, "Use of Special Prosecutor."
721. "The Hounding of Hayden Fisher," *Revolutionary Worker,* January 21, 1983.
722. "May 1st: Revolution and Internationalism," "Damián was assassinated by police agents in Los Angeles while building for May Day," *Revolution,* May 1, 2013, revcom. us. http://www.revcom.us/a/302/may-1st-revolution-and-internationalism-en.html
723. Avakian, *Ike to Mao,* 408.
724. "PDID officer Fabian Lizarraga—the pig who was standing five feet from Damián García when he was murdered in East L.A," "A Spy Story," *Revolutionary Worker,* January 28, 1983, 12.
725. "García was murdered while building for May 1st, 1980 in an L.A. housing project, as a police agent stood nearby." "Damián García ¡Presente!" *Revolution,* April 21, 2014. revcom.us. http://www.revcom.us/a/337/damian-garcia-presente-en.html

     "*It later came out that an undercover pig of the Los Angeles Police Department was on the spot when the assassination went down.*"[italics in original] "A Reflection on Piggery—Then and Now," *Revolution* #264, April 1, 2012, revcom.us. http://www.revcom.us/a/264/a-reflection-on-piggery-then-and-now-en.html
726. Paul DeRienzo, "McDonald's Private Spies," *Overthrow,* December 1983.
727. "The White House Crisis: The Tower Commission's Report, Appendix C: The N.S.C. Staff and the Contras," *New York Times,* February 27, 1987.
728. Joel Sappel, "Detective in Spying Case Linked to Birch Leader," *The Los Angeles Times,* May 24, 1983.
729. Ben Jacklet, "The Secret Watchers," *Portland Tribune,* September 12, 2002. http://portlandtribune.com/compone

nt/content/article?id=117580

730. Office of the City Auditor, Portland Oregon. Police - Historical/Archival - Police Historical/Archival Investigative Files - Revolutionary Communist Party. http://efiles.portlandoregon.gov/webdrawer.dll/webdrawer/search/rec&sm_anyword=revolutionary%20communist&sort1=rs_datecreated&count&rows=50
731. Ibid.
732. "The deepening economic crisis and the intensifying rivalry between the two superpowers propels them to redivide the world, to pump new life into their dying system. And if revolution doesn't prevent them from launching such a war, then such a war and the dislocations it wreaks will create unparalleled opportunities to strike crushing and perhaps decisive blow to U.S. imperialists and reactionaries everywhere." "Great Leap on May 1st," *Revolutionary Worker,* May 5, 1980.
733. "U.S., Soviet Delegates Splattered with Red Paint by Intruders at U.N," *The Associated Press,* April 30, 1980.
734. "Two Begin Serving Term For Paint Toss," *The Associated Press,* March 10, 1981.
735. *Revolutionary Worker,* May 5, 1980, Red Flag Edition.
736. Jerry Belcher, "Police, Leftists Clash Along Wilshire Blvd," *Los Angeles Times.* May 1, 1980.
737. "Scores Arrested, Injured in May Day Violence," UPI, May 2, 1980.
738. "Great Leap on May 1st," *Revolutionary Worker,* May 5, 1980.
739. "Judge Releases Maoists; U.S. 'Vendetta' Charged," *Washington Post,* November 16, 1979.
740. Al Kamen, "Plea Bargain Ends 3 1/2-Year-Old Case Of Violent Protest by Maoist Group," *Washington Post,* June 4, 1982.
741. Bob Avakian, "Conquer the World: The International

Proletariat Must and Will," *Revolution*, Revolutionary Communist Party, Fall, 1981.

742. Avakian, *Ike to Mao*, 339.

743. Bob Avakian, "Storms Are Gathering–Carry the Red Flag Forward!" *Revolutionary Worker*, Special National Edition, February 1979. Reprinted marxists.org. http://www.marxists.org/history/erol/ncm-5/avakian-speech.htm

744. Mao Tse-tung, "On the Ten Major Relationships," *Selected Works of Mao Tse-tung*, April 25, 1956. From marxists.org. http://www.marxists.org/reference/archive/mao/selected-works/volume-5/mswv5_51.htm

745. Karl Marx and Frederick Engels. *Manifesto of the Communist Party*. From marxists.org. http://www.marxists.org/archive/marx/works/1848/communist-manifesto/

746. Felt-Miller trial, 1980. Record Group 21, Records of the District Courts of the United States, District of Columbia, Criminal Case File 78-00179, *United States v. W Mark Felt and Edward S. Miller*. Location in NARA Stacks: 16W3/15/05/05-06. Box 30, 3993 & 4050-4051.

747. Ibid.

748. FBI file of Oliver Vincent Hirsch, member of the Revolutionary Union (Tacoma Branch), FBI case file 100-HQ-480681.

749. Seth Rosenfeld, "Anti-war activist Steve Hamilton dies." Quote from Hamilton's sister, Betty Metcalf. *San Francisco Chronicle*, March 20, 2009.

Notes: Interview

1. Our initial research was only able to identify six RU members, along with Pablo Guzman, a member of the Puerto Rican Revolutionary Workers Organization (formerly the Young Lords Party), who traveled with the RU's delegation.

2. Newton, who was due back in the US for trial, stayed only ten days. This came as a disappointment to the Chinese, who he says had offered him asylum. On the whole both Newton and Brown's accounts of the trip read as extremely self-focused. Newton's only reference to the actual tour being that he traveled "to various parts of the country, visiting factories, schools, and communes." The remainder of his reminiscence focuses on the important people he met, the embassies he visited, and the privileged treatment he received. Elaine Brown's account is even more self-focused. She writes almost nothing about her time in China, while sharing vivid recollections of her time with Newton, such as the following, this on the day before entering the PRC:"Nude under hotel terrycloth robes, Huey and I huddled together looking out on our [Hong Kong Hilton] suite's living-room window at the new day." Huey P. Newton, *Revolutionary Suicide,* New York: Random House, 1973, 323. Elaine Brown, *A Taste of Power,* New York: Pantheon, 302-303.

Index

Page references in *italic* indicate illustrations.

Aceves, Eduardo 238–9
ACLU (American Civil Liberties Union) 157–8
Ad Hoc Committee (AHC) of CPUSA 145–7
Adelman, Barnett 31
Alexander, Gertrude 32 60, 76, 199
American Communist Workers Movement (ACWM) 155
American exceptionalism 75, 246
American Friends Service Committee 124
America's Maoists 74, 83, 92, 98, 109, 172
Antioch College, Yellow Springs 82–3
Anton, Anatole 21
Arrellano, George 238–9
Asian Community Center (ACC) 189
Association of Communist Workers 155
Attica Brigade 8, 142, 173–5, *173*
 change of name to Revolutionary Student Brigade 175
authoritarianism 108, 113, 246
Avakian, Robert Bruce "Bob" 23, 24–9, 41–2, 43, 54, 58–9, *61*, 81, 88, 133, 138, 244, 252
 and the Attica Brigade 175
 and Bergman 29, 59, 76, 81, 127, 209, 211, 214, 244
 at the Bicentennial in Philadelphia 200
 and the Black Panthers 26–9, 60–61
 and the Boston busing plan 159
 and China
 after Mao's death 207–8, 209–10
 and the Deng demo and subsequent charges 225–6, 227–8, 230–31, 232–3, 243
 and the Mao memorial 220
 RU delegation to China 125, 126–7
 cult of 229–30
 epigraph 205
 in exile, self-imposed 224, 242–3
 and the FBI 64–5, 138, 169, 171
 on the formation of the RU 37–8
 and Franklin 93–5
 on García's murder 239
 From Ike to Mao and Beyond 252
 and the May Day farrago 235
 and Montgomery 171
 national speaking tour (1979) 232
 Nicosia on 179

and the RCP leadership 207
and split 210–19, 221–3
RCP rectification campaign 220–21
and RCYB 203
in Richmond 62
and Riesel 169
Secret Service investigation 233
and Stalin 76, 77 and the UFAF 60–61
and Wright 145, 147–8
Avakian, Ruth 24
Avakian, Spurgeon "Sparky" 24
Ayers, Bill 54

Barber, David 52
Bardacke, Frank 22–3, *23*
Bay Area Revolutionary Union 23–4, 32–3, 47–8, 83, 133, 153
Bayer, Abigail 236
Beaty, Ronald Wayne 101, 102
Bellow, Saul 21
Bergman, Anne 16
Bergman, Leibel 12–18, *17*, 41, 46, 59–60, 81, 133, 149–50, 222
and AHC 147
and Avakian 29, 59, 76, 81, 127, 209, 211, 214, 244
and China 18, 121–4, 207–9
epigraph of FBI informant report 205
RU delegation to China 125, 127
death 252
departure from RCP 211–14
epigraphs 5, 10, 205
and the FBI 12, 16, 17–18, 42, 59–60, 81, 96, 97, 108, 121–4, 149–50, *154*, 188, 205, 218, 249
and Franklin 87, 95–7, 108
and Hoover 39, 40, 123–4
and Israel 79–80
and the RCP leadership 207, 211–14
RCP re-assessment after split 213–14
and Riesel 170
Will We Remember? 252 and Wright 145, 148
Berkeley Asian American Political Alliance 189
Bernstein, Bruce 174
Bicentennial in Philadelphia 195–200
Biggin, Bill 197–8
Biggin, Judy 197
Bishop, Thomas E. 166, 169
Black Belt South 143–4
Black Nationalism 26–7, 37, 43 *see also* Black Panther Party
Black Panther Party 7, 17, 26–7, 53, 56
anti-working class and anarchist perspective 90
and Avakian 26–9, 60–61
under Cleaver 89, 90
delegation to China 124
and the Intercommunal Survival Committee To Combat

Fascism of the Black Panther Party 100
National Revolutionary Conference for a United Front Against Fascism 60–61
and the PFP 27–8
of Philadelphia 197–8
and the PLP 46, 180
and *Quotations from Chairman Mao Tse-tung* 119
and Riesel 168
and the RU/RCP 24, 33, 46, 62
and the Franklin split 89–91, 95
and RYM 50
and the SDS 53–4
sexism 53
Black student movement 175
Black Vietnam veterans 163
Black Workers Congress (BWC) 139, 140, 141–2, 153, 158
Blakkan, Renee, (epigraph) 132
Bond, Julian 21
Bonwell, Donald 232
Borock, Herb 171
Boston busing plan 158–9
Boston Globe 159, 181–2
Bown, Vern 32, 60, 202
BPP *see* Black Panther Party
Brisby, Kent O. 103
Brown, H. Rap (later Jamil Abdullah Al-Amin) 28
Brown Berets 98
Bundism 189
Burnham, James 92
Burt, Andrea Holman 101, 103
Burt, Benton 101
Burt, Douglas 101–2, 103
Burton, James 155, 157–8 epigraph 132
BWC *see* Black Workers Congress

California Communist League 79
Callahan, Mat 199
Callahan, Sandy 199
Camil, Scott 176–7
Canand, Russell F. 243
Cannon, Terry 22–3, 23
capitalism 15, 184, 244
and China 125
socialism's replacement and undoing results of 185, 186, 189, 222, 246
and the Soviet Union 193
and the Treiger faction 78
Carmichael, Stokely (later Kwame Ture) 28
Carter, Jimmy 224, 225
Central Organization of US Marxist-Leninist (COUSML) 155, 156
Chavet, Richie 174
Cherkos, Stephen 20
Chicago Democratic Convention police riot 36
Chicago Tribune 128
China 110–31
after Mao's death 8–9, 206,

207–10, 234
and Bergman *see* Bergman, Leibel: and China
and capitalism 125
Communist Party *see* Communist Party of China
Cultural Revolution 33, 52–3, 118, 126, 185–6, 208, 209
renounced by leaders after Mao's death 206
Gang of Four 206, 207–8, 209
and Hinton 110–14, 115–16, 117–18
Kissinger report on 128–30
Lin Biao Affair 126, 127
and the PLP 125–6
radicalism 53
and the RU/RCP
after Mao's death 205–10, 234
Deng demo 224–8, 230–31
and Maoist socialism 117, 139, 185–6, 194–5, 206, 210, 244, 245, 247
RU as China's representative in the US 132
RU delegation to China 124–31
Sino-American relations 108–9, 125, 126, 181–2, 234
Trading with the Enemy Act 118
and USCPFA 191–3
Sino-Soviet split 93, 97
schism between Chinese and Soviet communists 14, 44, 193–5
socialism *see* socialism: Maoist
Three Worlds Theory 194–5
US-China Peoples Friendship Association 8–9, 191–3, 203
China Books and Periodicals 118–21
China Reconstructs 120
Church Committee 166, 168
CIA 3
and *Ramparts* 25
Clark, Dave 203
Cleaver, Eldridge 25, 26–7, 28, 53, 60–61, 89, 90, 163
Cline, Dave 217–18
coalfields, West Virginia 160–65
Cockrel, Ken 142
COINTELPRO (New Left Counter Intelligence Program) 8, 49–50, 134, 249
Cold War 29–30
Collected Works of Mao Zedong 120
Columbia Spectator 174
Communist League 142, 155, 157, 158
Communist Party of China 14–15, 61, 114, 206
and Bergman 121–4
and the International Situation Conference 193–5
schism with Soviet communists 14, 44, 193–5
Communist Party of the Philippines 195
Communist Party of the Soviet

Union 13
schism with Chinese communists 14, 44, 193–5
Communist Party USA (CPUSA) 10, 11, 30, 60
Ad Hoc Committee (AHC) 145–7
and Bergman 12–13, 15, 60, 61
and the PLP 11, 16
and the UFAF 61
communist radicalism *see* radicalism
Communist Workers Party 231
Communist Working Collective 79
Community for New Politics (CNP) 25
COUSML (Central Organization of US Marxist-Leninist) 155, 156
CPUSA *see* Communist Party USA

Delano, Lewis "Skip" 163, 165, 170
Dellums, Ron 28
DeLoach, Cartha 167
democratic centralism 95, 105, 149, 248
Deng Xiaoping 208
RCP's demo over 224–8 charges against Avakian 227–8, 230–31, 232–3, 243
Dershowitz, Alan 100
Dewey, John 199
Dewey Canyon III, Operation 177
Didion, Joan 10
Dodge Revolutionary Union Movement (DRUM) 141
Dong, Harvey 190
Dunbar-Ortiz, Roxanne 84
Duncan, Donald 25
Dunham, Frank 122–3

Eastland, James 112
El Paso, Texas 133–4
Elbaum, Max 248
Eldon Avenue Revolutionary Union Movement (ELRUM), Chrysler 141
Erlich, Reese *23*
Ely, Mike 161, 162, 164, 234–5
epigraph 160
Engels, Friedrich 32
Epton, Bill 125
Equal Rights Amendment 185
Erlich, Reese 22–3, 23 (illustration)
Everybody's Books 189
Ewart, George 20

Falk, Winfield 240
Fall, Gina 161, 162
FALN (Fuerzas Armadas de Liberación Nacional 196
Farah textile company 133–4
FBI
and AHC 145–7
and China Books 119–20
and the Communist League 157
epigraphs 5, 34, 110, 205
files/documents 2, 3, 8, 20
and Garvin 110, 149
and Hinton 2, 110–12, 116–17

and Hoover *see* Hoover, J. Edgar
and Manganiello 103–4
and Mosher 68–9
and the *Movement* 62
New Left Counter Intelligence Program (COINTELPRO) 8, 49–50, 134, 249
and Noyes 119, 120 and the OL 155–6 and the PLP 56
and the press 165–73
and the Red Collective 155
and the Red Star Cadre 155
and the RU/RCP 46–8, 80–85, 132, 147, 153–4, 160, 245, 247–50
and Avakian 64–5, 138, 169, 171
and Bergman 12, 16, 17–18, 42, 59–60, 81, 96, 97, 108, 121–4, 149–50, *154*, 188, 205, 218, 249
and the Communist League 157
cover collective scheme proposal 83–4
early FBI interest 5, 6, 7–8, 42
and FBI dirty tricks 69–70
FBI overview of RCP 200–201
and Franklin 39–40, 86–7, 88, 96–7, 108, 171
and the Franklin split 91–5
under Gray 134–5
and Hamilton 20, 21
and Hirsch 161–2
informants 68–75, 76–7, 81, 84–5, 86–7, 88, 91–2, 93, *94*, 99–100, 117, 120, 127–8, 135–9, 140, 149–52, *152*, *154*, 156, 205, 248
and the journalists 165–73
and the LNS fake document 80
and the May Day farrago 235–6
penetration of RU's leading structure 68–75, 84–5, 151
and PLP 46–8, 56–7, 181
RCP seen as threat to US security 5, 7
and the RCP split 218–19
and the Schafers 155–6
and USCPFA 192–3
and VVAW 178, 179
and the Schafers 155–6 and SDS 34, 47–9, 54–7
Security Index 20
and Venceremos 103–4
and VVAW 178, 179
and the Weathermen 55–6, 122, 201
in Yellow Springs, Ohio 82–3
Felt, W. Mark 122, 123
Fencl, George 197
Fineman, Davida 79–80
Fisher, Hayden Steel 236, 237
Fitch, Bob 76
Fitzgerald, George 101
Foley, Michael 22
Fontancz, Gloria 148–9

Ford Revolutionary Union Movement (FRUM) 141
Forman, James 142
Franklin, H. Bruce 29–32, 41, 42, 60, *65*, 68, 84, 86–7, 252
and Avakian 93–5
Back Where You Came From (memoir) 102
and Bergman 87, 95–7, 108
dismissal from Stanford 100–101
expulsion from RU 97
and the FBI 39–40, 86–7, 88, 96–7, 108, 171
and Hoover 39–40
and Montgomery 171
From the Movement Toward the Revolution 98
under pen name of Will B. Outlaw 56
"Protracted Urban War" paper 86, 91–2, 104–5
RU rift over 86–95, 105–8 and expulsion of Franklin group 97
and Venceremos 98–104
Franklin, Jane 32, 81, 97
Franklin, Ted 80
Free Speech Movement 7, 17, 19–20, 22, 24
Free You 99
Freed, Jeffrey 88, 97

Gang of Four 206, 207–8, 209
García, Damián 236–9
Garrity, Wendell Arthur 158
Garvin, Victoria "Vicki" 3, 17, 149, 218
epigraph of FBI report 110
gay liberation 187
Ginsberg, Alan 163
Giuliani, Rudolph 196
Goff, Betty Sue 70, 71, 84, 98, 99–100
Goff, Lawrence "Larry" 6, 70–75, 84, 91, 24
and Hinton 117
and Venceremos 99–100, 102–3
Golden, Robert 137
Gomez, Rosalio 237
Gray, L. Patrick 134–5
Greenberg, Barry 32, 43, 67, 81, 133
Greenberg, Mary Lou 32, 60, 125, 127–8, 133
Guardian 139, 158
epigraph 132
forums 139–40, 142
Guzman, Pablo 125

Hall, K.K. 163
Hamilton, Steve 18–24, *23*, 38, 42, 60, 90, 91, 107, 143–4, 151, 153, 187, 188, 231
death 252
epigraphs 10, 58
later years 252
in Richmond 62
and the Stalin split in the RU 76–8
Hamlin, Mike 139, 142

Hampton, Fred 55
Hare, David 115–16
Harris, Larry 32, 76–7, 88
Heller, Lennie 22
Hilliard, David 61
Hinton, William 2, 110–14, *111*, 171, 191, 195
Fanshen 113–16, *115*, 118
and the FBI 2, 110–12, 116–17
and the RU 117–18
Hirsch, Oliver "OV" 161–2
HISC *see* House of Representatives Committee on Internal Security
Hobson, Bruce 102
Hobson, Jean 101, 103
homosexuality 186–7
Hoover, J. Edgar 11, 38–40, 69, 123–4, 134, 171–2, 181, 250
and China Books 119–20
press contacts 166, 167, 168, 171, 172–3
Veterans of Foreign Wars article 181
Horn, Joshua: *Away With All Pests* 115
Horner, Robert M. 92, 180–81
House Committee on Un-American Activities *see* HUAC
House of Representatives Committee on Internal Security (HISC): 71, 108–9, 171–2, 196
America's Maoists 74, 83, 92, 98,
109, 172
Hua Guofeng 206
HUAC (House Committee on Un-American Activities) 21, 33,171
anti-HUAC protests 7
and Bergman 15–16
Hume, Ellen 7
Hunt, Andrew: *The Turning* 179
Huston, Tom 121–2

I Wor Kuen 140, 143
Information Digest 135, 136, 139
Intercommunal Survival Committee To Combat Fascism of the Black Panther Party 100
International Black Workers Congress 139, 140, 141–2
International Situation Conference 193–5
International Socialist Club 43
Israel 79–80

Jackson, George 162–3
Jarvis, Mickey 207, 208, 211, 213, 218
Jiang Qing 206
John Birch Society 162

Kelly, Clarence 167
Kerry, John 177
Khrushchev, Nikita 13, 15
Kime, Teresa 232
Kissinger, C. Clark 128–30, 174–5, 191, 203
Klingel, Bill 67, 207, 212, 220

Klonsky, Mike 139, 157
Koziol, Ron 48, 82

LAPD *see* Los Angeles Police Department
League for Industrial Democracy 34–5
League of Revolutionary Black Workers 141–2
Lenin, Vladimir 44
What Is To Be Done 228
Materialism and Empirio Criticism 120
Leninism *see* Marxism-Leninism
Liberation News Service (LNS) 2, 79–80
Lin Biao Affair 126, 127
Lin Piao 209
Little, Malcolm (Malcolm X) 17
Liu Shaoqi 126, 208
Lizarraga, Fabian 237–8, 239
LNS *see* Liberation News Service
London, Jack 35
Los Angeles Police Department (LAPD) 237–8, 239–40
Los Angeles Times 233, 237–8
Loss in China and the Revolutionary Legacy of Mao Tse-tung 220
Lotta, Raymond 118
Lowell, Robert 21
Lyman, Richard 65, 66, 68, 100

Machtinger, Howard (epigraph) 58
Malcolm X 17
Mandel, Bob 22–3, *23*
Manganiello, Aaron 98, 102–4
Mao Zedong 8, 14–15, 25, 44, 77, 105–6
Collected Works of 120
death, and crisis in Maoist organizations 205–6
epigraph 245
"In Memory of Norman Bethune" (epigraph) 110
and Nixon 126
Quotations from Chairman Mao Tse-tung 119, 120, 126, 225
RCP memorials 219–20 Maoist radicalism *see* radicalism
Marcos, Ferdinand 195
Marx, Karl 32
Communist Manifesto epigraph 245
Critique of the Gotha Program 120
Marxism-Leninism 11, 15, 32, 43, 44, 51–2, 59, 69, 75–6, 96, 107, 228
Communist Manifesto epigraph 245
and the League of Revolutionary Black Workers 141
quasi-religious apprehending of 108
and the RCP's vision of socialism 185
and revolutionary nationalism 144
and urban guerrilla warfare *see* urban guerrilla warfare

Wei Min She 189–91
Maverick 99
May Day Brigades and campaign (1980) 231–42
Mayfair Photofinishing Company, Brooklyn 29–30
McCaffrey, John W. 151
McDonald, Larry 240
McGrory, Mary 6
McRae, Stewart 21
Miller, Bruce 163
Miller, Edward S. 122
Milton, Chris 52–3, 69, 171
miners, West Virginia 160–65
Mobutu Sese Seko 195
Mohammad Reza Pahlavi (Shah of Iran) 195, 231, 234
Monica, Doug 125
Montgomery, Ed 64–5, 77, 96, 170–73
Monthly Review Press 113
Moore, Arch 162
Morgan, David 236–7
Mosher, Tom 68–9
Mother Jones collective, Baltimore 82
Movement (newspaper) 22, 52–3, 62
Muslims 37
napalm 31
National Liaison Committee (NLC) 140–44, 148, 149–50, 152–3, 175
National Liberation Front 37, 46
  and RYM 50
National United Workers Organization (NUWO) 202–4
nationalism 37, 143–4, 189, 246, 247
  Black 26–7, 37, 43
    see also Black Panther Party
  and the PLP 125
  revolutionary 46, 144
  and the Sino-Soviet split 14
New Communist Movement (NCM) 155, 158
New Left Notes 23
New York Review of Books 21
New York Times 101, 116, 164, 166
  NY Times Magazine 32
Newman, Morton 102
Newton, Huey P. 26, 89, 124
  Free Huey! rally 28, 229
Nicosia, Gerald: *Home to War* 179, 180
Nields, John 248–9
Nine for Peace 161
Nixon, Richard 5–6, 121, 122, 126, 134, 167, 181, 208
NLC *see* National Liaison Committee
Noyes, Henry Halsey 118, 119, 120
NUWO (National United Workers Organization) 202–3
Oakland Seven 22–3, *23*
O'Connor-Rees, Sheila Louise 135–9, 140, 240
October League (OL) 138, 139, 155–6
  and the RU 132, 138, 157–8
Oil, Chemical and Atomic Workers

Union 63–4
OL *see* October League
Operation Dewey Canyon III 177

Pahlavi, Mohammad Reza *see* Mohammad Reza Pahlavi (Shah of Iran)
Palo Alto 32, 40, 41, 68, 83, 87, 101
Paul, Jay 240
Peace and Freedom Party (PFP) 7, 32
  and the Black Panthers 27–8
  and the PLP 41
  and the RU 38, 40–41, 62
Peking Review 72, 120, 208
Peninsula Observer 66–7
Peninsula Red Guard 32
Peery, Nelson 157
PFP *see* Peace and Freedom Party
Philadelphia, Bicentennial 195–200
Philadelphia Free Press 197–8
Philippines 195
Philosophy is No Mystery 120
Pinochet, Augusto 195
Plekhanov, Georgy 229
PL(P) *see* Progressive Labor Party
political violence, and the RU/RCP 86–91
Portland police intelligence 240–41
Prairie Fire duo 199
Prairie Fire Organizing Committee 196
Progressive Labor Movement 16
Progressive Labor Party (PLP) 11, 16, 20, 36–7
  abandonment of Maoism 125–6, 132
  and the Black Panthers 46, 180
  and China 125–6
  and the FBI 56
  Marxist-Leninist faction 43
  and nationalism 125
  and the PFP 41
  and the RU 41, 46–8, 56, 144, 180–82
  and the RYM 54
  and the SDS 47, 50, 54–7, 180
  and the WSA 37, 56
PRRWO *see* Puerto Rican Revolutionary Workers Organization
Psihountas, Joanne 125, 220
Puerto Rican Revolutionary Workers Organization (PRRWO) 140, 142–3, 153, 158
Puerto Rican Socialist Party 196
Pugh, David 67

Quotations from Chairman Mao Tse-tung 119, 120, 126, 225

Radical Action Movement (RAM) 71
radicalism
  balance between mainstream and 214–15
  Chinese 53
  and the League of Revolutionary

Black Workers 141–2
and political line 105–9
RAM (Radical Action Movement) 71
RU/RCP as inheritor of Sixties radicalism 7, 187–8
and bridge-maker for Seventies radicalism 246
see also Revolutionary Communist Party (RCP, previously the RU), USA; Revolutionary Union (RU)
student movement's engendering of radical Marxist-Leninists 11, 16
see also student movement
and urban guerrilla warfare *see* urban guerrilla warfare
and the Vietnam war 31, 35–6
see also Vietnam war: anti- war movement
and the Young Partisans, Richmond 62–3
RAM (Radical Action Movement) 71
Ramparts 25
Ransom, David 67
Rapid American Withdrawal 176
RCP *see* Revolutionary Communist Party (RCP, previously the RU), USA
RCYB *see* Revolutionary Communist Youth Brigade
Reagan, Ronald 22, 122, 167
Red Collective 155
Red Papers 1, 43–6, 47, 52, 143, 144, 193–4
Red Star Cadre 155
Rees, John Herbert 135, 136, 240
Rees, Sheila *see* O'Connor-Rees, Sheila Louise
Remiro, Joseph 103
Resistance, The 22
Revolution 1, 106, 120, 133, 158, 159, 174
Revolution and Counter Revolution 212
Revolutionary Communist Party (RCP, previously the RU), USA 1, 144, 245–8
Avakian cult 228–30
and the Bicentennial in Philadelphia 195–200
burnings of American flags 232
and the death of Mao 205–8
memorials 219–20
Deng demo 224–8
charges against Avakian 227–8, 230–31, 232–3, 243
development through mid 1970s 201–2
Equal Rights Amendment opposition 185
and the FBI *see* FBI: and the RU/RCP
founding of 183–5
growth into national organization 7, 205

and homosexuality 186–7
and the International Situation Conference 193–5
and the LAPD 237–8, 239–40
May Day 1980 campaign and "farrago" 231–42
and García's murder 236–9
and NUWO 202–4
organizational framework from the mid-Seventies 206–7
and split 210–15
Portland police files on 240–41
Programme and Constitution 184, 207
and RCYB 203–4
rectification campaign 220–21
Red Papers see *Red Papers*
redefining, and the Avakian cult 227–30
Revolution and Counter Revolution 212
roots of the RU/RCP 7
see also Revolutionary Union (RU)
and the Secret Service 233
and socialism 185–8, 194–5, 210, 217–18, 222, 245, 247
split under Avakian, with formation of RWHq 210–19, 221–3
and the RCYB split 216–17
and the VVAW split 217–18
Stalin split 75–8
and the UN 241
and the United Front 184
and USCPFA 8, 191–3
exit from USCPFA 215–16
and Wei Min She 189–91
and Western Goals 240
Revolutionary Communist Youth Brigade (RCYB) 203, 223
split 216–17
revolutionary nationalism 46, 144
see also nationalism
Revolutionary Student Brigade (RSB) 8, *173*, 175, 196, 200–201, 223
see also Attica Brigade
Revolutionary Union (RU) 6, 7, 37–42
Attica Brigade/Revolutionary Student Brigade 142, 173–5, *173*, 196
"B Paper" 87–8
Bay Area 23–4, 32–3, 47–8, 83, 133, 153
and the Black Belt South 143–4
and the Black Panthers *see* Black Panther Party: and the RU/RCP
and the Boston busing plan 158–9
in Chicago 85, 93, 133, 147, 152
and China *see* China: and the RU/RCP
and China Books 120
democratic centralism 95, 105, 149, 248

East Bay branch 76–8
expansion 132, 136, 160
and the Farah strike 133–4
and the FBI *see* FBI: and the RU/RCP
and the founding of RCP 183–5
Franklin rift 86–95, 105–8
expulsion of Franklin group 97
headquarters moved to Chicago 133
and Hinton 117–18
and homosexuality 186–7
and Hoover 38–40, 69, 123–4, 171–2, 181
and industry 160–65
joining collectives 81–3
key figures in creation and early evolution of 12–33
LNS fake document on 79–80
and Maoism 105–6
Miners Right to Strike Committee 161–4
and the National Liaison Committee 140–41
national organizing tour (1970) 81–2
and the NLC 140–44, 148, 149–50, 152–3
and the OL 132, 138, 157–8
"A Paper" ("The Military Strategy for the United States: Protracted Urban War (A Draft) ") 87–8
and the PFP 38, 40–41, 62
and the PLP 41, 46–8, 56, 144, 180–82
political line 105–9
political violence stance 86–91
and the PRRWO 142–3
and race and the working class 144, 158–9
Red Papers 1, 43–6, 47, 52, 143, 144, 193–4
Revolution 1, 106, 120, 133, 158, 159, 174
and the Richmond collective 61–4
RU/RCP *see* Revolutionary Communist Party (RCP, previously the RU), USA
and RYM II 51–3, 60
San Jose 6–7
and the SDS 42–3, 45, 54, 59, 60
and Sino-American relations 108–9
and the Standard oil strike 63–4
and Stanford University 65–8
Tacoma Chapter 162
and the Treiger faction 78–80
and the UFAF 60–61
and the United Front 78, 170, 178
and Venceremos 98–104
and the VVAW 175–80
in Washington, DC 136
and the West Virginia coalfields 160–65
and the West Virginia textbook strike 162–3

and the "What Road to Building a New Communist Party?" forum 139
worker-based modelling 60–64
and Wright 145–53
see also Wright, D.H.
Revolutionary Worker 227, 234–5
Revolutionary Workers Congress 189
Revolutionary Workers Headquarters (RWHq) 212, 216–17, 219, 222
Revolutionary Youth Movement (RYM) 50
and the PLP 54
RYM I faction 50–51
see also Weathermen
RYM II faction 50, 51–2, 60
Rich, Frank 116
Rich Off Our Backs (ROB) coalition 196, 197, 198–9
Richmond, California 61–4
Riesel, Victor 8, 165–70
epigraph 160
Rizzo, Frank 196, 197–8
Romaine, Paul 119
Rosenfeld, Seth 172
RSB *see* Revolutionary Student Brigade
RU *see* Revolutionary Union
RU/RCP *see* Revolutionary Communist Party (RCP, previously the RU), USA
Rubin, Jerry 20–21
Rudd, Mark 54, 118
RWHq (Revolutionary Workers Headquarters) 212
Ryan, David 16, 59, 85, 123, 193, 248–9
RYM *see* Revolutionary Youth Movement

Sale, Kirkpatrick 45
San Francisco Examiner 170
San Jose Civic Center 5
Sanchez, Jesus 101
Sanders, Donald G. 92
Savio, Mario 19–20
Scaling Peaks in Medical Science 120
Schafer, Harry E. "Gi" 155–6
Schafer, Jill 155–6
Scheer, Robert "Bob" 25
Scriber 13
SDS *see* Students for a Democratic Society
Seabok, Robert 101
Seale, Bobby 26
Secret Service, US 233
Segal, Jeff 22–3
Senate Internal Security Committee 112–13
Senate Select Committee to Study Governmental Operations with Respect to Intelligence Activities (Church Committee) 166, 168
Setzer, Curtis 164
Shah of Iran *see* Mohammad Reza Pahlavi

Shriver, R. Sargent 2, 116–17
Sinclair, Upton 35
Sino-Soviet split 93, 97
  schism between Chinese and Soviet communists 14, 44, 193–5
SLA (Symbionese Liberation Army) 103
Smale, Stephen 21
Smith, Mike 22–3, *23*
Smith, Windy 21
Smith Act 16
SNCC (Student Non Violent Coordinating Committee) 22
Snyder, Tom 232
socialism
  and the Black Panthers 26 Maoist 117, 139, 185–6, 194–5, 206, 210, 244, 245, 247
  and the RCP 185–8, 194–5, 210, 217–18, 222, 245, 247
  and the RCYB 203–4
  undoing of the results of capitalism 185, 186, 189, 222, 246
Socialist Worker 43
Socialist Workers Party 10
Somoza, Anastasio 231
Soviet Union
  and capitalism 193
  Communist Party *see* Communist Party of the Soviet Union
  Sino-Soviet split 93, 97
  schism between Chinese and Soviet communists 14, 44, 193–5
Spartacist League 79
SRI (Stanford Research Institute) 31
Stalin, Josef 13, 44–5, 107
  RU split under 75–8
Stallings, Herbert K. 145–6, 150–51, 155
Standard oil strike 63–4
Stanford Research Institute (SRI) 31, 65
Stanford University 17, 65–8
Stoned Rabbits Peoples Party (SRPP) 1
Stop the Draft Week (1967) 22
Student League for Industrial Democracy 34–5
student movement 11, 16, 174, 203–4
  Black 175
  see also Attica Brigade; Revolutionary Communist Youth Brigade (RCYB); Revolutionary Student Brigade (RSB); Student League for Industrial Democracy; Students for Democratic Society (SDS)
Student Non Violent Coordinating Committee (SNCC) 22
Students for Democratic Society (SDS) 22, 34–6, 175

and the Black Panthers 53–4
and the FBI 34, 47–9, 54–7
final convention (June 1969) 50–57
New Left Notes 23
and the PLP 47, 50, 54–7, 180
and the RU 42–3, 45, 54, 59, 60
and the RYM 50–51
at Stanford University 66, 67
and the US working class 58
and the Weathermen 50–51
Sullivan, David 79, 147, 148
Symbionese Liberation Army (SLA) 103

textbook strike, West Virginia 162–3
Thomas, Norman 35
Three Worlds Theory 194–5
Tomorrow 232
Trading with the Enemy Act 118
trashing 86
Treiger, Marv 43, 61, 78–80, 157
Tresidder, Donald 31
Trent, Jerry 237

UFAF (United Front Against Fascism) 60–61
Unemployed Workers Organizing Committee (UWOC) 196, 198-9
United Front Against Fascism (UFAF) 60–61
United Nations 241
United Technology Center (UTC) 31
urban guerrilla warfare 89, 246
Franklin's "Protracted Urban War" paper 86, 91–2, 104–5
US-China Peoples Friendship Association (USCPFA) 8, 191–3, 203, 223
RCP's exit from 215–16
UTC (United Technology Center) 31
UWOC (Unemployed Workers Organizing Committee) 196, 198-9

Vawter, Michael 171
VDC (Vietnam Day Committee) 20, 21, 24–5
Venceremos 98–104
and the Intercommunal Survival Committee To Combat Fascism of the Black Panther Party 100
Veteran, The 218
Veterans of Foreign Wars 181
Vietnam Day Committee (VDC) 20, 21, 24–5
Vietnam Veterans Against the War (VVAW) 8, 157, 175–80, *178*, *183*, 196, 199, 223
change of name to VVAW-Winter Soldier Organization 177
split 217–18
Vietnam war 31, 86, 175, 247

anti-war movement 5–6, 8, 17, 20–22, 24, 25, 31, 35–6, 37, 63, 72–3, 86, 100
and *Information Digest* 135
see also Vietnam Veterans Against the War
Village Voice 6, 102
voluntarism 55, 105–6, 247
VVAW *see* Vietnam Veterans Against the War

Wanamaker, Robert C. 103
Washington Post 226
Watson, John 142
Weathermen 7, 43, 50–51, 55–6, 165
and the FBI 55–6, 122, 201
news report on war council (epigraph) 58
Prairie Fire organization 196
and the Treiger faction 78
"War Council", Flint 58–9
Webster, William 167
Wei Min She (WMS) 189–90
Weiss, Janet 97
Weissman Steve 68
Welker, Herman, Senator 112
Wells, Lyn 54
West Virginia 8
and the May Day Brigade 232
miners 160–65
textbook strike 162–3
Western Goals 240
"What Road to Building a New Communist Party?" 139
Wilford, K.M. 118
Will We Remember? (Bergman's poetry) 252
Williams, Robert 37
Worker Student Alliance (WSA) 37, 56
Wright, D.H. 125, 139, 145–53
WSA (Worker Student Alliance) 37, 56

Yellow Springs, Ohio 82–3
Yip, Steve 189
Young Lords Organization 140, 142
Young Lords Party 125, 142
Young Partisans 99
Richmond 62–3

Zablocki, Clement J. 119
Zastrow, Peter 174
Zhou Enlai 124, 125

CULTURE, SOCIETY & POLITICS

Contemporary culture has eliminated the concept and public figure of the intellectual. A cretinous anti-intellectualism presides, cheer-led by hacks in the pay of multinational corporations who reassure their bored readers that there is no need to rouse themselves from their stupor. Zer0 Books knows that another kind of discourse - intellectual without being academic, popular without being populist - is not only possible: it is already flourishing. Zer0 is convinced that in the unthinking, blandly consensual culture in which we live, critical and engaged theoretical reflection is more important than ever before.

If you have enjoyed this book, why not tell other readers by posting a review on your preferred book site.

You may also wish to
subscribe to our Zer0 Books YouTube Channel.

Bestsellers from Zer0 Books include:

Poor but Sexy
Culture Clashes in Europe East and West
Agata Pyzik
How the East stayed East and the West stayed West.
Paperback: 978-1-78099-394-2 ebook: 978-1-78099-395-9

An Anthropology of Nothing in Particular
Martin Demant Frederiksen
A journey into the social lives of meaninglessness.
Paperback: 978-1-78535-699-5 ebook: 978-1-78535-700-8

In the Dust of This Planet
Horror of Philosophy vol. 1
Eugene Thacker
In the first of a series of three books on the Horror of Philosophy, *In the Dust of This Planet* offers the genre of horror as a way of thinking about the unthinkable.
Paperback: 978-1-84694-676-9 ebook: 978-1-78099-010-1

The End of Oulipo?
An Attempt to Exhaust a Movement
Lauren Elkin, Veronica Esposito
Paperback: 978-1-78099-655-4 ebook: 978-1-78099-656-1

Capitalist Realism
Is There No Alternative?
Mark Fisher
An analysis of the ways in which capitalism has presented itself as the only realistic political-economic system.
Paperback: 978-1-84694-317-1 ebook: 978-1-78099-734-6

Rebel Rebel
Chris O'Leary
David Bowie: every single song. Everything you want to know, everything you didn't know.
Paperback: 978-1-78099-244-0 ebook: 978-1-78099-713-1

Cartographies of the Absolute
Alberto Toscano, Jeff Kinkle
An aesthetics of the economy for the twenty-first century.
Paperback: 978-1-78099-275-4 ebook: 978-1-78279-973-3

Malign Velocities
Accelerationism and Capitalism
Benjamin Noys
Long listed for the Bread and Roses Prize 2015, *Malign Velocities* argues against the need for speed, tracking acceleration as the symptom of the ongoing crises of capitalism.
Paperback: 978-1-78279-300-7 ebook: 978-1-78279-299-4

Babbling Corpse
Vaporwave and the Commodification of Ghosts
Grafton Tanner
Paperback: 978-1-78279-759-3 ebook: 978-1-78279-760-9

New Work New Culture
Work we want and a culture that strengthens us
Frithjof Bergmann
A serious alternative for mankind and the planet.
Paperback: 978-1-78904-064-7 ebook: 978-1-78904-065-4

Romeo and Juliet in Palestine
Teaching Under Occupation
Tom Sperlinger
Life in the West Bank, the nature of pedagogy and the role of a university under occupation.
Paperback: 978-1-78279-637-4 ebook: 978-1-78279-636-7

Color, Facture, Art and Design
Iona Singh
This materialist definition of fine-art develops guidelines for architecture, design, cultural-studies and ultimately social change.
Paperback: 978-1-78099-629-5 ebook: 978-1-78099-630-1

Sweetening the Pill
or How We Got Hooked on Hormonal Birth Control
Holly Grigg-Spall
Has contraception liberated or oppressed women? *Sweetening the Pill* breaks the silence on the dark side of hormonal contraception.
Paperback: 978-1-78099-607-3 ebook: 978-1-78099-608-0

Why Are We The Good Guys?
Reclaiming Your Mind from the Delusions of Propaganda
David Cromwell
A provocative challenge to the standard ideology that Western power is a benevolent force in the world.
Paperback: 978-1-78099-365-2 ebook: 978-1-78099-366-9

The Writing on the Wall

On the Decomposition of Capitalism and its Critics

Anselm Jappe, Alastair Hemmens

A new approach to the meaning of social emancipation.

Paperback: 978-1-78535-581-3 ebook: 978-1-78535-582-0

Neglected or Misunderstood

The Radical Feminism of Shulamith Firestone

Victoria Margree

An interrogation of issues surrounding gender, biology, sexuality, work and technology, and the ways in which our imaginations continue to be in thrall to ideologies of maternity and the nuclear family.

Paperback: 978-1-78535-539-4 ebook: 978-1-78535-540-0

How to Dismantle the NHS in 10 Easy Steps (Second Edition)

Youssef El-Gingihy

The story of how your NHS was sold off and why you will have to buy private health insurance soon. A new expanded second edition with chapters on junior doctors' strikes and government blueprints for US-style healthcare.

Paperback: 978-1-78904-178-1 ebook: 978-1-78904-179-8

Digesting Recipes

The Art of Culinary Notation

Susannah Worth

A recipe is an instruction, the imperative tone of the expert, but this constraint can offer its own kind of potential. A recipe need not be a domestic trap but might instead offer escape – something to fantasise about or aspire to.

Paperback: 978-1-78279-860-6 ebook: 978-1-78279-859-0

Most titles are published in paperback and as an ebook.
Paperbacks are available in traditional bookshops. Both print and ebook formats are available online.
Follow us at:
https://www.facebook.com/ZeroBooks
https://twitter.com/Zer0Books
https://www.instagram.com/zero.books